Hopkins Academy

History of the Hopkins Fund

Grammar School and Academy

Hopkins Academy

History of the Hopkins Fund
Grammar School and Academy

ISBN/EAN: 9783337338664

Printed in Europe, USA, Canada, Australia, Japan

Cover: Foto ©ninafisch / pixelio.de

More available books at **www.hansebooks.com**

HISTORY

—— OF ——

THE HOPKINS FUND,

Grammar School and Academy,

—— IN ——

HADLEY, MASS.

PREPARED AND PUBLISHED UNDER THE DIRECTION
AND AUTHORITY OF THE TRUSTEES
OF HOPKINS ACADEMY.

1657--1890.

AMHERST, MASS.:
THE AMHERST RECORD PRESS.
1890.

PREFACE.

The pages that follow came to be in this wise. For about a hundred and fifty years the Hopkins Grammar School had a being and did a good work in Hadley, until its Trustees by charter from the legislature of Massachusetts became the Trustees of Hopkins Academy.

Under this name the good work has gone on seventy years and more until the present time. The Fund which has in part supported the school from the first, had its beginning in the bequest of Gov. Edward Hopkins, who left a considerable sum from his estate in aid and encouragement of good learning in New England, then newly settled. This Fund received increment, from time to time, from other sources. Its fortunes have been various. At different periods its concerns have deeply moved the minds of the people, and been a considerable factor in the life of the town and the community. This interest has left its impress in the record of town meetings, court proceedings, and the doings of President and Council who were in power in New England for a short time under the British Crown from May 25 to Dec. 20, 1686.

The work done by aid of this Fund has been benign. It has been a blessing to many. The story is rich in interest and worthy of record, that all who wish can read and possess. The materials for such a history were passing beyond reach. To make sure of them, before it was too late, was felt to be a demand of duty, that did not admit of longer delay. Questions as to this Fund, and its proper administration and use arising from time to time, deemed to be new, and to demand hearing and adjustment, were known to be questions long ago raised and decided by highest authority. It was proper that such knowledge should be within reach of all, and thus occasion for strife be wanting, and peace and good will prevail unbroken.

Hence at a meeting of the Trustees of Hopkins Academy held May 6, 1885, after discussion of the subject, it was voted that a committee consisting of Rev. Dr. Ayres, Rev. Dr. Dwight and Dea. Geo. Dickinson be chosen to investigate and arrange for publication the history of the Hopkins Academy Fund from its inception, its present standing, and its relation to the Board of Trustees and the public."

It was further voted that Dr. F. Bonney be added to the committee.

It was voted that the above committee be authorized and empowered to expend such sums of money as they may deem necessary to carry out the purposes of their appointment." Nov. 27, 1889, it was voted "that the committee having the matter in charge be authorized to go forward and publish the History of the Hopkins Academy Fund which has been under consideration for some years."

By authority of these earlier votes the chairman of the committee before named entered upon the work prescribed.

This proved to be no easy task. The materials of the history were out of sight. Records and papers supposed to be in being eluded search, hopelessly lost in some instances. Very valuable original papers belonging to the Academy had gone from its possession. Many of these were found among the private papers of the late Sylvester Judd, who probably had them in his possession by permission for the purposes of his History of Hadley, and failed to return them.

After his death these papers were purchased by J. R. Trumbull, Esq. and Dea. Geo. W. Hubbard, and by them held as their own to dispose and convey, until the death of Dea. Hubbard, who by his will conveyed them to be held by the Forbes Library in trust. These papers at present are with J. R. Trumbull, Esq., until the Forbes Library building is ready.

It would seem as if these papers were still the rightful property of the Trustees of Hopkins Academy, and that they might regain possession of their own by process of law. Should they reach the place of deposit intended for them, however, they may be in safer keeping than in the archives of the Trustees. Hints are now and then met of a book of records kept by the Trustees of the Grammar School, of which no trace has been found.

Printed catalogues published by the Trustees from time to time have yielded very valuable information. But some of these are still missing after all the search that has been made.

Much valuable information has been derived from persons living who were members of the Academy in its earlier years. Among these may be named Miss Thankful Smith (now deceased), Mrs. Charles W. May, Rev. Henry Seymour, Dr. Franklin Bonney, Rev. Addison Ballard, D. D., Rev. Ezekiel Russell, D. D., and many others.

It is hoped that this memorial of a noble institution and its work may be received and held in kind esteem by all among its pupils, teachers, guardians, patrons, and friends who may scan its pages.

Hadley, Jan. 15, 1890.

CHAPTER I.

EDWARD HOPKINS AND HIS WILL.

The school known as Hopkins Grammar School and Hopkins Academy has a history of nearly two and a quarter centuries. Nothing concerning this town is worthier of record than the story of this school, and its Fund. From its beginning until now it has given the town a name and memorial widely through the land, and beyond the seas. The dweller here is quite sure to think and speak of it as chief among the good things that give honorable distinction. It has been, and is, a power for good, in the town and beyond, far and wide. It has done a good work and made a record, which should be preserved in such form as to be within reach of all who feel an interest in these things. Such is the aim of the pages that follow.

The man whose name this school bears and perpetuates was not its founder, in the ordinary sense, though to him its being and such a history are due. Honor to whom honor is due. The name Hopkins should be held in grateful remembrance, (as it is largely), by all who are or have been dwellers in Hadley, or have been members of the school, and all who have enjoyed the fruits of his bounty elsewhere, or have felt the inspiration of his spirit and example. This influence has been benign and widely pervasive. The wise forethought of this man was remarkable in one living in his time, though like so many others before and since " he built more wisely than he knew."

Edward Hopkins began life with the seventeenth century. He was born in Shrewsbury, Shropshire, England, in the year 1600. He was a scholar in the Royal Free Grammar School in his native town. The Grammar School which he would establish in New England was after the pattern with which he was familiar in his youth, a school for boys, in which they were taught in the tongues and fitted for the University.

These schools were free, in that they were open, on the payment of such charges as were necessary to maintain them, to any who wished to enjoy such advantages.

Of his life previous to leaving England little is known. Engaging in commerce as a merchant he won a handsome fortune. In early life he joined the Puritans as a convert to their doctrines and observances. While living in London, he had worshiped in the parish church of St. Stephens in Coleman Street of which John Davenport was vicar. Here Theophilus Eaton was likewise an attendant. The relations of these men were close and confidential. With a company of friends, including the two just named, Edward Hopkins embarked his fortunes in 1637 to find, if not " a refuge and receptacle for all sorts of consciences," at least an opportunity to worship God in their own way and to administer their civil affairs " more according to the rule of righteousness " than was then the fashion in the Old World.

" 1637, Mo. 4. 26 Ship Hector and another arrived at Boston. In these came Mr. Davenport and another minister (Samuel brother of Gov. Eaton) and Mr. Eaton and Mr. Hopkins, two merchants of London, men of fair estate and good esteem for religion and wisdom in outward affairs." (Winthrop Hist. N. E. I, 226.)

" Edward Hopkins was one who would be a foremost man wherever he might be."

Declining many overtures to settle in Boston, after a short stay there he joined the settlement at Hartford, where he is at once found sharing in the administration of public affairs. The year of his arrival his name appears as one of the " committee " of the General Court at Hartford, so that it is deemed likely that he had part in that assembly of 1638 by which the " inhabitants and residents of Hartford, Windsor and Weathersfield, did associate and conjoin themselves to be one Public State or Commonwealth " " to maintain and preserve the liberty and purity of the Gospel of the Lord Jesus Christ, which we now profess, and in civil affairs to be guided and governed according to such laws, rules orders and decrees as shall be made, ordered and decreed " not by the King and Council—not even by Royal Parliament, but by the General Court, elected by the whole body of freemen, in which " *The Supreme Power of the Commonwealth*" was declared to reside. That constitution was the nearest approach to a republican organized democracy, in which the whole people of the several towns acted through representatives in a legislature elected twice a year by all the inhabitants, that the world had yet seen. Mr. Hopkins was elected first secretary of the Colony of Connecticut and deputy Governor under the Constitution of 1638, and succeeded Mr. Haynes as Governor in 1640, and again in 1646, 1648, 1650 and 1652. In 1654 he was again elected, though at the time of this choice he was in England, whence probably his return was looked for.

In alternate years he was usually Deputy Governor, and frequently chosen assistant and also one of the Commissioners of the United Colonies. In this last capacity he signed in behalf of Connecticut the articles of Confederation in 1643, by which the Colonies of Massachusetts, Plymouth, Connecticut and New Haven united for future help and strength, under the name of the United Colonies of New England, and was president of that body, when a settlement was made with the Dutch in 1650. In 1640 he was one of the committee appointed to negotiate the purchase from Mr. Fenwick of the port and appurtenances at Saybrook. And indeed, there was hardly a committee raised on the " foreign relations " of the Colony with Massachusetts, the Dutch or the Indians, in which he did not occupy a prominent place with Gov. Haynes, Capt. Mason, Mr. Whiting and Mr. Wyllis. In the interval of public duty he was diligent in business on his own account.

Gov. Hopkins went to England in 1653, on the occasion of his brother's death, intending to return to his family and friends in New England; but on his arrival there he was soon made warden of the fleet, (an office filled by his brother at the time of his death), Commissioner of the Admiralty and member of Parliament. Detained by these new duties, he sent for his family, and died in London in March or April, 1657.*

While he remained in this land he was still engaged as a merchant, and pushed his trading stations up the river and into the wilderness, and founded the commerce in American cotton.† This man, who busied himself with affairs both public and private, was one whose physical frame was frail. He was a man of feeble health. " He conflicted with bodily infirmities but especially with a bloody and wasting cough which held him for thirty years together." (Mather, Mag. § 5.)

He was eminent for piety, as well as wisdom and success in secular affairs. He and those with whom he came hither had as not the least of their reasons for removal " a great hope and inward zeal they had of laying some good foundation, or at least to make some way there-

---
*School Report city of Cambridge, for the year 1885, p. 35.
Barnard History of Hopkins Grammar School, Hartford.
Letter of Gen'l Court of the Mass. to Mr. Hopkins. Hutchinson Coll., p. 271.
†Bacon's Address.

unto, for the propagating and advancing the gospel of the Kingdom of Christ in these remote parts of the world, yea though they should be but as stepping stones unto others for performing so great a work." (Young's Chronicles of the Pilgrims, p. 47.) His intimate friend and fellow voyager hither, John Davenport, "a prince of preachers, and worthy to have been a preacher to princes," had been his spiritual teacher and counsellor in London. In the Hartford church he had for "his dear pastor" Thomas Hooker "the light of the New England churches," and received with meekness what they as ministers of Christ had to impart. He bore affliction to his dying day, taught by affliction to die daily as long as he lived. One expression of his heavenly mind, says Mather, among many others in a letter before his end was, "How often have I pleased myself with thoughts of a joyful meeting with my father Eaton! I remember with what pleasure he would come down the street that he might meet me when I came from Hartford unto New Haven, but with how much greater pleasure shall we shortly meet one another in heaven." With such men as these he was kindred in spirit, sharer in their sentiments, plans and counsels.

The wife of Gov. Hopkins was the daughter of the second wife of Theophilus Eaton, first and sole Governor of the Colony of New Haven. Mrs. Eaton was a prudent and pious widow of David Yale, daughter of the Bishop of Chester, Dr. Morton. Elihu Yale for whom Yale College is named, was the son of Thomas Yale, son of Mrs. Eaton by her first husband David Yale. Her daughter Anna was the wife of Edward Hopkins, named by him in his will as his "dear distressed wife," on account of whose condition his own life was marked by such sad and sore affliction. With all his property and honor, his sad spirit depressed by bodily disease and pain bore this added weight. "She was one that had from a child been observable for desirable qualities. But sometime after she was married she fell into a distempered melancholy which at last issued in an incurable distraction. Very grievous was this affliction unto her worthy consort, who was by temper a very affectionate person, and now left no part of a tender husband undone, to ease and if it were possible to cure, the lamentable desolation thus come upon the desire of his eyes." (Mather, B. II, Ch. 7, § 5.)

"Mr. Hopkins the governour of Hartford upon Connecticut came to Boston and brought his wife with him, a godly woman of special parts, who was fallen into a sad infirmity, the loss of her understanding and reason, which had been growing upon her divers years by occasion of her giving herself wholly to reading and writing and had written many books. Her husband being very loving and tender, was loath to grieve her; but he saw his error when it was too late. For if she had attended her household affairs and such things as belong to women and not gone out of her way and calling, to meddle in such things as are proper for men whose minds are stronger etc., she had kept her wits, and might have improved them usefully and honorably in the place God had set her. He brought her to Boston and left her with her brother, one Mr. Yale a merchant, to try what means might be had here for her. But no help could be had." (Winthrop, History of New England, I, p. 266 [217].)

Gov. Hopkins was a liberal man devising liberal things. He lived to serve and bless others. "He considered the poor and would put considerable sums of money into the hands of his friends to be by them employed, as they saw opportunity, to do good unto all, especially to them that are of the household of faith. In this thing he was like that noble and worthy English General, of whom it is noted that he never thought he had anything, but what he gave away, and yet after all with much humility he would profess, as one of the most liberal men that ever was in the world, often would, ' I have often turned over my book of accounts, but I could never find the great God charged a debtor there'." (Mather, Mag., B. II, Chap. 7, § 4.)

This man had been prosperous in business and gained a good estate. Having first made provision for the needs of his wife, and made such other legacies to relatives and friends, as he deemed proper and right, it was his concern that what remained of his property should be of use for generations and centuries to come, in helping young people of promise prepare themselves for the service of their country, and of mankind. Such had been his own character. His forecast of the future was far-reaching and wise, a sure instinct, inspired from above. He had no children of his own, and he made it a care and study that the children of others should have opportunity in the way of good learning for making themselves ready for such service. His character and spirit, in this regard, as in other respects, may be read in his will, here given in full.

EDWARD HOPKINS'S WILL.

[A copy of this will in manuscript is among the papers of the late Sylvester Judd, now in the keeping of J. R. Trumbull, Esq. The preface in Latin is omitted.]

The sovereign Lord of all creatures giving in evident and strong intimations of his pleasure to call me out of this transitory life unto Himself—it is the desire of me Edward Hopkins Esq. to be in readiness to attend his call in whatsoever hour he cometh—both by leaving my soul in the hands of Jesus, who only gives boldness in that day and delivers from the wrath to come—and my body to comely burial according to the discretion of my executors and overseers—and also by settling my small family, if it may be so called, in order and in pursuance thereof do thus dispose of the estate the Lord in mercy hath given me.

First my will is, that my just debts be paid out of my entire estate, where the said debts shall be found to be justly due, viz., if any debts shall be found to be justly due in New England, then they be paid out of my estate there. And if any shall appear to be due here in Old England, that they be paid out of my estate here.

As for my estate in New England (the full account of which I left clear in book there, and the care and inspection whereof was committed to my loving friend Mr. John Cullick) I do in this manner dispose. Item. I do give and bequeath unto the eldest child of Mrs. Mary Newton wife to *Mr. Roger Newton of Farmington and daughter to Mrs. Thomas Hooker, deceased, the sum of £30; as also the sum of £30 unto the eldest child of Mr. John Cullick by Elizabeth his present wife. Item. I do give and bequeath to Mrs. Sarah Wilson, the wife of Mr. John Wilson, preacher of the gospel, and daughter of my dear pastor, Mr. Hooker, my farm at Farmington, with all the houses, outhouses, buildings, lands &c. belonging thereunto, to the use of her and the heirs of her body forever. I do also give unto Mrs. Susan Hooker, the relict of Mr. Thomas Hooker, all such debts as are due to me from her upon the account I left in New England.

And the residue of my estate there I do hereby give and bequeath to My father, Theophilus Eaton. Esq, Mr. John Davenport, Mr John Cullick, and Mr. William Goodwin, in full assurance of their trust, and faithfulness in disposing of it according to the true intent and purpose of me the said Edward Hopkins, which is to give some encouragement in those foreign plantations for the breeding of hopeful youths both at the grammar school, and college, for the public service of the country in future times.

For the estate which the Lord hath given me in *this* England I thus dispose and my will is that £150 per annum be yearly paid per my executor to Mr. David Yale, brother to my dear distressed wife for her comfortable maintenance, and to be disposed of by him for her good, she not being in a condition to manage it for herself; and I do heartily entreat him to be careful and tender over her; and my will is, that this be paid quarterly by £37—10 each quarter and to continue to the end of the quarter after the death of my said wife, and that my executor give good security for a punctual performance thereof. My will also is that the £30 given me per the will and testament of my brother Henry Hopkins, lately deceased, be given to our sister, Mrs. Judith

---

*First minister of the church in Farmington.

Eve, during her natural life, and that it be made up to £50 per annum during her life.

I do give to my sister Mrs. Margaret Thomson the sum of £50, to be paid her within one year after my decease. I do give unto my nephew Henry Thomson £800 whereof £400 to be paid within sixteen months after my decease and the other £400 within six months after the death of my wife.

I do likewise give and bequeath to my neice Katharine Thomson, but now Katharine James (over and above the portion of £500 formerly given her) £100. I do also give and bequeath unto my neices Elizabeth and Patience Dalley, unto each of them £200, provided they attend the direction of their brother or aunts or such as are capable to give them advice in the dispose of themselves in marriage.

I give to my brother Mr. David Yale £200, to my brother Mr. Thomas Yale £200 and to my sister Mrs. Hannah Eaton £200.

My farther mind and will is, that within six months after the decease of my wife £500 be made over into New England, according to the advice of my loving friends Major Robert Thomson and Mr. Francis Willoughby, and conveyed into the hands of the trustees before mentioned, in further prosecution of the aforesaid public ends, which in the simplicity of my heart are for the upholding and promoting the kingdom of the Lord Jesus Christ in those parts of the earth. I do further give unto my beloved wife a bed, with all the furniture belonging unto it for herself to lie on, and another for the servant maid that waits on her, and £20 in plate for her present use besides one third part of all my household goods.

I give unto Mr. John Davenport, Mr. Theophilus Eaton, Mr. Cullick each of them £20, to be made over to them in New England where they are; and my will and pleasure is that £20 be put into a piece of plate, and presented in my name to my honored friend Dr. Wright to whom I owe more than that, being much engaged, desiring him to accept it only as a testimony of my respects. I do give unto my servant James Porter £10, unto my maid Margaret £5; unto my maid Mary 40 shillings. I do give unto my honored and loving friends Major Robert Thomson and Mr. Francis Willoughby £20 apiece in a piece of plate as a token of my respects unto them; and I do give unto my servant Thomas Hayton £20. I do give unto my sister Yale the wife of Mr. David Yale £20, as also to John Lollo, a youth now with my sister Eve £20 to farther him out to be an apprentice to some good trade and £20 more at the time of his coming to his own liberty to encourage him to set up his trade, if he continue living so long. I do give unto my nephew Henry Dalley, master of arts in Cambridge my land and manor of Thickol in the county of Essex; and for the payment of all debts, dues and legacies, do give unto him all my personal estate, and, by these presents, renouncing and making void all other wills and testaments. do declare, and constitute and make him my sole executor and my good friends Major Robert Thomson and Mr. Francis Willoughby overseers of this my last will and testament.

Signed sealed, declared, and published by the said Edward Hopkins Esq. at his home in London, on the 7th day of March in the year of our Lord 1657, to be his last will and testament.

CHAPTER II.

THE TRUSTEES UNDER THE WILL.

The persons named in this will as trustees, are worthy of larger mention. Only three of them appear in the execution of the trust. *Theophilus Eaton* died soon after the will was made. "This man had in him great gifts, and as many excellences as are usually to be found in any man. He had an excellent princely face and port commanding respect from all others." "He carried in his very countenance a majesty which cannot be described." (Mather I, 152.)

"No character in the annals of New England is of purer fame than that of Theophilus Eaton." (Winthrop, I, 277, note.)

In 1643 he was first designated by the title of Governor of the New Haven Colony, which office he held by annual and unanimous election till his death Jan. 8, 1658. He was an earnest friend of education. He was careful concerning the education of the sons in his own family. He kept up contributions for poor scholars at the college at Cambridge. He corresponded with teachers in different parts of New England, "that this town might never be without a suitable school master." (Barnard, Journal of Education, 1828, p. 276.)

Anne, the daughter of his second wife by her former husband, was, as has been seen, the wife of Gov. Edward Hopkins.

Another of these trustees was Mr. and Capt. John Cullick. He was a leading man in colony and church affairs. He was for several years one of the magistrates, and secretary of the colony. He was one of the aggrieved minority in the Hartford church when trouble arose in that body, "the withdrawers" as they were sometimes called. His name is found (as one not "*fully engaged*") among the original engagers, who met at Goodman Ward's house in Hartford April 18, 1659, and engaged themselves under their own hands or by their deputies, whom they had chosen, to remove themselves and their families out of the jurisdiction of Connecticut into the jurisdiction of Massachusetts." He was an active leader in promoting this migration.

May 20, 1658, Capt. Cullick and Mr. Goodwin, being in Boston for the purpose, petitioned the General Court there in their own and others' behalf, for leave to settle up the river "out of the jurisdiction of Connecticut, and within the pious and godly government of Massachusetts."

On the 25th of the month that Court gave them leave, but coupled the permission with the condition that they submit themselves to a due and orderly hearing of the differences between themselves and their brethren. (Walker, Hist. 1st ch. Hartford, 168, Judd, Hist. Hadley, 18, 19.)

Mr. Cullick removed to Boston in 1659, and died there Jan. 23, 1663. (Barnard III, 182.)

Among these Trustees the name of *John Davenport*, already mentioned, is second to none.

He was born in Coventry, England, in 1598, of which city his grandfather was mayor. In 1607 he was schoolmate of Theophilus Eaton in the Coventry Grammar School, admitted to Oxford before he was 14, called, as assistant to another, to public and constant preaching in London at 19. Here he won admiration and praise as a preacher, and for courage in visiting and residing with his flock in time of a dreadful plague. In 1624 he was vicar of St. Stephen's Church in Coleman Street, London, where his friendship with Gov. Eaton grew and ripened into a close intimacy, which helped to shape the future of both. Here Edward Hopkins was likewise his friend and parishioner. He ceased to be in sympathy with the Church of England in doctrine and polity, and became the object of suspicion to Abp. Laud. He suffered spoiling of goods and resigned his benefice, left England for Holland, whence, finding himself out of harmony with those with whom he was thrown, he returned to England in 1635. Having learned that civil and church affairs in New England were taking shape in accord with his own mind, he and Eaton became leaders in an expedition chiefly of Londoners who came in the ship Hector and another, and landed in Boston in 1637. Davenport and Eaton were chief agents in founding the colony of New Haven, where, with Davenport as pastor, the 1st church of New Haven was gathered and constituted Aug. 22, 1639.

In 1651 he was invited to remove to Boston and become pastor of the second church then newly formed. This invitation he declined, but later, when New Haven was no longer a colony by itself, but absorbed in Connecticut, he left his charge at New Haven to accept the urgent call to the first church in Boston. He removed thither and was installed Dec. 1, 1668, when more than seventy years of age, and died March 11, 1670, ae. 72. He was a very ardent friend of education. It was his strong desire that a college should be founded at New Haven. He corresponded with Gov. Hopkins concerning it, had hopes of aid from him concerning it, which failed of fruition by reason of the death of Gov. Hopkins, and he was the close, constant, confidential friend of the Governor, and of course earnest and hearty in the desire and purpose to carry out his plans as expressed in his will. (Barnard, Journal of Education, III, 280, 285.)

As has been noted, one of the trustees under the will of Gov. Hopkins was *William Goodwin*. Since through him chiefly any portion of this legacy found its way to Hadley, more extended notice of him will be in place in this history.

It is thought that he was probably an Oxford graduate admitted B. A. 1622—23. He sailed from London in the ship Lyon, Wm. Pierce master, June 22nd, and arrived in Boston Sept. 16, 1632. He is soon settled at Newtown (Cambridge), where from the first he was prominent in civil and in church affairs, as he was later at Hartford and Hadley. He was a man of character, of large means and great influence. Gov. Winthrop speaks of him as " a very reverend and godly man," but records the censure received by him in one instance in open court, for some " unreverend speech " to one of the assistants, as also Goodwin's humble acknowledgement of his fault.

He was made freeman in Massachusetts Nov. 6, 1632, and in May, 1634, deputy from Cambridge to the General Court. He was chosen ruling elder of the Newtown church as early as 1633.

As ruling elder he and some other laymen, (among them probably, Dea. Andrew Warner) laid hands in ordination on Mr. Hooker, pastor, and Mr. Stone, teacher in that church. He was one of the foremost in furthering the removal from Newtown to Hartford. When land was to be bought in Hartford in 1636 by the emigrants from Newtown, the agents in the negotiation were Mr. Stone, teacher, and Mr. Goodwin, ruling elder of the Hartford church. In the office of ruling elder he was next in dignity to the pastor and teacher. He was moderator of church meetings. It pertained to the office to propose the admission and dismission of members, prepare all matters of business in the church, to keep watch of the private conduct of church members, to bring incorrigible offenders before the whole body for hearing and judgment, to pronounce censure when determined, to call the church together and dismiss its meetings with the benediction, to visit the sick, to ordain persons elected by the church to any office therein, to preach in the absence of the pastor and teacher. Thus in one instance he "exercised," as the conduct of public religious service was called, for two months continuously in the absence of pastor and teacher at a synod in Boston in 1637.

Mr. Goodwin lived in close and happy intimacy with his pastor, Mr. Hooker, until his death, July 7, 1647. To Mr. Goodwin and Gov. Hopkins Mr. Hooker in his last will committed the care of his property and the custody of his children.

He lived in happy relation with Mr. Stone and his brethren in the church until about six years after the death of Mr. Hooker.

Then came a time extending from 1653 to 1659 of sore and bitter quarrel in the Hartford church, which drew the attention of all the New England churches, and fills large space in the early ecclesiastical history of this colony.

It has been taken for granted that the question at issue in this strife was one of baptism and the rights of the children of baptized church members. Of late this view is called in question. It is now thought that the large element in the controversy was personal. It was a struggle concerning the rights of the minority of the church, "the withdrawers", and the majority led by Mr. Stone, a man of strong individuality, disposed to magnify his office, as in his turn was Mr. Goodwin likewise.

The convictions of the two parties concerning each other's rights and prerogatives were strongly opposed. Mr. Goodwin's feeling was strong that the rights of the brotherhood were disregarded.

It is generally agreed that this church difficulty began in antagonism between Teaching Elder Stone and Ruling Elder Goodwin, both men of strong character, firm conviction, unbending will, staunch and steadfast in maintaining truth and right as they saw them.

This difference, it is thought, is very much one concerning a pulpit candidate. On one occasion Mr. Stone hindered a vote of the church concerning the fitness of Mr. Wigglesworth for office in the place of Mr. Hooker.

There were stormy church meetings one after another, in which Mr. Goodwin charged that the act of the teacher infringed the prerogatives of others.

The majority was with the teacher and acquitted him, but the charge, though rejected by the church after debate in two meetings, was again preferred in a formal paper by Mr. Cullick, to which the church sent a reply which is lost.

These two men were much heated. But Mr. Goodwin felt most keenly his practical deposition from the office of ruling Elder in the church and its official headship, by the choice of a moderator. This was done by the advice of Mr. Stone, who had resigned his office. Mr. Goodwin was a man " fond to rule ", for whom it was not easy to accept graciously the loss of such a position.

The minority apparently withdrew from the communion of the church, refused to recognize Mr. Stone as an officer of the church, and asked for a council to consider the whole case.

After hindrance and delay such a council was held June 11, 1656, resulting in the substantial vindication of the minority as against the arbitrary course of Mr. Stone and the church. They did not accept the decision. Mr. Stone went to Boston to consult the elders there, five of whom wrote to the withdrawers, deploring their differences, and offering their offices of help toward a settlement.

A Council of nine churches and seventeen members held at Boston Sept. 26, 1659, in its result reproves both parties, expresses the hope that mutual satisfaction may be given, that there be a return of the dissenters into communion with the church of Hartford as formerly. But if any still desire to remove, the council's advice and determination is, that the church forthwith give their dismission "and that such as have joyned themselves to another church doe solemnly renew their covenant." The council ends with a pathetic exhortation to love and unity, and not to turn again to folly.

This result was graciously received by the representatives of both parties, of which they gave proof before they left Boston for home. Most of the withdrawers, led by Mr. Goodwin and John Webster, soon removed to Hadley, (had already virtually done so). and the great quarrel in the Hartford church was over.

"On the whole respecting this controversy the impartial verdict of history must be that in spite of many irregularities and doubtless a good deal of temper on both sides, the general weight of right and justice was with the defeated and emigrating minority.". (Walker's History, First ch. Hartford, pp. 146—175.)

We know this man by the goodly company in which we find him. Mr. Goodwin was of like mind with Theophilus Eaton, John Davenport and John Cullick. They were one in spirit, in principle, thought, aim and purpose. They walked together because they were agreed.

Gov. Hopkins chose Mr. Goodwin as one of the trustees of his estate for he knew him and believed in him. He had been with him in the conduct of affairs with the Indians. He was fellow member with him in the church in Hartford. Gov. Hopkins was a man of peace, and yet it is thought that he was in sympathy with the minority in the Hartford church. The trouble had begun, as he was leaving the country, and he was aware of its progress as it went on, and with this knowledge chose Mr. Goodwin as one to exercise this trust.

Mr. Davenport of New Haven likewise was in sympathy with the minority withdrawing, among whom Mr. Goodwin was a leader. He opposed their course in propounding themselves for admission to the Wethersfield church. Papers drawn up and signed by Rev. John Higginson of Guilford in answer to inquiries of the Weathersfield church concerning the propriety of admitting the withdrawers to their fellowship, served greatly to strengthen and encourage them in their course. (Walker, p. 166.)

The troubles in the Hartford church had this outcome. Mr. Goodwin and those with him, deeming that in no other way they could gain their hearts' desire, first meditated removal, planned it, carried out their plans. These withdrawers from the Hartford church, with others of like mind in the churches of Weathersfield and Windsor, were the first white settlers of Hadley, with whose coming hither the church of Christ in Hadley as such began its life.

On this wise was the coming of Mr. Goodwin to Hadley, who was among the first to come, and in it is found the answer to the question, how any part of the Hopkins legacy found its way hither, since Edward Hopkins himself had been dead more than two years, when the "engagers" held their meeting in Hartford in April, 1659, and knew little, it is likely, of this region as the probable site of an emigrating colony from Hartford. In considering the disposition of the estate, there will be occasion to take further notice of Mr. Goodwin and his part in these transactions.

CHAPTER III.

THE DISPOSAL OF GOV. HOPKINS' ESTATE.

The trustees were delayed in the execution of their trust six years. The General Court of Connecticut was in sympathy with the majority in the Hartford church and with the town as well. Hence the Court sequestered the estate and directed the payment of all rents and debts not to the trustees, but to the Selectmen of the several towns where the property was situated, who were also held accountable to the General Court. This fund must be kept in Hartford. Such was the feeling, desire, purpose, study. Mr. Goodwin's removal with a colony to Hadley meant the loss of the fund to Hartford. Aug. 23, 1658 the Court " ordered and required that the several towns where any part of the estate of either Edward Hopkins Esq. or George Fenwick Esq. be known to remain shall speedily take inventory of said estate and present it under the hands of those who order the prudentials of the town to the Court in October next." (Conn. Col. records.) This was not done for the aid or at the request of the trustees, for they were "hindered" by it. They had already an inventory of the estate. Mr. Hopkins says in his will, that he had left a clear list of it with Capt. Cullick. (Bacon, Appendix 48.) (Barnard.)

This order was neglected as would appear from a vote of June 15, 1659 " that whatever person or persons in this Colony have, in their present possession or improvement, any estate that either is, or has been reputed the estate of Geo. Fenwick or Edward Hopkins Esq. that they secure and preserve the said estate in their own hands, or the value thereof, (casualties accepted) to be accountable to this court, when required thereunto, until the wills and inventories of said gentlemen be exhibited into this court and right owners to the estate appear and administration be granted according to law." The effect of this vote, says Bacon, would naturally be what Mr. Davenport complains it was, to make those indebted to the estate refuse to pay their debts to the trustees and to lock up the whole estate for safe keeping until a satisfactory share of it was allotted to Hartford.

Oct. 6, 1659 "The last will of Edward Hopkins Esq. being exhibited into this court it is thought meet by this court that the former restraint laid upon the estate should be taken off and that the debts due the estate should be required and gathered in to prevent damage to the estate." This order, says Barnard, probably originated in the fact that owing to a council held at Hartford in June, 1659, to compose the difficulties in the church in Hartford, Elder Goodwin and his friends temporarily gave up the design of removing to Hadley, but resuming their intentions to leave, the sequestration was renewed by the following order of the General Court. "Feb. 23, 1659—60. Whereas there hath been a repealing of the former restraint laid upon the estate of Edward Hopkins Esq. that debts due the estate might be taken in. Upon further consideration, this court orders that the estates aforesaid be secured within *this colony*, until the said estate be inventoried and the inventory be presented, and administration granted by this court."

By an order passed May 17, 1660, it appears that an inventory of the estate had not been presented, whereupon individuals holding the estate and the selectmen of the several towns were required to make presentment thereof at the next court on penalty of £5 for each neglect. By a subsequent order dated June 8, 1661, the treasurer was required to take the custody or the rents of portions of the estate occupied by John Cole and William Hills. In pursuance of this order (May 17) Joseph Mygatt, John Allen, James Steele and William Kelsey, "Townsmen of the town of Hartford," presented to the General Court, June 18, 1660, a month after the order was passed, an inventory of the Hopkins Estate, amounting to £1382—03—06, "Besides the *negar*." On the back of this inventory is the following endorsement:

"Hartford, June 16, 1660. Concerning Mr. Hopkins estate we underwritten having presented the order of court to Dea. Stebbing and Lieut. Bull desiring their return; they answered as followeth: that the inventory on this paper, was a true inventory, as far as they knew, only his farm at Farmington and some trifles excepted, come to hand since, and they do engage to preserve the said estate and make return of it to the court at any time it is demanded, until the will and inventory of Mr. Hopkins be proved in the Court at Hartford."

In this inventory "His housing and land in Hartford and Weathersfield" are set down at £629, which deducting £84 for Weathersfield, leaves £545 for the value of his real estate in Hartford.

On the 3d of October, 1661 "'The will and testament of Edward Hopkins Esq. being presented to this court legally attested, is accepted as authentic. This court do likewise order and impower Edward Stebbing and Lt. Thomas Bull, to take the management of the estate of Mr. Hopkins deceased into their hands and the gathering in the debts due to the estate, and to be accountable to the court for the same, when called thereunto." *

Dea. Stebbing and Lieut. Bull had the charge of the estate of Gov. Hopkins' estate in Connecticut, not only by appointment of the General Court but by a prior appointment of the Trustees in 1659, under authority given by Henry Dalley, sole executor of the will.

"Upon a proposition from Mr. Goodwin, in reference to *the legacy belonging to* THIS COLONY by the last will of Mr. Hopkins, and whereas there was by a writing a tender of £350 to this colony out of that estate: this court doth declare that they do not reject the tender. And further, this court doth appoint Major Mason, Mr. Matthew Allyn, Mr. Wyllys and Capt. John Talcott, as a committee to treat with the trustees of Mr. Hopkins's estate about foresaid legacy, and what the major part of those that meet do conclude, shall stand as the issue of that business and the secretary is to write a letter to the Trustees to appoint time and place of meeting."

This committee corresponded with Mr. Goodwin, desiring the Trustees to appoint a time and place to meet with this committee, "to put a final issue to the business respecting the legacy." But Mr. Goodwin under date Feb. 24, 1661 wrote that the committee have ordered £350 to be allowed on conditions named,—a characteristic letter herewith given entire.

Letter from Mr. Goodwin to the Honored Court that is to be held in Hartford in March next following the date hereof.

MUCH HONORED.

We received writings from you signed by the secretary, wherein you desired the Trustees to appoint a time and place to meet with a committee which you have chosen to treat with them and to put a final issue to the business respecting the legacy. I am desired in the name of all the Trustees to inform the Court that we cannot entertain that motion, both for that we are not able to undertake such travel, nor do we see any use at all of it (if we were able) for we have ordered three hundred and fifty pounds set out of Mr. Hopkins' estate committed to our trust to be allowed to Hartford upon these conditions and terms following. (1) That it be by them improved according to the mind of the donor expressed in his will. (2) That this court do also engage to remove all obstructions out of our way that we may not be disturbed nor any way hindered from, by, or under them, in the management of the rest of that estate, according to our trust, that so love and peace may be established between us. (3). That you will deliver us back the attested copy of the will sent us from England or else a true copy of it under the seal of the colony.

Now if it please the honored Court or their Committee to accept of this tender of £350 as is aforesaid, and shall deliver unto us, or to our attornies an instrument drawn up in writing and sealed with the seal of the Colony wherein all the conditions of the tender aforesaid shall be fully and plainly expressed and confirmed by the Court as aforesaid before the last of **March** next ensuing the date hereof, that then this grant of £350 to Hartford as abovesaid shall be settled upon them, to be improved by them according as is expressed in the will of the donor. But if the Court do not plainly declare their acceptance according as is above expressed, then we hereby declare our grant to them here inserted to be a nullity and void; and thus I humbly take leave of you, subscribing myself, Your worships in all due observance,

WILLIAM GOODWIN,
In the name of the rest of the Trustees.

Hadley, February, 24th, 1661.

It could have been no easy matter for these Trustees to meet and confer with the committee in Hartford as requested, since Mr. Goodwin must make the journey from Hadley, Mr. Davenport from New Haven and Capt. Cullick from Boston.

From a writing presented to the General Court at New Haven by Mr. Davenport resigning the donation of Governor Hopkins to their care, dated the fourth day of the fourth Moneth, 1660, it appears that the three Trustees and legatees then surviving, viz.: himself, Capt. Cullick and Mr. Goodwin, " met together to consider what course they should take for the discharge of their trust, and agreed that each of them should have an inventory of the aforesaid testatour's estate in New England, in houses and goods and lands, which were prized by some in Hartford, intrusted by Capt. Cullick and Mr. Goodwin, and in debts, for the gathering in whereof some attorneys were constituted, impowered and employed by the three surviving trustees, as the writing in the magistrate's hands will show.

Afterward, at another meeting of the said Trustees, they considering that

" by the will of the dead, they are joyned in one common trust, agreed to act wth mutual consent in performance thereof, and considering y^t by the will of the testator two of Newhaven were joyned with two of Hartford, and y^t Mr. Hopkins had declared his purpose to further the Colledge at Newhaven, they agreed that one half of that estate wch should be gathered in, should be paid vnto Mr. Davenport for Newhaven, the other half to Captain Cullick and Mr. Goodwin to be improved for the vses and ends forenoted, where they should have power to perform their trust, wch because they could not expect to have at Hartford they concluded it would be best done by them in that new plantation vnto wch sundry of Hartford were to remove and even now gone. yet they agreed that out of the whole an 100^{li} should be given to the Colledge at Cambridg in the Bay, the estate being 1000^{li}, as Captain Cullick believed it would be, wch we now see cause to doubt, by reason of the sequestrations laid upon that estate and still continued by the General Court at Hartford, wherevpon some refuse to pay their debts and then forsake the purchases they had made, to their great hinderance of performing the will of the deceased according to the trust committed to them, and to the endamagement of the estate."

The following letters, written near the same date, having reference to the same matter may best interpret themselves.

1660, 20 d. of the 2^d m. in the closing paragraphs of a letter to Gov. Winthrop, Mr. Davenport wrote as follows: "The course that the General Court take about Mr. Hopkins, his legacie, seems to me very strange, viz.: that they would know what portion of it they shall have and yet keep his trustees from receiving what belongs to that estate by sequestracions one after another whereby the estate will suffer no small loss, some being ready to deliver up what they had purchased, because they will not have a litigious title, and one hath waved his bargains upon that account. Others who were ready to have paid what they owe to the estate now refuse to paye, pretending the Courts order, whereby when the sequestration shall be taken off, there is danger that through loss of the season when they were prepared to paye, there will be loss of the payment itself the debtours pleading their disabilitie now. And the pretence whereupon the sequestracion is the 2^d time laid on is that the inventory is not given in, whereas some of the Court it seems knew that it was left with our Attorneys in Hartford by Capt. Cullick with a trust to be by them presented to the Court which they also acknowledge and take the blame to themselves. But I do not love contentions. We have agreed in the answer which I send enclosed, Yours ever obliged, &c.

JOHN DAVENPORT."

The following was enclosed in the foregoing:

"HONORED SIR:

Captain Cullick and Mr. Goodwin have been with me, by whom I understand that some were appointed both from the General Court and from the Towne of Hartford to know what portion of Mr. Hopkins, his Estate (with the disposal thereof for the ends specified in his will we are entrusted) shall be allowed unto the said Colonie or Towne.

Our joynt answer thereto is, that the General Court be pleased to declare

1. That they accept of that copie of Mr. Hopkins his will which is delivered unto the Court already, as authentical and sufficient for the end whereunto it is produced.

2. That the said Court acknowledges us three to be invested with power by virtue of said will to dispose of the estates bequeathed unto us according to the mind and intent of the Testator to our best understanding.

3. That all the sequestracions, encumbrances and disturbances whatsoever from the General Court be so taken off, that we may prosecute and settle the business that concerns our trust without impediment or interruption. These things being done to our satisfaction we shall seriously consider what answer we may give to the praemised question according to God and the trust committed to us.

In witness thereof we subscribe our names at Newhaven the 19th day of the 2^d month in the year 1660.

JOHN DAVENPORT,
JOHN CULLICK,
WILL. GOODWIN.

Indorsed by Gov. Winthrop, Mr. D., Capt. C. and Mr. G. about the Hopkins legacie." (Mass. Hist. Coll. IV. Series, vol. VII. pp. 513, 514.)

"TO THE HONORED COURT AT HARTFORD.
Much Honored.

Yours of Nov. 16, 1663, I received and not to trouble you with my answer under your second motions to induce us to be of your minds my final return to all is this. That as I have no cause, so I do in no sort consent to that which you were pleased to move me unto but do desire that you yourselves would return the estate unto us, who only have the right to dispose thereof with due satisfaction for all damage that shall appear to be done unto it since it hath been taken out of our hands, which being timely performed, I doubt not but the three hundred and fifty pounds tendered unto you in February 1661 may yet be settled upon Hartford, on such like conditions as be therein expressed tending to the securing of the estate from any further obstructions by your means, and ordering of the improvement of it according to the donor's end expressed in his will, as our duty bindeth us to do.

Now hereunto I do humbly desire the Honored Court speedily and plainly to declare themselves to me (or our attorney) whether they do now accept of this tendery or not without any further agitations about the disposing of it, which it hath already been a great wrong to the estate and the donor thereof, as also to us the Trustees and the whole country besides, the which if you shall decline to do betwixt this and the end of March next ensuing the date hereof, this tendry also is to be judged a nullity and we shall forthwith endeavor the freeing of the estate elsewhere* as the great betrustment committed to us in all respects considered, in duty bindeth us to do thus. Hoping and heartily wishing that you would accept of my motion though I cannot accept yours I rest Yours to love and serve as I may,

WILLIAM GOODWIN.

Hadley, Feb. 1, 1663."

(Bacon's Address, appendix 6.50).

Another letter of the same date as the foregoing is herewith given.
"TO THE MUCH HONORED GOV. MR. WINTHROP AT HIS HOUSE IN HARTFORD,
PRESENT THESE:
MR. GOODWIN TO JOHN WINTHROP.

Honored Sir.—I received a writing from the honored Court at Hartford wherein they are pleased to move me to such a disposal of

---

* NOTE. The English Court of Chancery is probably intended.

Mr. Hopkins trust committed to us the Trustees, as we cannot consent vnto, I have sent by the same hand which bringeth this unto your worship my answer therevnto; and the which I do desire may be a fynale issue of these agitations between vs and the Honored Court which have been very prejudicial to that pious act of the worthy donor as also to vs the Trustees and almost all the country besides, by thus long and without cause detaining the estate from vs who only have right to dispose thereof and thereby hindering the vseful improvement of the same for the glory of God and the good of His people.

They are pleased to speak much of vnity, peace, love and friendship between yourselves and us. I conceive that this which I do now offer to the Court is a nearer way to attain to that than that which is propounded by them to me and also be for the prevention of further trouble which is not like to be avoided, for we ought not in duty to the estate and the worthy donor thereof, but forthwith vse our utmost endeavor to free the same, that it may be vnder the improvement the worthy donor bequeathed it vnto.

Thus, Worthy Sir I commit you and all my good friends with you to the holy guidance and blessing of heaven and rest yours most willing to live the little remainder of my few days in love and peace with you all.

WILL. GOODWIN.

HADLEY, Feb. 1, '63.
Endorsed by John Winthrop jun.
Mr. Goodwin Rec'd Feb. 9, 1663."

(Mass. Hist. Coll. Vol. VIII, 4th Series, pp. 50, 51.)

During the year 1663, when Gov. Winthrop was in England, Mr. Dalley, the executor of Gov. Hopkins' will, "dealt with him" for the restraint put upon the estate, and the Governor promised that on his return it should be set at liberty. Mr. Winthrop came over in 1663, and Oct. 8th of that year, the Court appointed the Governor (Winthrop), Mr. Matthew Allyn, Mr. Wyllys and Capt. Talcott, or any three of them, to consider what is next to be attended in reference to Mr. Hopkins and his estate, by him bequeathed for to be improved for the promotion of learning and to make report of their thoughts at the next Court.

Their thoughts found expression in the record of the Court 1663-4, March 10th. "This Court, upon good advice, do see cause to take off the sequestration formerly laid upon the estate of Edward Hopkins, Esq., which for several good reasons was laid under restraint, partly because an authentic copy of the will of the said Edward Hopkins did not appear for the orderly discharge thereof, and partly because an attested inventory of the will of the said estate hath not as yet been exhibited into this Court, yet it now being hopeless because of the decease of Capt. John Cullick to obtain such inventory, This Court doth order as before mentioned."

The subject is not again introduced in the records of the General Court, but in the records of the Government Council, under date Jan. 13, 1664-5, we find the following order: "This Council doth hereby declare that the estate of our honored friend, Edward Hopkins, Esq., shall not be molested by sequestering in behalf of the country."

April 28, 1664, Mr. Davenport tendered Gov. Hopkins' donation to the town of New Haven in a paper reciting the difficulty and embarrassment of the Trustees by reason of the restraint laid upon the estate. Now Mr. Winthrop has returned from England and his promise made to Mr. Dally has just now been made good, and at length the estate is free. "He further stated that though the estate was something damnified, yet it is thought that when all is paid there will be a thousand pounds in the whole, of which Hartford had gained four hundred for a school—now the rest was in their trust and he had writ to Mr. Goodwin about it and he thought it was meet New Haven should have more than Hadley and *so Mr. Goodwin agreed* to pay the one hundred pounds out of his part to the college in the Bay which they had purposed before to give it." (Bacon's Discourse, Appendix, p. 53.)

In this partition Hartford receives a sum larger than had been named in the former tendry, sharing equally with New Haven, and by Mr. Goodwin's own suggestion, the hundred pounds paid to Harvard College should be taken from Hadley's share.

THE FINAL SETTLEMENT OF THE ESTATE.

The estate after such long and annoying delay is set free. The two surviving Trustees, Davenport and Goodwin, proceed to divide it among the three towns, New Haven, Hartford and Hadley. But for the troubles in Hartford *church* the fund would have been shared equally by New Haven and Hartford. This distribution was made in writing and is preserved in two papers, the same in substance, though some particulars found in one are wanting in the other.

One of these papers* is found in the Records of the Hopkins Grammar School in New Haven, entitled:

The Agreement Between Mr. Davenport and Mr. Goodwin about Disposing Mr. Hopkins his Estate.

The closing paragraph is this: "Hereunto, as to our last order, dispose and determination touching the said estate, we have set our hands and seals

---
*Copies of both papers are in the Judd collection with J. H. Trumbull, Esq.

in several instruments before witnesses, the far distances of our habitations and our unfitness for such a journey denying us opportunity of a joint action otherwise than by writing. Therefore with mutual consent we thus declare our agreement. I the said Wm. Goodwin do sign and seal this instrument as my true agreement for Mr. John Davenport of New Haven.

WM. GOODWIN. [Seal]

The 13th day of the 4th Month, 1664.
Signed and sealed in the presence of us   HENRY CLARK,
WM. WESTWOOD.

On the records of the Trustees of Hopkins Academy is found the following paper, differing as already noted from the foregoing, copied from the manuscript among the papers of the late Sylvester Judd in the keeping of J. R. Trumbull, Esq.

Messrs. Davenport and Goodwin's Agreement, April 30, 1664.

"Be it known unto all men, that whereas the worshipful Edward Hopkins Esq. a faithful servant of the Lord, and our honored friend, hath by his last will and testament (which is proved according to law in England, and demonstration thereof made to the General Court at Hartford in New England) given and bequeathed all his estate in New England, his debts and legacies there being first paid out of the same; *together with £500 that are to come from Old England after the decease of Mrs. Hopkins;* unto Theophilus Eaton Esq. John Davenport Sen'. Pastor of the Church of Christ in New Haven, Capt. John Cullick and Mr. Wm. Goodwin sometime of Hartford, since of Boston and Hadley in the Colony of the Massachusetts in New England; confiding in their faithfulness for their improvement of the same towards the education of youth in good literature for the service of Christ in these foreign parts. We therefore the said John Davenport and William Goodwin (being the only survivors of the said Trustees) for answering the trust committed to us by the last will and testament of our worthy honored friend, do order and dispose of the said estate as follows viz.

The debts and legacie being paid, we do give to the town of Hartford the sum of 400£ of which Hills his farm shall be a part, at the price at which it was sold by us, and payment ready to be delivered if there had been no interruption, the rest of the 400£ in such debts or goods as we or our agents see meet, provided that this gift be improved according to the true intent of the donor (viz for or towards the erecting and promoting of a grammar school at Hartford. Provided also that the General Court at Connecticut do grant and give to us the said Trustees a writing legally confirmed so that neither themselves will, nor any by from, or under them shall disturb or hinder us in our dispose, or executing our dispose of the rest of the estate, which being done this gift is in all respects valid. We do also desire and request that the school house may be set upon the house lot which was lately in the occupation of Jeremy Adams, where our worthy friend did much desire that a school might be set. Further our desire is, that the management of the said estate at Hartford may be in the hands of Dea. Edward Stebbing, Lt. Thomas Bull and their assigns.

We do further order and appoint that the rest of Mr. Hopkins his estate, *both that which is in New England and the 500£ which is to come from Old England when it shall become due to us, after Mrs. Hopkins her decease* be all of it equally divided between the towns of Newhaven and Hadley, to be in each of those towns respectively managed and improved towards the erecting and maintaining of a *Grammar* School in each of them. And the management thereof to be in the hands of our assigns, which are for that at New Haven for the present and so to continue (except some other way may be by us agreed on) the Town Court of New Haven, consisting of magistrates and deputies, and the officers of the church at Newhaven. And for that at Hadley John Russell Jun. Pastor of the church of Christ at Hadley, Lt. Samuel Smith, Andrew Bacon and Peter Tilton. These we the said John Davenport and William Goodwin do appoint, and constitute to be our Trustees, for ordering the said estate and carrying on the work, wherein it is to be employed each in their several towns respectively.

Hereby committing to them and investing them with full power to act in the same in their several towns respectively; in all respects as ourselves, both in managing this trust themselves and in choosing successors from time to time, as they shall see meet, who, or the major part of whom, or (in case at any time the Rest of the Trustees be taken away before others be chosen) any of whom may and shall have full power to perfect and put in execution the pious end and intendment of the worthy donor, yet reserving to ourselves while we live, the full power of a negative vote for the hindering of anything that may cross that end. Only provided that one hundred pounds shall be given and paid to Harvard College out of that half of the estate which Hadley hath*, which also is to be ordered as we or our assigns shall judge most conducible to the end intended by the donor.

Hereunto as to our last order, dispose and determination we have set our hands and seals.

Signed and sealed by William Goodwin at Hadley April 30th 1664 in presence of Henry Clark and Nathaniel Dickinson Senr And at New Haven by the Rev. John Davenport Sen, 8th 3d, 1664 in presence of William Jones and John Davenport Jun.

WILLIAM GOODWIN and Seal.

JOHN DAVENPORT Senr and Seal.

This is a true copy of the Instrument made by Mr. Davenport and Mr. Goodwin for the disposition of Mr. Hopkins his estate committed to them.

HENRY CLARK,
Constable and Commissioner.
Sept. 23 1672.

*NOTE.—It was at the suggestion of Mr. Goodwin that the one hundred pounds to be paid to Harvard College should come from Hadley's part in the division. It is worthy of note, likewise, that £400 were assigned to Hartford, while it was not yet sure that the value of the estate would reach £1200. Is not this spirit magnanimous?

CHAPTER IV.

THE FUND AT HADLEY.

To the part of the fund (arising from the Hopkins legacy, as before related) assigned to Hadley, additions were made from time to time by several individual donors, and by the Town of Hadley. One of these, *John Barnard*, removed from Cambridge to Hartford, was one of the first settlers of Hadley, where he was buried May 23, 1664. He must have been acquainted with Gov. Hopkins and Mr. Goodwin. He had been with them in the church at Hartford. Moved by a common impulse he and Mr. Goodwin had come hither to lay foundations for many generations.

In his will, bearing date May 21, 1664, shortly after the foregoing agreement of Mr. Goodwin and Mr. Davenport, occur the words that follow, as copied in the records of Hopkins Academy, from the original in the Probate office at Northampton.

JOHN BARNARD'S BEQUEST, MAY 21, 1664.

John Barnard hath bequeathed and given in his last Will and Testament unto the Town of Hadley in Hampshire, for promoting and advancement of a school for learning, twelve acres, one rood and nine pole of meadow land, perpetually to be and remain to the use aforesaid, lying within the bounds of the township of Hadley.

Six acres, two roods and twenty-nine poles lying in the meadow called Hockanum, bounded by Mr. Wm Goodwins land, north east, Francis Barnards land, south west, abutting on the river, north west and the swamp south east. Another parcel in the meadow, called the great meadow, containing five acres, two roods and twenty poles; bounded by the land of Phillip Smith east and William Partridge west, abutting on the highway north, and the adjoining furlong south.

By the same supposed to be in a codicil May 21, 1664.

John Barnard, I do give (viz.) to the use and toward the maintenance of a school, I give perpetually my piece of land lying in the Forlorn; as also my piece of land that lies in Hockanum, and also that land I have given to a school if there be not a school in Hadley at the decease of my wife, then the land to be improved by four of the poorest men in town till there be a school set up.

Another donor was Nathaniel Ward, an early settler of Hartford, a gentleman of good standing, in the colony of Connecticut. He was among the first that came to Hadley, where he was made freeman March 26, 1661. He was buried June 1, 1664. He is called Goodman Ward. At his house in Hartford "the engagers" met, April 18, 1659, and engaged themselves under their own hands, or by their deputies whom they had chosen, to remove themselves and their families out of the jurisdiction of Connecticut into the jurisdiction of Massachusetts. He died childless. His will is dated May 27, 1664, just after the Hopkins estate was set at liberty. He gave a piece of his home lot, on the street, with his house, for the use of the school. A part of this building was used for many years as a school house. From a vote of the town March 30, 1709-10, it appears that an appendage to this house, an outhouse is "ready to fall down." The spot is the site of the present residence of Mr. L. S. Crosier.

This gift was made near the time of the agreement of Davenport and Goodwin, before any school was established in Hadley, and yet it is by no means improbable that such a prospect was in his mind.

The extract from his will conveying this gift is herewith given:

MR. WARD'S GIFT, MAY 27, 1664.

"Nathaniel Ward. Item to the town of Hadley I give after the decease of my wife, my now dwelling house with about five roods or an acre and a half of land on which it standeth, and my lot of five acres more or less in the north meadow and my lot in Hockanum containing nine acres more or less, to be improved toward maintaining a school ever. Provided that whereas I have taken up twelve or thirteen pounds of the estate of Mr. Hopkins if any of that be by me to be repaid it shall be out of the estate given by me to the town."

Another benefactor of the school was *Mr. Henry Clark*, Windsor 1640, representative 1641-1650, Assistant 1650-1651, a first settler of Hadley, a wealthy and distinguished man. He was one of the commissioners for holding the courts at Springfield and Northampton, (Associates as they were called after 1669) from 1663-1676. He died s. p. Dec. 23, 1675.

There is reason to think that he was intimately acquainted with Wm. Goodwin, shared his confidence and his views in matters of education, especially as related to Hopkins school, which at the time of his death had begun its work and which it was in his mind to promote by this bequest.

April 30th, 1664, he witnessed the paper signed by Davenport and Goodwin, directing the disposition of the legacy of Governor Hopkins, dividing it between Hartford, New Haven and Hadley.

Here is given out of strict chronological order Henry Clark's donation, Dec. 15, 1675, more than ten years later than the two other gifts already mentioned, and after the Hopkins school began its work.

"I do give my nine acre lot in Hockanum in the town of Hadley and two acres and a half of my lot in the lower end of the great meadow, in Hadley, on the nether side of the lot, I give to the town of Hadley, committing it to the care, disposing and ordering of Lieut. Samuel Smith, Ensign Cook, Dea. Tilton, and Mr. John Russell, Jr., to be by them disposed of, (in case they quietly keep and remain in their committeeship for Hopkins school) unto Hopkins School for Hadley. But if they be put out of, or disturbed in that committeeship—then to be otherwise disposed of, as they or the survivors of them, see meet for the good of the town." (Record of Hopkins Academy.)

It is worthy of record that John Barnard, Nathaniel Ward and Henry Clark, who left something from their estates (about forty acres of land in all) for a school, was each of them without children, like Gov. Hopkins himself, whom they had known and whose spirit they seem to have caught. They made the children of others, in long succession, their heirs, thus furnishing a worthy example, which since their time none have been found to copy in the matter of gifts to this school. Is it too much to hope that some such may yet appear after so long a time?*

The town of Hadley made grants of land from time to time to and for the use of a Grammar school—as appears from votes in the town records as given herewith.

JANUARY 14, 1666.

"The town have granted to and for the use of a Grammar Scoole in this town of Hadley and to be and remain perpetuallie to and for the use of said Scoole the two little meddowes next beyond the Brooke commonlie called the mill Brooke and as much upland to be laid to the same as the comittee chosen by the town shall in their discretion see meete and needful provided withall it be left to the Judgment of the said Committee that so much of the 2nd meddow shall be excepted from said grant as that there may be a ffezable and convenient passage for cattel to their ffeede."

The committee, chosen for the occasion aforesaid, are Mr. Clark, Lieut. Smith, William Allis, Nathaniel Dickinson and Andrew Warner. This meadow tract contained sixty acres, more or less, with considerable upland, bounded north and west by the great river, and by the fence south and east.

---

*Dea. Geo. Dickinson who died Aug. 10, 1889, left in his will $200 to the Trustees of Hopkins Academy in trust for the benefit of the young men's Library Association, and in case that Association should cease to exist, to be employed for the benefit of Hopkins Academy and library.

Marginal note by Peter Tilton. These meadows are the round neck of land and the little long meadow that was reserved by the Indians in the first sale and afterwards purchased by itself.

(Original Town Record, p. 40.)

THE TOWN OF HADLEY'S GRANT, OCT. 16, 1671.

"The town have granted a piece of land near the corn mill for the erecting and setting a dwelling house upon the same (for the use of a miller) with this proviso that whatever land or estate, with the said house and mill, &c. that hath been given by the Town of Hadley or by any other, for the maintaining of a Grammar Scoole there be ordered, managed and disposed by the present school committee in being and after them by their successors whom they shall chuse, provided they be still pious discreete ffaithful men, otherwise the said grant to be void and Invalid to the ends and purposes aforesaid." See Town Record.

A true copy compared with the original this present 8th of Oct. by us.

JOHN RUSSELL, AARON COOKE.

The above preserved in the Record of Hopkins Academy.

June 3, 1678, the town voted and granted a parcel of ground adjoining to the mill perpetually as a house lot for the miller, not exceeding four acres, to be laid out by the committee appointed for the purpose.

Gifts for the School which became its Fund were seven in number, and all made during the fourteen years, from 1664 to 1678. They were these:

1. By Davenport and Goodwin from the Hopkins estate in 1664.
2. By John Barnard in 1664.
3. By Nathaniel Ward in 1664.
4. By the Town in 1666.
5. By the Town in 1671.
6. By Mr. Clarke in 1675.
7. By the Town in 1678.

All these gifts were made within twenty years after the settlement of the Town. In the order of time they followed the lead of the Hopkins donation and seem both in intention and in fact to have constituted one fund and under one management, though somewhat vaguely and loosely defined.

TOWN VOTE, MARCH 14, 1666-7.

"The town have voted Mr. Clark, Lieut. Smith, Nathaniel Dickinson, Andrew Warner and William Allis a committee for and in behalf of the town to order, dispose, set and lett according to their best judgment and discretion the parcels of land lying about the mill brook, granted and given to and for the use of a Grammar scoole in this town of Hadley and for the advantage of the same."

At this time the school had begun its course, under the direction of Mr. Goodwin with such counsel as he was inclined to receive from the others named in the agreement, to act with him. It is likely that he had in his mind his own retirement from such direction and control and his removal from town, and wishing to see the school and its affairs settled on a secure and durable footing, he made the following proposal to the town:

MR. GOODWIN'S PROPOSAL TO THE TOWN, MARCH 20, 1668-9.

"Mr. Goodwin proposes as that wherein he is willing to concur (viz) that as to the ordering of that estate, distributed and given by Mr. Davenport and himself (as trustees to Mr. Hopkins) to the town of Hadley, donour of the said estate both for the present and the ffuture; he the said Mr. William Goodwin hath chosen three persons (or will chuse them) to have power in the premises. He is willing allsoe that the town should give their aprobation of the said persons. As allsoe that the town shall make choice of two more able and pious men which ffive persons together with himself shall have the sole and ffull dispose and management of the estate above expressed, in all respects for the end to which it is bequeathed.

2nd. As allsoe the said five persons together with himself while he liveth shall have the *sole dispose and management of all other estate and estates given by any donor or that may be whilest they survive* to this town of Hadley for the promotion of literature or learning.

3rd. Those ffive persons to continue, abide and remaine in the work above expressed till death, or other Providence of God remove any of them and the surviving to chuse to themselves the full number aforesd.

4th. Mr. Goodwin desires the name of the Scoole may be called Hopkins Scoole."

TOWN VOTES IN ANSWER TO THE ABOVE, MARCH, 26, 1669.

"Mr. Goodwin being sent to by the town to know the persons he would make choice of, as respecting the premises, he returns he had chosen Mr. John Russell, pastour of the church at Hadley, Left. Samuel Smith and Aaron Cooke. The town voted their aprobation of Mr. Goodwins choice. The Town allsoe voted Nathaniel Dickinson Senr, and Peter Tilton to Joyne with the three persons before mentioned as a Joint committee who with Mr. Goodwin while he lives, and after his decease shall Jointly and together have the ordering and ffull dispose of the estate or estates given by Mr. Davenport and Mr. Goodwin (as trustees as aforesaid to Mr. Edward Hopkins) to this town of Hadley, *or any other estate or estates that are or may be given by the town itself or any other donour or donours*, ffor the use, benefit and maintenance and promoting of a Gramar Scoole to and ffor the use and in this town of Hadley. As allsoe Jointly and together to doe, act and conclude and execute and ffinish anything respecting the premises ffaithfullye according to their best discretion.

Voted Allsoe by the town that as to the fiive persons before expressed, if any decease, or be otherwise disabled through the Providence of God, the rest surviveing shall have the sole choice of any in the roome and place of those surceasing, to the full number of five persons, provided they be known, discreet, pious, faithful persons.

The Town hath ordered Mr. Clarke and Peter Tilton to present the premises to the court to be recorded."

(The above is from the original town record, p. 44.)

"A true copy compared with the original by us,

JOHN RUSSELL and AARON COOKE."

The above note is appended to a copy taken by the above named, and preserved in the records of Hopkins Academy.

AGREEMENT BETWEEN MR. GOODWIN AND THE TOWN AS PRESENTED TO THE COURT MARCH 30, 1669.*

Whereas John Davenport Sen. Sometime of New Haven, now of Boston, in the colony of Massachusetts; and Mr. William Goodwin of Hadley in Hampshire, in the same colony; the only surviving Trustees to and for that part of the estate of Edward Hopkins Esq. given and bequeathed by that worthy and much honored donor, in his last will and testament; for and to the promoting and advancing of literature or learning in these parts of America called New England as his said trustees authorized and empowered by his last will and testament or those surviving of them, should, according to their discretion, care and faithfulness, see cause to order and dispose, the abovesaid Mr. John Davenport and Mr. William Goodwin, making a clear and absolute gift and disposal, of a considerable sum, or part of said estate, to the town of Hadley in Hampshire, in the colony aforesaid; for and to the end and use above expressed (viz) for the erecting and maintaining of a Grammar School, as by an instrument jointly sealed and subscribed, by the said Trustees appears; the said sum amounting to about three hundred pounds, *as also two hundred and fifty pounds more ordered and given by 'the Trustees to the Town of Hadley at the decease of Mrs. Hopkins,* And whereas the said Trustees have by both their assents constituted a committee of four persons, chosen by Mr. William Goodwin as respecting the estate as above expressed given and disposed to the town of Hadley; for the ordering and managing the same for the end aforesaid. Two of the said persons not accepting the said trust, the aforesaid Mr. William Goodwin in consulting with the said Town, about the further choice of persons upon whom the management of the above estate might be perpetually settled, and the will of the honored donor in all respects fulfilled. He acted in and about the same with the town as follows, viz. Mr. William Goodwin hath made choice of three persons to the end aforesaid, viz. Mr. John Russell Jun., Samuel Smith and Aaron Cook Jun. of whom the town have voted their approbation. The town also made choice of two persons, viz. Nathaniel Dickinson Sen. and

---

*NOTE.—At a County Corte holden at Northampton ye 30th day of ye 1st month 1669, the affairs of the School were presented, and these papers ordered entrance at lengthe on the record with warm approval "*in perpetuam* rei memoriam." (Court Record in Probate Office, pp. 205, 206.)

Peter Tilton, which five persons viz. Mr. John Russell Jun. Samuel Smith, Aaron Cook Jun., Nathaniel Dickinson and Peter Tilton shall be and are a joint Committee authorized and empowered clearly to act and jointly and together as also with the said Mr. William Goodwin while he lives, and after his decease, having full power, jointly and together, to order and appoint, dispose, manage, act, finish and conclude according to their discretion, care, and faithfulness, anything in respect to the premises; and for the benefit, furtherance, and advancement of the end or ends before mentioned, intended and expressed, by the worthy donor of the said estate, and likewise, by the Trustees in the gift of the same to the said town of Hadley.

Also the said Committee of five persons above expressed, shall have full power and authority, jointly and together to order, dispose and manage, *any other estate or estates* given and bequeathed to the town of Hadley; either *by the town itself*, or by any other donor, or donors or *that may* or *shall be* given, to the use and benefit, promoting and advancement of the school aforesaid, and learning for and in the town of Hadley.

The town hath ordered, that the five persons before mentioned surviving Mr. Goodwin, if any of them shall decease, or otherwise be disabled, the remaining persons of the said Committee shall have the sole choice of other or others in their room or place still continuing the number of five, provided their choice be of known discreet, pious, faithful persons."

Wm. Goodwin, who has been so prominent in this history, now ceases to be active in these matters. He was, as has been seen, elder in the church at Newtown, afterward at Hartford, and still later at Hadley. After him neither of those churches had another ruling elder. After a residence of ten years at Hadley he removed, about 1670 to Farmington, Conn., where he died March 11, 1673*

In 1672, Sept. 24th, at the County Court held in Springfield, he was plaintiff in an action agt. Peter Tilton Defdt. Thus runs the record :

" Mr. William Goodwin late of Hadley Plaintiff contra Peter Tilton of Hadley defdt in action for the case for intruding himself upon the committeeship about ye estate of Edward Hopkins Esq. (improved in Hadley) upon the schoole contrary to the mind of the said Mr. Goodwin Trustee to the sd estate. Also ye sd. Mr. Goodwin is Plaintiff agt. Mr. John Russell Jun. Lieut. Smith, Ensign Cooke all of Hadley Defdts in action of the case for associating withe sd Peter Tilton in acting upon sd schoole affairs and for all just damage."† (Court Record in Probate Office, Northampton, pp. 140, 141.)

Mr. Tilton challenged the Court as unqualified to hear the case for the reason that the members of the Court had some of them individually been advised with concerning the matter. At the dictate of a wise expediency they did not hear the case. Hence it was dismissed. Two of the Judges declinind to act because of defendant's objection.

---

*NOTE.—Inquiry has risen of late whether Elder Goodwin did not marry Mrs. Susanna, the widow of Rev. Thomas Hooker.
†The dean of the Court "exonerates and discharges Mr. Goodwin as having performed his engagements concerning the estate," though no exact and detailed account is given.

This record further takes notice of the "trouble and harshness" to which Mr. Goodwin had been subjected in the matter of the school estate and commends him for his zeal and fidelity.

"The Corte considering the admirable intenseness, the indefatigable care and paynes that Mr. Goodwin hath expressed to promote and advance the affairs of the schoole both for its foundation and progress Doe thankfully accept thereof." "They acknowledge the good hand of God in sending those Reverend ffathers, and worthy Gentlemen the said Trustees to dispose such an estate to these remote parts of the country and of this colony, for so worthy and eminent a work. (See Record at large pp. 140, 141.)

This record is illuminating as respects the character of the men concerned in this business. We have had occasion to notice the strong individuality of Mr. Goodwin. A like strong individuality was characteristic of the defendants. Peter Tilton was such a man. Between two such men rivalry, antagonism and even collision were possible. Difference there surely was, involving some degree of feeling. For his comfort's sake Mr. Goodwin may have felt that it would be well for him to leave Hadley for Farmington, that he might close his days in peace remote from strife. He went and thither his troubles followed him, as has been seen. It must have been a sore trial to his spirit that with the chief defendant were associated Lieut. Smith, Ensign Cooke, and, more than all, Mr. Russell, who afterward was at such pains and cost to vindicate his memory and secure the ends he had at heart, with odds against him. Mr. Goodwin lived on the lot occupied by the late Dea. Geo. Dickinson, on which earlier stood the house of Dea. Jacob Smith.

Wm. Goodwin had one daughter, Elizabeth, who married John Crow. One of the Trustees of Hopkins Academy, lately deceased, was a lineal descendant of Wm. Goodwin.*

TROUBLES CONCERNING THE SCHOOL PROPERTY IN THE CORN MILL.

At the date of the agreement of Mr. Davenport and Mr. Goodwin, April, 1664, the part of the Hopkins estate assigned to Hadley was in trust with Mr. John Russell, Lieut. Samuel Smith, Andrew Bacon and Peter Tilton in conjunction with Mr. Goodwin himself, who would seem to have had the management of matters very much in his own hands. This prominence was conceded to him so long as he continued to reside in Hadley. He is spoken of as disposing of the property with the consent of the other Trustees, investing a considerable share

*Deacon Rodney Smith, died February 2, 1890.

of it in a corn mill, on the mill brook a little south of the school lands. There is no known record of the year in which the mill was built, nor of any grant by the town for the use of the stream. A vote of the town Oct. 16, 1671, granted a house lot for the use of the miller. (Town Records). The mill may have been built that year. In Philip's war the mill was garrisoned at times and was preserved until Sept., 1677, when it was burned by the Indians who had made an attack upon Hatfield. The miller's house, the farm barn, fences and other property were likewise consumed. The committee, through lack of ability and fear of the Indians, did not rebuild the mill. They resigned and remitted their right to the place and remains of the dam in consideration of ten pounds voted by the town Nov. 7, 1677. The town likewise voted and granted to Robert Boltwood the remains of the dam belonging to the mill aforesaid. He, encouraged by the town, rebuilt the mill about 1678 or 1679. The committee of the Grammar school obtained it in 1683, Samuel Boltwood son of Robert had it in 1685; and it was again delivered up to the Trustees of the Hopkins school in 1687 in whose possession it remained.

The school committee was not at one in respect to this surrender. Mr. Russell never gave his consent. It caused him sore trouble and on the 30th of March, 1680, he presented to the County Court at Northampton the estate of the school and what had been done by the other Trustees, the Town and Boltwood. The Court decided that this transaction of the Trustees was illegal, "we may not allow so great a wrong." They judged that Goodman Boltwood should be repaid what he had expended and that the mill should belong to the school. (Judd, p. 58.)

ORDER OF THE SESSIONS, MARCH 30, 1680.

At a Court held at Northampton March. 30, 1680. The languishing estate of the school in Hadley being presented to this Court, by the Rev. Mr. John Russell, one of the committee for the said school, the Court taking the same into their serious consideration and finding by the records of this Court that there hath been three hundred pounds of Mr. Hopkins his estate disposed and ordered to Hadley for erecting and maintaining a Grammar school there, the management whereof for the school was to be by a committee appointed to that end viz. The Rev. John Russell, Mr. Samuel Smith, Mr. Peter Tilton and Capt. Aaron Cook, and finding in the records of the Court holden at Springfield Sept. 24, 1672; that by the accounts then presented to the Court and by the then acknowledgement of the committee for the school, the aforesaid three hundred pounds, which was disposed to Hadley, out of Mr. Hopkins his estate; was then actually in the hands of the committee, and under improvement there for the said school; which that Court then ordered should be continued, and improved towards the maintenance of a grammar School in Hadley forever. And accounting it our great duty to use all just endeavors to promote, as all schools of learning in general, so in particular, and more especially, this school, that had such a foundation and fair beginning, it becomes matter of inquiry of the committee, what was become of the said three hundred pounds, and which way it was laid out and improved for the school, who gave this answer.

That it was most of it, by Mr. Goodwin in his life time laid out upon a corn mill standing upon a stream or small river about two miles or more upward from the town of Hadley, which mill brought in annually a considerable income to the school whilst it stood, but in the time of the Indian war, the said mill and house were burnt down and ruined, whereby, the school is brought into a low condition. Hereupon it being further inquired into concerning the remains of the said mill and dam, and it appears that three of the committee (for the others knew not the act of the rest till afterwards and they did not consent to it) At the motion of the town of Hadley for the encouragement of Robert Boltwood to rebuild the corn mill in the place where it formerly stood the committee had in consideration of the promise of ten pounds from the town, for the school, resigned the place and the remains of the Dam to the town for that end, whereupon the remains of the Dam belonging to the mill above said were by the vote of the town of Hadley granted to Robert Boltwood, who built thereupon, and thereon, as the said Boltwood present in Court says, he now improves the mill to his own use and as his own.

This Court well considering the premises and observing several oversights, and irregularities in the aforesaid proceedings, and that there is no legal alienation of the mill from the school, nor may it according to right thus pass from the school, for which it was first built, and to which it was settled, do therefore declare that the said mill ought to revert and continue to the Grammar School in Hadley, and the maintenance thereof; all which, although forced to declare in answer to a case and query propounded, referring to the school estate, that *we may not allow of so great a wrong*, and evident prejudice to so good a publick matter, yet do it with great tenderness and respect to the town of Hadley that voted; to those of the committee that acted (knowing what a day of temptation and discouragement it was done in, through fear of the enemy and uncertainty of any estate) as also with respect to Goodman Boltwood, and his estate, which we would not be wasted or suffer in the least degree. And therefore that we may do him all the right, which being true to the public interest will allow us, we judge that Robert Boltwood be fully satisfied and repayed what he has now laid out or disbursed upon the said mill and may be justly due to him upon that account. And this being done the revenue and profits of the said mill, to be continued and improved according to its native and original constitution of it, toward the maintenance of the Grammar School in Hadley (which is in part a resolve of the other query, or case propounded) and the income from the said mill, with the rents of the land, Mr. Henry Clarke gave to this school and the farm or lands given by the town of Hadley with other donations; this Court hopes will after a little time set the school upon its legs again, especially if the two hundred and fifty pounds that is to come to this school from Mr. Hopkins estate in England can be gained. And in the meantime we advise that what shall come in from the land, mill, and otherwise (till a schoolmaster be got) be imployed toward payment of Goodman Boltwood, for that he hath been out upon the mill and to putting of the farm, belonging to the school, under a way of improvement, so as to bring in a yearly rent or income for the end aforesaid. Yet we see not but that something of the donations may be to a school at Hadley for the present (if the committee see cause) be allowed for an English school there." The soundness of this opinion was afterwards called in question in that without warrant it relaxed the requirement that a Grammar School must be maintained. (Records of Hopkins Academy.) Copied from the Record in Probate office pp. 207, 208. The same record is found in the office of the Clerk of Court.

In the records of the County Court in the Probate Office at Northampton is found the following, pp. 224, 225. Sept. 26, 1682, the committee rendered an account of the school estate to the County Court.

REPORT OF THE SCHOOL COMMITTEE TO THE COURTE HELD AT SPRINGFIELD, SEPT. 26, 1682.

The Committee for the Hopkins School in Hadley p'sented to the Corte a Return or an accompt concerning the school which is as follows.

Whereas the Worshipful Edward Hopkins Esq. who sometyme dwelt at Hartford upon Coneticot and afterward removed to Old England where finishing his course hee in Testimony of his sincere affection to the work of ye Lord in forraigne partes and as an expression of his zeal to the glory of God therein, bequeathed a considerable estate to be improved for ye educating of youth in good Literature and intrusted the same to be disposed by the Wisdom and fidelity of Theophilus Eaton Esq. Mr. John Davenport the Rev. Pastor of the church at New Haven, Capt. John Cullick and Mr. Wm Goodwin Sometymes of New Haven and Hartford.

Bee it known that ye sayd Mr. John Davenport and Mr. Wm Goodwin did as by Deede under their hand and scales Bareing date at Hadley and New Haven Aprill 30, 1664 and May 30, 1664 having first made over the sum of 400£ to ye Town of Hartford for the erecting and maintaining a gramer school there appeares made a free donation of all ye rest of ye sayd estate given by sayd Edward Hopkins Esq. to be disposed as above sd, viz both y^t of which was in New England and alsoe 500£ which was after Mrs. Hopkins her decease to be sent over to the Towns of New Haven and Hadley to be equally divided between ye sd Towns excepting one hundred pounds that was to be payd out of that part which belonged to Hadley unto Harvard Coledge. This was to be improved in each Town for ye erecting and maintaining of a Gramer School and committed to the management of their assignes and their successors which they should from tyme to tyme Chuse for the prsuance and putting in execution ye will of ye Pious and Worthy donour. The assignes first nominated and appointed by Mr. Davenport and Mr. Goodwin in their original

Deede were ye Rev. Mr. John Russell, pastor of ye Church of X in Hadley Leuft. Sam¹ Smith, Andrew Bacon and Peter Tilton, of whom Andrew Bacon not excepting and Mr. Tilton delaying his acceptance until some further overture had passed between Mr. Goodwin and the Town of Hadley, afterwards he accepted of sd work and Aaron Cooke Jun. was Chosen by Mr. Goodwin with the consent of the Rest in the Roome of the sd Andrew Bacon he accepted the same March 26, 1669 and the school by a joynt vote and agreement was called the Hopkins School. These Remayned ye Assignes or Committee for ye sd Hopkins School untill ye 7 dec 1680 when Leuft Sam¹ Smith lyeing sick and p'ceiving his approaching end the sd Sam¹ Smith and Mr. Peter Tilton the Reverend Mr. John Russell Capt Aaron Cooke chose his son Leuft Phillip Smith in the Roome in sayd Trust. Hee the Sayd Phillip Smith delayed his acceptance of the said Trust untill April 13, 1682 and then he accepted and acted with the Rest. Likewise Mr. Peter Tilton have long desired to lay down the burden of that service and being unwilling after all entreaties to continue ye same on ye sd 13 Aprill 1682 he layed down the said place. The Rest of the Comittee yielding thereto, he having for it together with ye sd Mr. John Russell Capt. Aaron Cooke and Leuft Phillip Smith made choice of Sam¹ Partrigg to succeed in the Roome of ye sd Mr. Tilton on the sd 13 of Aprill 1682 the sd Sam¹¹ Partrigg accepted the sd service and acted therein so that ye present comittee for Hopkins School in Hadley are ye Rev John Russell Capt Aaron Cooke Leuft. Phillip Smith and Sam¹¹ Partrigg.

The estate of the Hopkins School prsented by the comittee was

	£	s.	d.
By Mr. Goodwins account as in the particulars thereof it appears	308	01	11
Item Given by Thomas Coleman	05	00	00
Item Given by Wᵐ Westwood	013	17	02
Item Given by Widow Barnard	002	00	00
	328	19	01

Item Given by the Town of Hadley to the School two small meadows lyeing about the mill commonly called the school meadows by estimation about 60 acres of meadow

Item Given by Nathaniel Ward of Hadley to ye schoole one house with about an acre of Land and about twelve acres of meadow Land

Item Given by John Barnard twelve acres of meadow

Item Given by Mr. Henry Clarke about eleven acres and a half of meadow Land

These Lands have not been brought to any particular valluation.

Item There is by ye sd Deed of Mr. John Davenport and Mr. Wᵐ Goodwin the one half of 500 li which Mr. Hopkins by his last will ordered to be sent to New England given to sd Hopkins School in Hadley the which has not yet been received and we feare is never like to be. The account of Hopkins School in Hadley as Mr. Goodwin gives an account of charges expended by him to settle the estate £10—00—00

Item loss in the price of a house and land bought by Mr. Goodwin and allowed	25—08—00
Item building a cellar, Craine, Chimney, and oven while the mill was building.	3—00—00
Item building a house over the mill	12—03—00
Item building a house for the miller to dwell in	43—19—03
Item building a Barne for ye ffarme	10—00—00
Item fencing in ye farm at first	26—04—00
Item fencing twice more after the war	20—00—00
Item pd to clearing a debt of Mr. Hopkins which was condition at of clearing a debt to Mr. Hopkins	17—00—00
Item to Wm Markham for a rood of Land and Repair of a Barn	05—00—00

The Remaynder of this School Estate except House and Land was all of it expended in Building a mill and Damm and repairs of the houses and in setting up and maintaining the school master in ye beginning of the work princiuply by Mr. Goodwin before the Comittee had any considerable influence in the work. The mill thus erected and fitted yielded at first five or six and twenty pounds per annum, afterward about twenty, which all of it that could be spared from necessary repairs was improved towards the maintaining the school master for ye sd Gramer School until in the Indian Warr it was burnt and consumed by the enemie except ye irons and some small remaynes.

These with the house and Land continue of the school estate, the farm being now fenced again and the last yeare Lett out to tenants hath yielded some small rent which is imployed towards the maintenance of the School master.

This is the true account of ye state and estate of Hopkins School in Hadley this present 25 of Sept. 1682

JOHN RUSSELL
AARON COOKE

This Corte having p^{r}used this return or account for ye Comittee of Hopkins his school in Hadley doe accept and allow thereof soe farr as it is at present and doe take notice of ye p'sent comittee for Hopkins School in Hadley to be Mr John Russell Pastor to the Church of Christ in Hadley Capt. Aaron Cooke Leuft Phillip Smith and Sam^{ll} Partrigg all of Hadley whom this Corte do allow and approve of all and doe desire and expect their further management and carrying on of ye affairs of sd schoole from tyme to tyme which this Corte will be always ready to promote and encourage as need may require.*

---

*NOTE.—Record probate office, pp. 224, 225. The same in the office of Clerk of Court.

CHAPTER V.

DOINGS CONCERNING THE SCHOOL, MILL, &c. FROM 1683–1688.

Aug. 8, 1683, Robert Boltwood agreed to surrender the mill and appurtenances to the school committee in consideration of their paying him £138 in grain and pork. They took possession about Nov. 1, 1683.

In 1684 hindrances arose. The town challenged some right in the stream and land, and the committee would not consummate the bargain. Robert Boltwood died in 1684.

March 30, 1685, John Pynchon and John Allis heard the case of Samuel Boltwood and the school committee, John Russell, Aaron Cooke and Samuel Partrigg, by choice and consent of the parties, respecting an agreement and bargain with Robert Boltwood made Aug. 8, 1683. They decided that Samuel Boltwood should give the committee a clean title to the mill and its appurtenances or else make them good in the sum of £44, 13s, 5d, since to this extent was he under obligation to them. (See the original award in the papers with J. R. Trumbull.) In consequence of this decision Mr. Judd says the mill was delivered up to Samuel Boltwood about May 1, 1685.

At a new county court appointed by Andros, held at Northampton, June 6, 1687. The order of the President and Council was read and a petition and statement from the Trustees of the school. Samuel Boltwood was summoned to appear and show cause why he detained the mill. He presented a paper giving a regular account of his father's building and selling the mill and of the award of Pynchon and Allis, which put the mill into the Boltwood's hands. Referring to the award, he says, "it seems rational, especially for those who profess religion, to stand by what was done, or make good their bond. What is my just right I plead for and no other." The next day the court ordered those persons in Hadley, who had taken the school estate into their hands for an English school to return it speedily to the former committee the feoffees of the Grammar school viz. Mr. John Russell, Aaron Cooke, Joseph Kellogg and Samuel Porter to whom they added Chileab Smith in room of Samuel Partrigg removed.

They also ordered that Samuel Boltwood should deliver up the school mill and appurtenances to the same feoffees for the maintenance of the school. If the feoffees and Boltwood could not agree the matter was to be submitted to arbitrators agreed upon by the parties. Judd's Hist. Hadley, pp. 61, 62.

Apr. 10, 1688. The difficulty between Samuel Boltwood and the school committee as to what should be paid sd. Boltwood for his own and his father's expenses on the mill, was submitted to arbitration by mutual agreement and choice, to William Clarke, Esq., Joseph Hawley, Esq. and Samuel Partrigg, two of these agreeing to decide. If no two agreed, then Lieut. Allis was to agree and determine with two of the aforesaid, and this judgment was to be approved by the members of the Hon. Superior Court. The committee were John Russell, Aaron Cooke, Joseph Kellogg, Chileab Smith.

Apr. 26, Wm. Clark, Joseph Hawley and John Allis signed a decision that Goodman Boltwood should be alowed for what he and his father hath expended in or about the mill now in the hands of the committee above sd, seventy-one pouns, ten shillings; toward which we find the committee hath already paid sixty-two pounds, eleven shillings and eleven pence, half-penny, so there is due still to Goodman Boltwood 08-19-11 1-2, which we order the committee to pay unto Goodman Boltwood in wheat, peas and indian and pork at equal proportions, or such other pay as may be to his satisfaction, which being performed they shall give full acquittances and discharges each to other and this to be a full and final issue betwixt them of all differences for or about the school estate.

That this is our determination we have hereunto subscribed o^r names, the day and year above sd.

WILLIAM CLARKE,
JOSEPH HAWLEY,
JOHN ALLIS.

Apr. 26, 1688. Sam^{ll} Partrigg alsoe agreed to the above sd except only, that he apprehended that there was a consciencious due to Robert Boltwood or his heirs, with refference to his Building these mills in a tyme w^rin he exposed himself and family and the estate he layed out on the aforesaid accoumpt in eminent Hazzard by reason of the Indian enemy, the war not being at an end and defended principally at his own charges as alsoe the Bargaining y^t was made with him by the town pt. of the committee etc., though now it proves illegal in law, yet something he apprehended due from them that Bargained with him

SAM^{ll} PARTRIGG.

(Original paper with Judd collection with J. R. Trumbull.)

In such wise this prolonged trouble and strife were composed and a period of quiet ensued lasting many years.

The period during and following Philip's war for more than ten years was full of trial and discouragement. Population diminished. Values shrunk. The school revenues, especially, had suffered serious loss, whose repair seemed not very hopeful. The hearts of the people sunk. The school was kept up with difficulty. It was, in fact, intermittent. It was not easy to get and keep a master competent to teach the Grammar school. It was felt that in the situation, an English school would answer all demands and obligations. The Court had given encouragement to this sentiment. In the controversy that sprung up at this time and showed much heat, the great majority were on this side of the question. Mr. Russell, though his sense of right and duty in the other direction was strong, found only a few to stand with him. The general feeling found expression in the action of the Town given herewith.

Aug. 23, 1686. Voted by the Town that all the estates of Houses and Lands bequeathed and given by any Donor or Donours In their last will and Testament to this town of Hadley or to a schoole in said town, or to the promoting and furtherance of learning in said town as the legacie of Nathaniel Ward, John Barnard and Henry Clarke Gent, they would look on said estates and donations to belong nextly to the town to be improved according to the will of the testators and therefore take it into their own hands to manage order and dispose, to the use of a school in the Town of Hadley, this had a full vote in the affirmative.

Voted by the Town that Ensign Nash, Henry Barnard, Nehemiah Dickinson, Thomas Hovey and Samuel Barnard are a committee from the Towne to make demand of the school committee of all the produce Increase and rents of lands and estates above said, and accrueing thereto which at present are in their hands undisposed of.

Voted that the Selectmen shall have full power to Sett and Lett out the lands abovenamed for the use abovesaid.

Voted by the Town that Mr. Partrigg, Ensign Nash, Nehemiah Dickinson and P. T. are a committee to look out for the procuring a school master, and to determine, conclude and Agree with him with refference to his salary according to their best discretion. Voted and granted." First Town Record p. 26. A true copy compared with the original Oct. 8, 1686 By us

JOHN RUSSELL and AARON COOKE.

In such a vote Mr. Russell could by no means acquiesce. He must have been deeply and strongly moved. The general feeling in the town was one of strong opposition. One of the committee, a man of influence and power, was the leader on that side. This was a kind of proceeding under which it was not in Mr. Russell to remain quiet and make no protest and seek no relief. Hence he submitted the case at the earliest moment to the county court held in Springfield, Sept. 28, 1686. The order of the Court is here given. p. 260 Probate Record*

ORDER OF THE COUNTY COURT SEPT. 28, 1686, AT THE COUNTY COURT HOLDEN AT SPRINGFIELD.

The declining estate of Hopkins School in Hadley, being presented to this Court by the Rev. Mr. John Russell Aaron Cook Joseph Kellogg and Samuel Porter the committee of the said school for that some of Hadley, do disturb or obstruct the management of the estate of said school; therefore this Court doth declare and order that the whole donations to a school there, from the charitable donors, be all employed and improved, for and towards the maintenance of the Grammar School there in Hadley, it appearing that the intent of Mr. Henry Clarke in what he gave to the school was, that it should go and be employed to the said school, called Hopkins School, also the like doth appear as to goodman Wards gift, and goodman Barnards may as well be taken to and for that school as any other.

Wherefore this Court orders that all said gifts and others with the land given by Hadley town be all accordingly improved by the aforesaid committee And that Mr. Samuel Partridge, one of the committee who dissented from the rest, ought to concur and join with them in it. We further declare that some former concessions of the County Court at Northampton March 30, 1680, which were suited to gain a compliance of all, and to ease some spirits, were not so warily expressed, and therefore, those concessions or expressions may not and are not to be understood to the disadvantage of the said school. But that the mill, farm and all the donations, are notwithstanding to be improved for and to the said Grammar School and not to an English disjunct and separate from a grammar school.

We further advise, that the said committee, as trustees for Hopkins estate do jointly improve all, for the ends aforesaid and do propose it to the town of Hadley, to add something and help forward a school, which may suit and answer both the committee's trust and the town's end also, of having children taught to read and write. And Mr. Peter Tilton not concurring, but alledging that one party, viz. the town of Hadley, were not present, (though Mr. Partridge spoke in the Court in their behalf; therefore further this Court orders that in case the trustees of Hopkins school and the town of Hadley, do not sodder or come to an agreement about said estate, and school, that then it be further considered at Northampton Court.

This act, made in Court Sept. 28, and Sept. 30, 1686 and ordered to be entered.

As attest JOHN HOLYOKE Clerk.

Oct 2, 1686 extracted out of the acts of the abovesaid Court, examined and compared therewith, and a true copy.

Attest JOHN HOLYOKE Clerk.

---

*This Record is found both in the Probate office and in the office of the Clerk of Courts at Northampton.

The following paper, sent probably at the same time with the act of the Court, Sept. 28, 30, is in place here, immediately after the decree of Court.

LETTER OF JOHN PYNCHON TO MR. RUSSELL.

Springfield, Oct. 2, 1686. To the Rev^d Mr. Russell p to ye Ch. in Hadley.

Revd Sir I am hartily sorry Mr Partrig is so cross in ye businesse of the school and so averse as to obstruct all p'ceeding but it will be the duty of the committee and nothing will be done as it ought till he be removed wh I suppose Predt and council may do and sea good reason for it. Its soe hard for the County Court to do any thing Mr P. being present and a justice of the P. in some degree one of the Cort. And Mr. Tilton fully falling in with him and is as strong and full in all his notions as Mr. P. himf, that hereby it is a wonder y^t any th passed it being strongly urged y^t ye Cort had not to do in it &c. that ye Cort might not however take cognizance unlesse y^t I had been sumoned.

Mr. Cl. tho, a friend in ye businesse and was almost, &c. But I am glad we gott passed so mh as to recover and regain the ground lost formerly as you will see by the inclosed wh. in truth Mr. P. desired Hadley might not see or know at least awhile and Mr. Tilton said it would kindle such a flame yt would not be quenched. But if to do right and secure publick wright, kindle a flame the will of the Ld. be done. And yet I beg his leading all concerned to act with moderation &c. To gett the paper and order passed I was enforced to declāre y^t if Mr. Clarke did not assent with me I would alone have it on record myf. But he concurred in the order and it is the act of the Court and now it is exprssed an order of the Court.

Mr. Partr affirmed the Court never ordered any th. only approved &c. The latter part of it is advising—Spossing the T. wd join and add someth. bec. noth. also passed and the last is by way of Advice. The former is an order wherein is an exprsn declaring yt all ye Comittee ought to Joyne together And then if one will obstruct it is necessary and must come to it yt he be removed by the Psid &c who must do this businesse we are too weak in ye c Court and I am full for it to leave all with ye Presd and glad it is like to be in the hands of ym who will powerfully order.

And I pray Gd ye sc may stand upon its right basis and all may run in the old Channel bec * * it is right so to be however I h been Somewhat forced to yield But now I hope have gott upon even if not the higher ground and bottom or standing already, I am highly ambitious of having the countenance of the Prsidt in setting the sch and all matters in Statu quo with most humble sarvice   Yo^r most Cordiale
    JOHN PYNCHON.

That Exp^{r}sion y^t ye committe to act joyntly and together was most unhappily done by &c. and must be attended.

The order of the Court Sept. 28, 1686, is found on the same paper and was probably sent to Mr. Russell with this letter.

About this time it would seem that the offices of the President and council in this business were invoked. In what sort they responded can be learned from what follows. Joseph Dudley was now in the office of President under a commission of King James II, and with a council had jurisdiction over the King's dominion of New England. Dudley held this office till Dec. 20, of this year, 1686, succeeded by Sir Edmund Andros who was deposed by a vote of the people, April 20, 1689. This was an an arbitrary government in which the voice of the people was not heard, which they disliked, and yielded to it with ill grace. From Pres't Dudley Mr. Pynchon received an order. What came of it is told herewith.

MAJOR PYNCHON AND COMMITTEE,S RETURN TO THE PRESIDENT AND COUNCIL IN BOSTON, 1686.

To the Honorable the President and Council in Boston.

In obdience to an order received from the Hon[ble] Council bearing date October 21, 1686, on Thursday, November, 18, 1686 I went to Hadley and sent for Capt. Aaron Cooke Sen. and Mr. Hawley. On the same day, I acquainted Mr. Partrigg that I was come up, on the Councils order to examine, and make report of the school affairs. Therefore, I desired a town meeting the next morning that the town might depute some persons to give us an account of things; and after divers words was fain to order, that there should be a town meeting at sun a quarter of an hour high. After this some hours in the night, some of the towns men came tome, and made sundry cavilling objections, that they were surprised and that it was not the way to make good blood etc. Next morning Capt. Cooke and Mr. Hawley came over to Hadley and having waited till towards noon, some men came to us as a committee from the town viz. Mr. Tilton, Mr. Partrigg with some others who objected against the Councils order, in that it expressed a free school and they had no controversy about any such school and that there was no particular complaint; and therefore they should refuse to declare aught. We told them we should proceed to hear the school committee and were willing to give them opportunity of answering.

Towards night (we waiting all this while) the same committee with some others, coming from the town, said that not being willing to show themselves surly, they came and were willing to hear and discourse with us, as gentlemen and friends; but not in attendance to the councils order, that they should utterly refuse.

The Committee for the school, readily gave in the inclosed account of their reasons, why they could not consent to the taking the estate given to Hopkins's school to any other use, and presented to us, the orders of the town, and county courts, proving that the estate was by the Town *all* given to Hopkins's school; to be ordered by the committee chosen by Mr. Goodwin and the town and their successors forever. Neither do we find anything by the town presented. that doth any way invalidate the reasons and plans, presented by the committee; notwithstanding, the town, by their act here presented have taken away a great part if not all the estate.

The Towns committee after they heard what was presented, drew out two or three long papers in a way of answer, and therein labored to prove an English school was a Grammar school, therefore improving the estate, that way answered the end of the donors, but they utterly refused to let us have their answers or to send them to the Council; alledging that they had no power to do so. They further said: that no council nor county had anything to do with the estate, but in a court of law, that it was their property, therefore at their dispose; for property and use were inseparable, they were in possession and could not be ousted, but by a trial by their peers, (tho they themselves, without the using any such way, or method, had taken it from the committee, although they had possessed it, these twenty years.)

The committee humbly beg, they may be convinced of their error, or strengthened in their work, or freed from it, and from the great complaints of their acting by will—not being peaceable and well wishers to the town—and that they may be directed what to do with respect to the mill, which the County Court ordered to return to the school, and how they should act in regard of that clause of their commission, that saith, that they should act jointly and together. Mr. Partrigg, one of the committee, acting against them. We humbly propose whether the clause, jointly and together, may not refer, only to the committee that was chosen partly by Mr. Goodwin and partly by the Town, and not to any successors, which are otherwise chosen—also whether it be not necessary to remove Mr. Partrigg from being one of the committee, he being so strongly against the estates being improved for a Grammar School; which is sufficient to maintain one, with a little addition from the town. Also whether it be not necessary, speedily to order, the return of the estate again, into the hands of the school committee.

We should have sent your Honors copies of the settlement of the estate upon Hopkins,s School, but that we understand by Mr. Russell, they are already with the President.

Humbly requesting that some speedy course may be taken by an act from the council, for the quieting of the hot and raised Spirits of the people in the town; and setting of this on its right basis, we subscribe ourselves

Your Honors, most humble Servants

JOHN PYNCHON
AARON COOKE
JOSEPH HAWLEY

Nov. 19, 1686. Voted by the Towne that Mr. Partrigg and Ensign Nash and P. T. shall be sent to the gentlemen whom the President and Council have ordered to appeare and examine some applications made to themselves by some of Hadley, respecting a free school, to signify to said gentlemen that the Town think themselves not concerned in said order, there being no difference about any such thing as a ffree schoole, there being no such schoole among us. Voted by the town, nevertheless, that Mr. Partrigg, Ensign Nash, Nehemiah Dickinson, Daniell Marsh, Tho. Hovey and P. T. be a committee from themselves to treat with said gentlemen or to give Answer to what may be Aledged in a difference betweene some of the comittee for our Towne schoole and themselves that so, if possible, there may be an Amicable compliance.

The Reasons of the School Committee which were given in to the Committee and by them sent to the Council.

WRITTEN BY MR. RUSSELL.

We cannot consent to the taking the estate belonging to Hopkins,s School in Hadley, from the said school, and putting it to any other use; because to us, this is 1st. Against the gift to the good work, therefore not right 2nd Against our trust, therefore not faithfulness 3rd Trust committed to us by solemn and solemnly ratified covenant—therefore against truth and truth that that we are betrusted with the execution of. 4th against the will of the deceased therefore not according to the principles of humanity and piety 5th Against the law of not removing ancient landmarks, therefore brings the curse 6th Against the Lord in His right, therefore Sacrilege 7th Against authority, managed by disowning, denying, opposing and misleading, (that we say not seducing) others thereto, therefore against the ordinance of God, against peace—therefore against holiness &c. against the welfare of the town for the present and the future, in all generations therefore unkindness to them and their publick good, against the rule of prudence, exposing us to sin and folly, as well as the hazard of our estates, thus we say it is to us. If any can show us that we err herein, we shall we trust willingly attend to, and led by better light than our own, but till then, we look on what is done, as the taking away all the school estate, and overthrow of that work.

These seven heads of argument are elaborated at much length with abundant appeal to scripture and no little iteration. The fifth head is argued as follows:

" 5th Against the law of land marks, Deut. 27: 17, Cursed be he that removeth his neighbors land mark." These land marks between God, and the town and all others, were set in the lot March 20th and 26th 1668-9 by Mr. Goodwin for himself and Mr. Hopkins; and by the Town and by the Court March 30th and by the Committee. Now for any of these parties to alter these land marks, without the consent of all the rest, is against the law and against right. Mr. Goodwin doth not consent, the committee consent not, the Court consent not, and if all these, who shall consent for God? This is also done without any trial by law, even by those who say, they can be touched in no other way. Shall we remove land marks because men, or a Town will be angry if we do not? If it be objected that the estate taken by the Town and which we are required to surrender was given to a school, not to Hopkins,s therefore no wrong. The answer is

The Town hath given it to Hopkins,s School forever; upon serious consideration; by a solemn covenant with Mr. Goodwin; ordered it to be enrolled in the Court, the Court have added their sanction to it; the Court, the Town and Mr. Goodwin, have betrusted the execution of this covenant with the Committee and they have undertaken it. Who shall now warrant the execution of this covenant (tho' an error) with God and His property.

That act especially of pious and publick minded men, which is capable of a double interpretation a better or worse. Charity and piety binds us (leaves us not at liberty) to interpret in the best manner.

If a pious man gives to a school; and there is not one word to distinguish what school; piety and Charity bind to refer it to the best its capable of; else I wrong the good man, and do not him the right which a rule and Charity call for. Here is not such a mere evenness for charity to cast the balance, but there are casting circumstances added to the rule of piety, and charity in general viz. 1st here was a school promoting, set on foot, and making by his friend, that was as his own soul, where shall we think a man meant to act in such a work; but where a beginning was and with such a friend.

2nd The School spoken of by John Barnard was not at the making of His will; but expected to be at his wife's decease or soon after, and to this it was given; this was Hopkins,s School.

3rd. The Town, the then town, and the Court judged this the school and put it into the committee's hands, to be by them ordered forever, and there it hath been now about twenty years.

What reason now to deny or question the school's right? or what other can have more or equal right? It's known that goodman Ward and Mr. Clarke's donations were intended to a Grammar School, with Mr. Hopkins's donations.

4th If the Town keep the property and use, they give nothing and if use and property are inseparable, then the school having the use, have also the property, or nothing. If you say the property and use is theirs (the Town's) and they have given neither use nor property it's a poor gift."

The seventh head is argued thus:

"7th It is against authority. The ordinance of God, Rom. 13: 18. 1st. Against the law I. 8. a most good and wholesome law, and according to God. 2nd Against the County Courts order formerly. 3rd Against the new order when they have again considered and reviewed it. 4th Against the President's letter, for you put the committee upon that, that not only yourselves have regulated the contrary, but you know it's against the law, against that, that is done by law. All the authority in the country demands one thing—you command the contrary—and commanding the contrary, say there is no law against it, no Court,s act about it.

When this comes into a publick Town meeting, some question the order, some deny it, others lead to the denying it, who must we obey now? God or man? all the authority in the country, or you? Should we now do this thing we must say as you, no law, no act, or else, th.o there be, we will not. need not attend it. If no obedience to authority, how can there be any peace or order? or any man have his own? if men will take without law, against law, against Courts, and teach others so to do, and set towns in a flame? Was then one word spoken by you, for the asserting and maintaining authority, when it Spoke, so as it can no plainer or louder, in such cases, by the officer at Clarke,s arrest and this by justice of the Peace, to act that, that is not justice nor prudence, and teach and lead others so to do.

Should not we be seditious, if we should do so? and make others so. It is against the Town, not only as rushing them on all these rocks of sin and sorrow or punishment compelling them to break the hedge, that so the serpent may bite them whereby all the sin and blame of the town would be ours; but is also against the Town profit for there is no such way of ease, and cheapness to keep a school, as this, and the great advantage of some poor men to bring up their sons to learning; as we see in Bro. Barnard,s which may be much to the glory of God, and their profit.

We should count it sinful and simple for us to do these things and hazard our estates, should we do it and when called to account for promoting the estate answer? the Town were angry, or would have us do it—would that excuse or secure us? Simple it is because sinful, and also because if we, and every one in the Town, should have joined with you we could not but have added to your sin; but have been no help.

Ques. If the question be how doth it appear that the estate of goodman Ward and goodman Barnard is the Grammar School or Hopkins,s School seeing the testators, in their wills, name not Hopkins,s School or a Grammar School, and the town hath nowhere given it to Hopkins,s or a Grammar School; or if given it—not given it forever as appears by their act.

Ans. As to goodman Ward I know his expressed mind was, to join it with Mr. Hopkins,s estate And goodman Barnard, given to a school if any one in Hadley, at his wife.s decease. When he died there was an English school; but that was accounted none; or none as to his will an end; but it must be some higher; and the highest one that came before his wife's death, was this Grammar one, Hopkins,s School; to which it was then due as an inheritance by will; and is not now to be pluckt from this true heir, to be given to another born about twenty years after, of another kindred and inferior rank to the causeless prejudice of this. Goodman Barnard,s heart, was one with Mr. Hopkins. His will saith, if a school in Hadley, at his wife,s death (having been much spoken of before, by Mr. Hopkins,s estate) then his estate is to that school, but this Hopkins,s School, was in Hadley at her decease (and no other but that he accounts none).

But secondly. If the will of the donors have not determinately fixed it to what school, then what doth reason Speak? There is somewhat given to a school in a town and not fixed to what school, is the voice of reason now, and the publick good, that it should be an higher school or an inferior one? to one that is in the place, when the will saith it shall become due; or to one that is not of twenty years after; and we know not whether ever will be settled. Is it to that which this man,s friend set up, with whom his heart was, or to another, of which he never heard, and quite opposite to the mind and heart of his friend? Religion and Charity, require one to interpret in the best part I may. If it was not fixed by the donors, nor the voice of reason and the publick good, and union of men,s hearts in friendship not the right of being the first born, do settle it to a Grammar School, not the having the first orderly possession of it, yet the town hath given it to and settled it on Hopkins,s Grammar School, forever. This appears by their act March 26, 1669 and by their consequent practice which we evidence by these.

1st. It is evident by the whole frame of the town act, as well as by testimony, that the very device, and good work aimed at, was the conjoining of estates for a Grammar School in Hadley.

This was what Mr. Goodwin was betrusted with, had on his heart and expressed to the town; with this the town joined giving to it choosing committees and ordering the way of managing it.

2ndly. It is evident that in this good device devised by Mr. Goodwin and the town, the estate devised and given to carry on this good work was all the estate which Mr. Goodwin had given of Mr. Hopkins,s his donations or that should be given, or was to come after her decease viz. two hundred and fifty pounds, this was the estate on Mr. Goodwin,s part, And on the town,s part, it was the school meadows they had given, and any other gifts by any other donors that had been or should be given. The thing devised or the end of the device was that these estates all of them should be to the school.

3rdly. It is evident, that the device and End of these agents, was the uniting to pursue the very end and same work of Mr. Hopkins and his trustees. This is first and last Expressed as the end of all this device and conjunction. Mr. Hopkins and Mr. Goodwin,s device was a Grammar School forever in Hadley. This plain end of the donors, they make their own; and in express words say again and again their device is to satisfy and carry on and perfect that device.

4thly. The device or end of this good work was, that the managing this estate, and the care and ordering of this whole concern; should be in the hands of the Committee, by them chosen.

The Town and Mr. Goodwin, devised and ordered, that these should manage the work.

This is their commitiee—Mr. Goodwin and the town do it by them. They devise to carry on this work, which is to be forever by this committee. To choose a committee, with power to choose successors for this end. This end was the Grammar School perpetually or forever; when it is said, if any decease, the surviving ones shall have the sole power of choosing others and all this for a perpetual settlement.

All these estates are, by Mr. Goodwin and the Town, put into the hands of the Committee, for prosecuting Mr. Hopkins and Mr. Goodwins end perpetually or forever.

5thly. It is evident, the device was, that all the parts of this estate, were alike fastened, and made sure to this work.

1st. All were conjoined with Mr. Hopkins his estate, and Mr. Goodwin,s donations

And 2nd All was in the hands of a Committee by succession; and solely in their hands and choice.

3rd This was for perpetuating a perpetual settlement

6thly. It is beyond question, this was the device, as appears by their practice. It is so put into the hands of the committee as this order impowers and appoints, so hereby the committee take and improve for this school, on these terms, as a perpetual settlement so it hath been improved the biggest part of twenty years. It is understood by the Court, so presented to them—so they call for; and hear accounts of it, and ratify the same—and now must we hear, that it is nor so?

7thly. All this is to Hopkin,s School. And now after all this acting and possession, and improvement, must we hear that it is not the School,s? or not the Grammar School,s? or not forever? Sure we must needs say, that we have heard a language that we understand not, hence altho it be not in such words, as some would have said, in some of these men,s wills " we give it to a Grammar or Hopkins,s School : nor by the Town, we give the estate of Nathaniel Ward &c. to a Grammar School in Hadley forever." Yet it is said in words that are equivalent—they are all given, by the testators to a School in Hadley. No other School (Except some by women) hath ever been settled in Hadley. The Town and the court have understood this, the School and both of them, put this estate, and all the parts of it, into the hands of this successive committee for a perpetual settlement.

What shall now warrant the taking this from the same? The Court also calls for the Committee,s attending the management of all this estate, for Hopkins School. This we understand to be their regulating of it."

More follows to the same effect chiefly in the way of recapitulation. The paper unabridged is found in the Book of Records of Hopkins Academy.

Here may be introduced Mr. Partrigg's Reasons, drawn up at this time and perhaps offered at the hearing beforenamed.

MR. PARTRIGG'S REASONS.

Reasons of my dissent from the Committee in their tyeing up the School Estate (Hadley,s right) to a Grammar School only ; viz.

1st. Because the school estate in all the parts of it, is the town of Hadley,s right and property.

The first part I shall speak to is, that given out of Mr. Hopkins,s estate on Court Record, Folio 105, 1st Book.

The Honor^d Court sitting March 30th, 1669 have entered upon record their favorable acceptation and approving such work as the promoting learning, and thus they enter the deed, which the Trustees to Mr. Hopkins,s estate made for the disposure of said estate, such and so much to be equally divided to each; viz. New Haven, Hadley ; and to be disposed and managed in each town to a Grammar School etc. and appointed and impowered committees to act upon it as they shall see meet, or as ourselves might do etc. They have also the Court,s Sanction ; this in the deed.

When Hadley Committee come to act, as by agreement entered upon record 1st, they explain their meaning in the deed aforenamed, that said estate is a gift to Hadley. See their agreement p. 107 of that aforesaid book of record. In page 141 in said record the said estate is declared, as the Court,s sense, to be to the Town of Hadley two or three times over.

2udly. The town of Hadley act upon it, either as having a right aforesaid, or being intrusted, all the aforesaid shows rather, that they acted upon their right; as also they improve part of the Committee (by their choice) and said Committee receive and make discharges to as to said estate which the Court confirms. See p. 141.

3rdly. The Town act accompting said estate their own right; and therefore add some of their own estate to the completing of their design; which, doubtless, they would not, nor could not, in prudence have done, had they no right, and disposure as aforesaid. See the lands and payments they made following.

2nd. Pt. of School estate, is those meadows given by the town to said use of a Grammar School, is the town,s right for the ends aforesaid; because it is not liable to be carried out of said town, it is to be improved in the town for a school. 2nd Town grants or appointments of any estate to their own use must be considered as they are; which seems to be no otherwise than a living man,s will; subject to alteration, especially the grant being made to no other use or right but their own. See their Grant folio 107 of said record.

3rd Pt. Nathaniel Ward,s grant of estate (in his last will) to learning in Hadley is Hadley,s right, because the words in his will on the aforesaid record folio 39 are (I give to the town of Hadley after my wife,s etc. for a school etc.) his will being an approved will, according to the law of this jurisdiction; and the words positive makes it a firm right. A condition there is, but it no ways weakens but strengthens the right; the debt to Mr. Hopkins,s estate being satisfied and issued.

4th. Pt. Goodman Barnard,s gift (in this last will) to learning in Hadley, is Hadley,s right, which is in these words (in his will on record folio 37) to the use and towards the maintaining a school, and further explains his words and also that land I give to the school in Hadley; but if not a school in Hadley at my wife,s decease, then to four poor men in Hadley, till a school is set up. It is true the words are dark in the grant giving it to a school and not mentioning what school, but in the latter clause ties it to a school in Hadley, if a school is set up, or to four poor men. So that it is clear the intent and meaning of his will is giving it to Hadley in case they set up a school.

5th Pt. Widow Barnard,s grant, on her will is Hadley,s right. The grant is in these words; I do also give to the use and furtherance of learning in this town of Hadley £4. Here, no doubt, but the intent was to the town for that end and no other—they having the dispose of those concerns within themselves.

6th. Pt. Mr. Henry Clarke, Gentleman, his grant for his part of his estate to learning or otherwise, is Hadley,s right, and it is declared in these words in his will, folio 165. I give my nine acre lot in Hockanum and two acres and an half of my lot in forlorn etc. to the town of Hadley, and upon conditions etc. it is to Hopkins,s School. These conditions are: if the committee meet with no disturbance; but in case they do, then he doubles his grant to the town; saying then it shall be improved for the good of the town, and thus the trustees are bound—though there is a respect to Hopkins,s School; but in case that be not promoted, or flourish not, then; once and again he says it shall be to Hadley town, and it seems there was engagement to it by Mr. Clarke. And would Hadley in reason have laid out so much as they have besides their land aforesaid added from time to time had it not been their own concern? viz.

When Mr. Watson was school-master £20 per annum for three years   £60.
To Mr. Younglove for seven years an addition upon scholars, about
    £10 yearly   70

Towards building the mill at	50
To Mr. Russell two years at least £10 per annum	20
More helping at mill several times at	10
	£210

In answer to this that said estate was tied to a Grammar school and committed to the School Committee for that end. It is true Mr. Hopkins,s estate, by them that gave the deed to Hadley was so tied; but it is questionable whether the first donor did so tie it; and as to this estate bound to be improved as aforesaid it seems to be spent and by Providence lost viz. This estate, at first delivered to Hadley by Mr. Goodwin, was in specie as followeth.

Imprimis in a house sold them which Mr. Watson had accompted for and work done for himself at	£113–9–7
In a mill built and work about it and the mill house besides the £50 the town allowed	175–0–0
In fencing at	26–4–0
	£314–13–-7
Goodman Coleman Leger	5
Wid. Barnard Leger	4
Mr. Westwood Leger	13
	£336–-13–-7

PER CONTRA

Said House and work alienated to Mr. Watson	113–9–7
The mill and all work about it some of it lost and sold to the Town except £15 in Irons and Stones	160
The aforesaid allowance by the town at	210
seven years rent of the school land at £20 a year	140
School land rent, since for 3 years besides rents of the mill at £10	30
	653–9–7

By the aforesaid account it appears that Mr. Hopkins,s estate and all others that gave moveable estate, as to the specie of it, is wholly spent and lost and almost double the money with it; which the town and the town,s land hath allowed to that use.

And name the thing within the limits of Hadley that can be called Mr. Hopkins,s Estate, and hath and doth bring in an income to said school or to Hadley; except the rents of the mill, which being lost and spent as aforesaid —and I make no mention of it in the aforesaid account. As also £15 which is yet due from the mill, for the old irons and stone, which if it be or be not the town,s right, it is by them dearly bought, being but £15 for £50 they laid out upon said mill. But if it be said there is £44 due from the mill and it is an intermixed estate the aforesaid £50 will balance, if not, let the balance of the abovesaid accompt; viz. £316—16—0 do it. So that the remaining estate that brings in any income towards schooling, is the town,s land and those lands in Hadley given by the aforesaid donors.

Hereupon the town have applied themselves to the Committee of the School, to improve the estate, viz. the income of it, to English schooling, till said estate, or the town be in a capacity to obtain and procure higher learning. And the Committee all but myself, refuse; and as to myself I would have yielded for reasons following.

R. 1st. Our Pastor lays it down from that 9 Heb. 16, 17 There is no alteration the testator being dead, And the donors of Hopkins,s Estate tyeing his estate up to a Grammar School; and therefore it must be improved to no other school, to this I answer and make use of it as a reason aforesaid. Mr. Hopkins,s Estate and the estate of those other donors that gave moveable estate is spent and lost as in the abovesaid accompt. And consider all sums more of other estate and when the thing given is wholly gone, the conditions as to the using of it is also gone and of no strength, there being nothing to use.

R. 2nd. As to Goodman Ward,s, Goodman Barnard,s and his wife,s Mr. Clarke,s donations aforementioned, no one of them is absolutely tied to a Grammar School; but to learning, or a school in general. And therefore if the using the Estate be to an English school that is tied to a Grammar School, is a breach of the same rule. The tye to a Grammar School was only in Mr. Hopkins,s estate by the donor which is ended with the estate; and the estate given by the aforesaid donors under no such tye. See my aforesaid recital of their grants

It is pleaded yet further, that the town have passed over their own land, and all these donations to a Grammar School and to the use of the Committee in succession forever. To this I answer (as a reason also)

1st. if the town have done so, by the aforesaid argument taken from 9 Heb. 16, 17 they sinned in it because the donations are not given to a Grammar School. But whether it be a sin or not, I hope the repentance which seems to be evident may be accepted and the estate set at liberty, according to the will of the donator and the earnest desire of the Town. But here see what the town have done as to their donations and their own land, in passing them over to a Grammar School as is pleaded.

In January 14, 1666 the town did grant the school meadows to a Grammar School, as an addition to Mr. Hopkins,s estate for the ends aforesaid; but inasmuch as Mr. Hopkins,s estate is gone, and there is no estate left but these lands and the lands the aforesaid donors gave, the town may have reason to alter their order, and if they do I know not any sin in it in as much as it is their own concern.

The Town of Hadley never gave away their School land so as it can be commanded away from a School or learning in Hadley. And if a Grammar School that they first order cannot be obtained according to their judgment; they may put it to any other learning; viz. an English School and this is plain from the words in this grant, that they have put it into the Committee,s hands for the use of the School aforesaid or learning; therefore if the Committee do not keep up a Grammar or other School for learning the town may have just cause to regulate the business to such learning as can be obtained, which is all the town have desired, that if we cannot have a grammar with the income of the estate, let us have such schooling as it will obtain.

2nd And as to the other lands, it seems by the order to be tied to a Grammar School neither by the donators nor the town; for the town say they pass over all gifts and grants that shall be given from time to time to the use of the school aforesaid. These donations were not so given

Further the order says or learning for and in the town of Hadley and if it be for and in the town of Hadley, then it is nor given from themselves I know no more binding in a town or for concerns of the town, when the propriety is given to no particular in the town, nor no other, but to the use of the town, but said orders may be and are usually, altered according to the order of the town, as well as any particular person may alter his design, and no account to be given. Especially when the alteration is very small, if any thing from the order; viz. they having reserved for learning; to improve it so if need be; and as to passing it to the Committee successively, it is not their propriety thereby but for the ends and use aforesaid, in which if they fail the town and no other may call them to accompt for it. Especially when Mr. Hopkins,s estate which called for a mutual choice of a Committee by the Town and his Trustees: that part is gone; and that only left upon which the town instructed their part of the Committee; and when by their order there can be nothing acted but by both parts of the Committee jointly and together and to the number of five persons so and so qualified &c. which is three or four times mentioned. And if said Committee do nor act according to the mind of the town for learning, or jointly again, the town may lawfully take care, and give further orders about it. Especially when they answer the law of the Commonweath in Grammar or English Schooling, their families being but about fifty

R. 4th This reason is from the former State of the town considered with their present State since which order was made between thirty or forty able householders (to promote learning in the highest degrees here mentioned) are now in their graves and the greater part of their survivors in a poor condition to do anything towards a school; and nigh one third of the lands in the town in tenants hands which take little care to promote such designs, as also the greatest part of the children, such poor men,s, that cannot pay anything towards schooling the children; much less bring them up to Grammar learning, so that there is not one that I Know of now that pretend to Grammar learning except two that are brought up at their parents particular charges; the school having been so uncertain as is we Know, Grammar School masters so hard to settle, that as soon as ever one is settled, one place or other calls them off, and so it hath been ever since the first, except with Mr. Watson who I understand went away upon some difference betwixt him and our pastor

That we have been in danger several times to be presented for want of a school, notwithstanding the great provisions that hath been laid in upon that accompt in Hadley as aforesaid.

And now the town only desire to use their own estate, in the vacancy of a Grammar School, for an English, as I suppose their order will bear them out in it, as aforesaid. It is now twenty years it hath been improved, I do not desire to reflect upon the success it is so well known. But the improvement of the school estate upon English learning by a grammar school master, and by an English school master, I cannot see the difference as to the end if that

be viz. English learning or writing. But this, he that can teach grammar, is surely better fitted to teach English, than he that hath no grammar in him. But the ground of all this is: if no grammar, such poor help as we have, when better cannot be obtained; that we have not half years and whole years vacancies, under pretence of grammar schooling; and so schooling fail in a great measure. For I suppose it will be granted that the learning of any trade or science, is best insinuated by constancy in attendance to it.

If we cannot have polishers for the stone let the ruff hewers set to it, to prepare while polishers come.

A letter was written concerning these matters by Governor Dudley to Mr. Russell, without date, but it must have been sometime between May 27th and Dec. 26th, 1686, as follows:

GOVERNOR DUDLEY'S LETTER TO MR. RUSSELL.

Revd Sir

I lately received your very solicitous letter referring to your free school in Hadley; and am very sorry that, while your inclination and opinion is so good and well rendered, you should seem to stand like Athanasius, contra totum mundum. But right is too strong to suffer any force or compulsion long; but it will break loose and prevail. In the meantime I am deeply sorry that, the pious and charitable device of Mr. Hopkins should be in any manner perverted or allayed, or the occasion of a difference or misunderstanding in that good place.

My opinion such as it is I am willing to offer you, and as willing that you communicate to those who may either value it, or to whom it may be a service. However you need not in this matter care upon the reputation of any person; but upon known maxims in law and valid cases which I presume, no good man with you will be so hardy as to oppose. However I am sure such can harm none but themselves. Those rules that occur without the turning to authors for the very words are such as these: the words of a deed are the deed; but the intent of a will is a will. And the true intent and meaning of the donor, in every device, is carefully to be required by the ordinary and pursued by the executor. That devices and bequests to pious uses are, of all others most sacred, and to be pursued and advanced by persons entrusted; and in no case or manner to be slipt or narrowed but to be extended and enlarged both for serviceableness and manner of improvement, as far as the good and sound construction of the will, will in any way bear.

That executors or Trustees being thereto impowered making their declaration and particular designation to a device at large to pious uses, is to be holden good; and being once done and reasonably determined is not by themselves to be altered.

That all such trustees and managers of estates bequeathed to pious uses, are from time to time accountable to the ordinary or their superior: (in whose room our County Courts have always stood) and in case of breach or deviation are to be regulated and restored into the right way. That whatever such trustees shall do contrary to law, to embezzle the estate, lower the profits, divert the use, or in any case whatever part with the freehold, whence the maintenance of the pious use should arise, and upon which it is now legally settled, 'tis of itself perfectly void and of none effect. And they themselves for such breaches are liable to censure for their reformation; and finally for a removal; and other meet persons betrusted, who shall more faithfully manage the same. That when gifts to publick uses are originally impracticable and afterwards useless or unprofitable in the place from the manner of the donation, they shall now neither be diverted to any more private or less profitable use; but to more publick and greater; and that often by the authority of the King and Parliament. That gifts and grants of particular persons or Committees to any publick pious use, when the grant is duly and effectually made in law, cannot by any means by themselves be ever revoked, but will abide and remain in all respects effectual; and are thenceforward become a publick estate, liable to all the rules and methods of management accordingly.

From all that is above: I am of opinion that the trustees of Mr. Hopkins,s Estate, have descended to the lowest and most restrained exposition of the bequest, of the most pious and charitable donors in assigning the same to a free Latin School; and have conveyed it as far up the river as could modestly be desired when they brought it to Hadley.

And what they have done therein and the town have added in disposing it into lands streams and mills can by no legal methods ever be altered. And that therefore the order of the County Courts, in all points is good and just and of authority; save in the last little hanck thereof viz. in the meantime to be improved &c. which I am of opinion saving always a great deference to the gentlemen of that Court, was an inconvenient as well as illegal concession, devised to have given a present easure to your earnest people, which therefore hath the usual effect and issue of such method, to put forward the irregular desire of the less thinking people to obtain their impetuous resolve th'o thereby to the after destruction of the gifts and which without any threatening, will end in the perfect removal of its improvement in your town: And perhaps bring it here to this College, or some less profitable foundation: all which I pray God to prevent for the honor of the Donors, Trustees, Town of Hadley and the good and sound profession of the true religion.

If anything in this hasty paper may be of service to your good people, I shall be glad. If any rest not in it, at your next desire, I may further proceed to communicate the matter to the Council while out of true respect to your good neighbors, and unwillingness to discover their present ill humor I have foreborne. I humbly ask your prayers and blessings and am Sir

Your faithful servant,

J. DUDLEY.

Original in Judd papers with J. R. Trumbull.

PRESIDENT AND COUNCIL,S ORDER DECEMBER 8, 1686.

By the Honorable, the President and Council of His Majesty,s Territory and Dominion of New England, in America. Upon the perusal of the return made by Major Pynchon and the Committee for Hadley School. The President and Council do order that the Committee for the Hopkins,s school, be and remain the Feoffees of the Grammar School in said town. And that Mr.

Partrigg be and is hereby dismissed from any further service in that matter. And that the said Committee make report of present Estate of said Mr. Hopkins,s and other Donations to the school (which having been orderly annexed to the Grammar School and hereby continued to that) unto the next County Court of Hampshire; who are hereby impowered, to supply the place of Mr. Partrigg, with some meet person, in Hadley, and that the said Court do find out, and order some method for the payment of Boltwood,s expenses upon the mill; that the the mill, Farm and other land given to the school may return to that publick use. The President and Council, hereby declaring it to be beyond the power of the Town of Hadley, or any other, to divide any of the lands or estates or the said mills, streams or privileges thereof (which are legally determined to this said Grammar school) to any other use whatsoever.

The President and Council judging the particular gifts in that Town a good foundation for a Grammar School both for themselves and the whole Country.* And that the Grammar School can be no otherwise interpreted, but to be a school holden by a master capable to instruct children, and fit them for the university.

Council House Boston, December 8, 1686.

By order EDWARD RANDOLPH, Secretary.

This is a true copy of the order of Council, sent me by Mr. Randolph, taken out of the original, which is to lodge with myself, till the County Court and then to be there presented.

Attest, JOHN PYNCHON.

Found in the records of Hopkins Academy.

This order of the President and Council moved the school committee to make report to the next County Court in Hampshire. The doings of the court are found in the paper that follows.

ORDER OF THE SESSIONS JUNE 8, 1687.

The Honorable the President and the Council by their order of December 8, 1686, having taken cognizance of the estate of the Grammar School in Hadley, called Hopkins,s School; ordering that the Committee for the said Hopkins,s School to be and remain the feoffees of the Grammar Scool in said town; except Mr. Partrigg, whom they dismissed from that service; and ordered the next County Court in Hampshire, to take care for supplying the place of Mr. Partrigg, with some other meet person, referring the case of the School and particularly the Committee to make report of the estate of Mr. Hopkins and other donations thereto, to the next Court in Hampshire which the said Committee have now accordingly done. And the Honorable the President and Council, declaring the Donations to have been orderly annexed to the Grammar School in Hadley, and that they are to be continued to that service. And having ordered the said Court to find out, and order some method for, the payment of Boltwoood,s expenses, upon the mill, that the mill with the Farm and other lands given to the school, may return to that publick use.

---

*It is in question whether, in the original of which this is a copy, the word was country or county.

The premises considered, and the committee of the said Hopkins,s School viz. Mr. John Russell, Capt. Aaron Cooke, Joseph Kellogg and Samuel Porter (now settled by the President and Council the Feoffees of the said School) appearing at this Court of Quarter Sessions for the County, as the County Court in Hampshire and presenting the Estate of Hopkins and other donations to said school, that they be settled to it as formerly they have been, by order of former County Courts in Hampshire, and particularly by the last County Court in Springfield in September, 1686. All which this Session will approve of, and considering the President and Council judges the gifts a good Foundation for a Grammar School for the whole Country, and having the concurrence of his excellency, our Honorable Governor, therewith, as hinting the same to the worshipful Judge of this Court, that it is not in the power of the Town of Hadley, or any person to divert any Donations, Lands, Mills, Streams or Estates, given, determined or employed to the Grammar School there; to any other use whatsoever. Wherefore this Court do advise the Town of Hadley, or such as acted in their behalf (only one alone viz. Mr. Partrigg appearing) who thr'o inadvertence or precipitancy have entered upon the school estate taking part of the donations into their own hands, for an English School (which may not be allowed disjunct from a Grammar School) to return and restore the whole profits thereof to the former Committee viz. Mr. John Russell, Aaron Cooke, Joseph Kellogg and Samuel Porter now the Feoffees of the Grammar School called Hopkins,s School. Mr. Hopkins,s given by him to promote humane literature, and declared by his Trustees, to be for and to a Grammar School which can be no otherwise interpreted, as the President and Council have declared; but to be a school holden by a master capable to instruct youth for the university. And therefore it is misapplied, and abused by such persons in Hadley, who have acted in it, to employ it otherwise and so ought speedily by them to be returned. And Mr. Partrigg saying: they desired to be understood, as not detaining, or holding the estate; but leaving to the Court to order. It is therefore, hereby ordered, that those persons in Hadley, who have anyways meddled, or intrenched upon the school estate thereof, which ought to be managed by John Russell, Aaron Cooke, Joseph Kellogg and Samuel Porter, the Feoffees of the said school, (to whom this Court of Sessions [according to order] have now by the consent and choice of the rest of the Committee, added Chiliab Smith of Hadley, to make up the number of five Feoffees) do deliver up all the estate they have entered on forthwith; into the hands or ordering of the Feoffees on penalty of all damage that may come to themselves by neglect thereof. And that Samuel Boltwood, who hath the school mill in his improvement, which was firstly built by Mr. Hopkins's estate, for the school, do likewise deliver up said mill and appurtenances, to the Feoffees aforesaid; who are to take it into their hands and improvement, for the maintenance of the school to which it belongs. And for what Samuel Boltwood hath expended upon the repairing or new building of it, he yielding to resign it in case he be paid what he hath lien out; if the toll or rent since it hath been in his Father,s and his hands have not sufficiently paid their just expense upon a moderate due accompt. Then the Feoffees of the school to allow further, according as they shall see just and reasonable; by continuing the rent of the mill to him, or otherwise, till he be paid what is meet he should have. And in case the Feoffees and Samuel Boltwood come not to an agreement concerning it between themselves within thirty days, That then the consideration of what the said Boltwood should and ought to have; for what estate he or his Father expended upon the rebuilding of the said school mill be determined by Mr. John Allis, (whom this Court appoints) and one such man as the Feoffees of said school shall choose and appoint together with one such man as Samuel Boltwood shall choose or appoint; which three men or, at least two of them are to give in their award concerning it, at the next Quarter Sessions, on the first Tuesday of September, which if neglected, we advise and direct the Feoffees to a prosess in a course of law, that they may be in a capacity, to settle a school master there according to the intent of the Donations; which if the whole estate be all got together and all improved, we hope may maintain a Grammar School, with a small yearly addition thereto, by the Town of Hadley who may be well beneffitted by the same school master to teach their children.

Further, in case the Town of Hadley or those that acted for the Town, do actually deliver up the estate they entered upon, unto the Feoffees and do forthwith declare it by delivering it into their hands, we propose it to the Feoffees to allow them the half of sixteen pounds they engaged to a school master or otherwise as the Feoffees see meet.

This is also a true Copy of the original at Quarter Sessions Court held at Northampton in his Majestys territory of New England Northampton, this 8th of June. 1687.

Attested by James Cornish, Clerk.

The Town in compliance with the order of the court passed this vote in which it is easy to read the spirit of the voters.

TOWN VOTE AUGUST 29, 1687.

Voted by the Town that the Lands seized and taken into their own hands with reference to an English school by their vote August 23rd, 1686, wanting that formality in the seizure, as might have been, the Town do now let fall their said seisure leaving said lands in the hands of the Committee as formerly; withal reserving a liberty to themselves and successors to make claim and plea according to law at anytime for the future, for what may appear to be their right in the Premises.

After the vote of the Town Aug. 29, 1687, the court of sessions sent the following letter to the selectmen of Hadley, March 7, 1688, to be communicated to the town. The members of the court were John Pynchon, John Holyoke, Joseph Hawley, Capt. Aaron Cooke of Hadley, Lieut John Allis.

HONORED FRIENDS:
Having had a sight of the vote of the town of Hadley of Aug. 29, 1687, in way of compliance (as we suppose) with the advise of the Court of Sessions, held at Northampton, June 7, 1687, we judge meet to let you understand our sense of it, that it is far short of what we expected and advised to being at best lean in itself, if not a justifying of yourselves in

your former precipitant, illegal entering upon the school estate, rather than a delivering it up to the committee as you were directed actually to do, and forthwith to declare it under the hands of those that had acted in entering thereon; and presuming upon your readiness so to do it, we proposed it to the committee or feoffees, if they saw cause, to allow one-half of the £16 that was engaged toward a school master. But what you have done being so short of that directed to and so worded as speaks your insubjection to authority, especially in conjunction with your other actings, we must declare it no ways convenient the committee should allow any part of the said 16£ and that you are accountable for your perverseness toward the school affairs, and for your slighting of such who have had more regard to your own good and interest than yourselves. Such a spirit we see breathing forth from you as will necessarily call for some further animadverting thereon, if you do not retract some of your actings which we earnestly desire you to overlook and rectify. We would not particularize and yet in way of caution to amendment, might mention your unkindness and sourness in not granting the use of a house that stands empty and your illegal rating of the school estate, contrary to the declared direction in all our books, of schools, hospitals etc. are not to be taxed, which we do particularly insist on, for your speedy rectification of what you have disorderly done (that we may not have occasion to lay it before his excellency.) Several other things are before our consideration which we do not mention, hoping and expecting you will revise your own actings and amend, which is the (scope) of these lines to prevent anything that may prove uncomfortable to yourselves being assured that a sense of your own crossness, perverseness, unsubjection to order and repentance for what is done amiss, will but become yourselves, and is the plainest path to your own comfort, which we pray God to direct you in and are

YOUR ASSURED FRIENDS.

We let you know and hereby declare that we forbid the constables and all officers from levying or collecting any particular tax toward any town affair, upon the school estate

Springfield March 7, 1687-8. By order of this Session

JAMES CORNISH.

(Clerk under Andrus.)

The selectmen replied to this letter and in June, 1688, and the Court sent another to Hadley "enjoining them to seek their own peace."

Judd Hist. pp. 62, 63.

Mr. Russell's part in this controversy is worthy of careful note. It caused him serious trouble. He was a staunch friend of the grammar school in distinction from an English school and earnestly intent on its secure establishment. There is reason to think he had the hope of something still higher. In his mind's eye was a college to grow up on this foundation.

Mr. Russell stood stoutly for the right as he saw it, against strong opposition led by a man of large ability and influence (Mr. Partrigg) and the leading man in the county after the death of Major Pynchon.

His position and course on this question had the effect to cool and estrange many of his people, so that after the decree of the court, Sept. 28, 1686, only twelve persons could be found to sign a paper adhering to Mr. Russell and the Grammar school, and accepting the order of the court. All but this small number seem to have favored an English school. This paper is as follows.

We whose names are underwritten hearing of a court order about Hadley school which some do oppose, we for our parts fearing and the disorder of opposing authority, declare that we neither oppose nor deny the said order, but do accept the same, and submit to it, giving all due honor to authority and would have it attended.

Oct. 18, 1686.

Samuel Gardner
John Ingram
Chileab Smith
Joseph Kellogg
Samuel ———
John Preston
Samuel Porter Senior
Aaron Cook
Widow Mary Goodman
William Marcum
Hezekiah Porter.

This was a time of great trial for these people. They were poor, suffering from the waste of war and much discouraged. The school estate had suffered serious loss. The school was intermittent. A school-master suitable for a Grammar school was hard to find and harder to retain on such terms as could be offered. The feeling on either side was intense. Once heated it took time to cool.

The town seem to have given their feeling expression in votes to reduce Mr. Russell's salary for several years. After his death in 1693 votes were passed which were a confession of wrong and made good to his heirs the dues they had witheld.*

Among the Judd papers with J. R. Trumbull the following is found which may be in place here:

TESTIMONY OF CHILEAB SMITH.

We whose names are undersigned do testify y^t ye Town of Hadley upon Mr. Goodwin,s motion did give liberty to sett a mill for the school in the place where ye corn mill now is.

Oct. 15. 1687

SAMUEL GARDNER
CHILIAB SMITH   his mark

---

*Mr. John Russell, the first minister of Hadley, was graduated at Harvard, in the third class, 1645, at the age of eighteen, born in England, the son of John Russell. He was ordained when twenty-two years of age, four years ater graduation, pastor of the church in Weathersfield, Conn. In 1648, he was school master in Hartford. He remained in Weathersfield about ten years, when he appears on the scene fifty miles up the river, as pastor of the flock of Christ in Hadley, to whom he was a faithful shepherd until his death. He toiled and suffered for his people in all the hardship and suffering of their lot. The regicides Goffe and Whalley found harbor in his house. As a writer he was wordy and full of repetition. He was the leading name in the school committee during his life, though for a time there was some difference between him and Elder Goodwin.

CHAPTER VI.

THE BEGINNINGS OF THE SCHOOL, AS LEARNED FROM TOWN RECORDS, COURT PROCEEDINGS AND OTHER PAPERS.

The school, as has been seen, began its work as early as 1667. How it went on for some time in its earlier years is learned from no clear, continuous record, but is somewhat matter of inference from an occasional vote of the town, proceedings in the County Court, and sundry papers relating to troubles and differences that arose from time to time and their adjustment. Some of these votes are given, covering some years, as follows. Dec. 21, 1676, some ten years after the school began its work, the town record has this vote :

It is ordered and voted by the town for the upholding and maintaining of the Scoole that the Scoole master shall have thirty pounds p^r Annum, which shall be paid part from the Annuitie of the Scoole Estate and the rest made up by the scholards and Towne.   (Old Record, p. 55.)

It is also voted that whereas the scoole masters salerye the last year was much diminished that therefore they will give on their next Town rate fifteen pounds to the said scoole master.

Allsoe with respect to the great ffailure of persons in not sending their children to scoole it is ordered and voted by the Towne that the present Selectmen and the Selectmen Annuallye shall take a list of all children ffrom six years ould to twelve, which shall be compellable if not sent to scoole to pay Annually according to and equallye with those that are sent, only some poore men,s children which shall be exempted as they shall be Judged by the Selectmen ; And ffrom six yeares ould, to continue till twelve at scoole except they Attain a ripeness and dexteritie in Inferior learning, as writeing & reading which shall be Judged by the Scoole master.   (Original Record, p. 55.)

From these and other votes it would seem that scholars from six to twelve years of age paid for schooling if able, whether in school or not. The income of the school estate paid only part of the expense. It was within reach of all of suitable age on payment of such cost as was not met by the income of the school property and the Town's allowance. The management, employment of teachers, and the like, was in the hands of the school committee for the most part.

Jan. 22, 1677. Voted by the town that Mr. Younglove shall have for his teaching school the next year the use of the House and Homestead belonging to the school with twelve Akars of land given by John Barnard and thirty pounds besides which shall be raised by the remainder of the school land the scollards and the Towne.

Voted by the towne that for the year ensuing all male children ffrom six yeares ould to twelve shall be compellable to pay to the scoole such as goe after tenn shillings by the year and they that goe not ffive shillings by the year and all others above the age expressed that are found Illiterate and go not to paie ffive Shillings by the year, this order to begin its date May 1st next ensuing. (Original Record, p. 58.)

Oct. 15, 1678. Voted by the town unanimously respecting the scoole and scoole master and his maintenance that Mr. Younglove showing himself willing and desirous yet to remain scoole master the Towne voted as aforesaid to Improve him in this work for one whole year from the time viz some time in May when his year expires that he now is in, and have voted that with the produce of the scoole land the scollards and the Towne in General shall be raised 30 pound for Mr. Younglove,s Sallerye and he accepts of the same.
(p. 59.)

Feb. 7, 1680. Voted by the Towne that they are willing to endeavor the procuring and provideing a scoole master that shall teach the Latin Tongue; as allso the English to any that are entered with writeing and Cyphering

Voted that the Said Scoole master shall have thirty pounds for this yeare ensuing and so for the next If he continue which summe shall be raised by the school estate and the scollards and what is wanting to make upp the said Complement to be paid by the Towne and that the said payment shall be no worse than other payments for service.

Voted that Every Latin Scollard shall paye twenty shillings pr Annum or by ye yeare and Every English Scollard sixteen shillings and so proportionably and all that are of Age that is from six to twelve yeares though they come not yet shall paye eight shillings by the yeare and all that doe but Enter shall paye for the Quarter.

Voted that the scoole Comittee with Luft Joseph Kellogg and Samuel Partrigg are Impoured to procure, provide and Agree with a Scoole master that may be suitable for the worke of said scoole on the Termes aforesaid.
(Original Town Record, p. 65.)

1682, Jan. 11. Voted that for the raising of 10 pound to make up the scoole masters Sallerye all that goe to scoole Shall paye and all that come to Scoole from 6 yeares to 12 shall paye alike and those that come not yet of the same Age halfe so much and 'Tis left with the Selectmen to proportion out of said persons for the making up of said Complement.
(Original Town Record, p. 70.)

Jan. 1685. Voted that Mr. Partrigg shall Teach schoole this winter three months or longer. (p. 75, Town Record.)

Aprll 28, 1686. Voted that Samuel Partrigg have eight pounds paid him for his services in keeping schoole in Hadley the last winter.

Voted that the Selectmen with Ensigne Nash, Chileab Smith and Nehemiah Dickinson, doe forthwith treat with the Schoole Committee and Desire the payment of eight pounds to Mr. Partrigg (out of the Schoole estate in their hands) for his keeping schoole the last winter.

Ap^{rtl} 1st, 1687. Voted by the Towne that a motion be made to the School Comittee to lend the Towne 16 pounds of the School estate to pay Mr. Mather the present School master   Voted by the Towne their aceptance of said motion by the Comittee and Mr. Partrigg Ingages to the Comittee in the Townes behalf the return of said estate.

April 7, 1692. The School Committee moving to the Town that they may remove the corn mill, that now is below the bridge to a more convenient place for the use of the school.   Hereupon voted by the Town that they do grant the place they desire so long as they maintain a mill there for the Town,s use

March 30th, 1709-10.   Whereas the School Committee in Hadley desire the advice and approbation of the Town with respect to their exchanging one acre and half of land with an out house ready to fall down thereon, which was given to the town by Mr. Ward deceased   Voted by said town that the committee can see it their way and can exchange the same for meadow land or let a long lease of said acre and 1-2 of land so as may be of encouragement to any to build thereupon, so as to bring in a better income to the school. This town hath approved thereof.   Voted in the affirmative.

These votes covering a period of more than thirty years, are largely the history of the school at this time. From them it is gathered that school matters were conducted somewhat loosely. The province and function of the Committee as related to those of the Town were not clearly distinguished.

CHAPTER VII.

NAMES AND DOINGS OF THE SCHOOL COMMITTEE. NAMES OF TEACHERS OF THE GRAMMAR SCHOOL.

A record of changes in the Committee is still in being. They seem to have kept a record of their other doings, which is lost. The names of the Committee are those that follow. Those chosen by Mr. Davenport and Mr. Goodwin in their agreement in 1664, were Mr. John Russell, pastor of the church in Hadley, Lieut. Samuel Smith, Andrew Bacon and Peter Tilton.

In 1669 when Mr. Goodwin made his proposal to the town to name three trustees, to whom the town should add two more to serve with himself while he lived, Mr. Goodwin made choice of Mr. John Russell, Lieut. Samuel Smith and Capt. Aaron Cooke. The town chose Nathaniel Dickinson, Sen. and Peter Tilton, the latter of whom was named in the agreement of Mr. Davenport and Mr. Goodwin, and for some reason seems to have fallen out of the number and came into it again by choice of the town. The name of Andrew Bacon also disappears. It was agreed that this board of five persons should fill vacancies in their number and thus make the committee perpetual. Thus Lt. Philip Smith was chosen in 1680,

 Col. Samuel Partrigg in 1682, removed 1687 by the County Court;
 Samuel Porter in 1685,
 Joseph Kellogg in 1686,
 Chileab Smith in 1687, by the Court with the concurrence of the other members of the Committee.

In 1720 the Committee were:
  Chileab Smith,
  Thomas Hovey,
  Samuel Porter, Esq.,
  Sargeant Joseph Smith and
  Dea. John Smith.

Nov. 5, 1733 the Committee were Westwood Cooke, John Smith, Eleazar Porter. Under this date occurs the following minute in the records of the Committee:

"We the subscribers, Lieut. Westwood Cooke Lieut. John Smith and Eleazar Porter of the Scool Committy in Hadley have made choyce of Dea. Samuel Dickinson to serve as a committy man in the room and sted of Lieut. Thomas Hovey, one of the scool Committy: he being aged and crazy and declines the service any longer. And we have also made choyce of Mr. Job Marsh to serve as a committy man, in the room and sted of Mr. Joseph Smith, one of our late scool com^{tt} men now deceast."

In 1745 Capt. Moses Cooke was chosen,
" 1746 Dea. Joseph Eastman and Ensine Moses Marsh,
" 1750 Dea. Enos Nash,
" 1757 Mr. Eleazar Porter to succeed the Honorable Eleazar Porter, deceast,
" 1758 Mr. Samuel Gaylord,
" 1768 Dea. David Smith,
" 1769 Mr. Elisha Porter,
" 1772 Mr. Edmund Hubbard,
" 1781 Mr. Charles Phelps,
" 1783 Dea. Oliver Smith,
" 1785 Lieut. Enos Nash,
" 1793 Capt. Elisha Dickinson,
" 1796 Dea. Seth Smith,
" 1797 Doct. William Porter,
" 1804 Dea. Jacob Smith,
" 1812 Dea. William Dickinson,
" 1815 Col. Moses Porter.

These five last named were in office when the General Court was petitioned for the act incorporating Hopkins Academy, and were the original Board of Trustees of that institution when incorporated. This Committee was sometimes criticised by men of views opposed to each other concerning a more or less liberal way of managing school affairs. They were censured and even threatened with deposition for failing to maintain it as a Grammar School. On the other hand, they were blamed for too strict adherence to the Grammar School idea, and for forgetting that the school was Hadley's sole and exclusive right, thus stirring anew the embers of the controversy of 1686—7.

TEACHERS OF THE GRAMMAR SCHOOL.

Just when the Grammar school began its work cannot be exactly determined. Materials for its early history are scanty. The school committee, as has been said, seem to have kept no record now to be found but one that noted little but the filling of vacancies in their number as they occurred. Such accounts as the Treasurer kept are confused and blind, and often baffle rather than satisfy inquiry. An occasional vote of the town sheds a little light, but leaves many questions of interest without answer. The roll of the names of the committee from the first is preserved nearly, if not quite, complete. The names of many of the teachers are known and something of their character and later history.

It was understood from the beginning, and for the most part kept in mind, that the school was a Grammar school, a school taught by a master competent to give instruction in the tongues, and fit young men for the university. Only for a short time an English school was kept, while the committee was put out of their stewardship by the town. With this exception the Grammar school was maintained not wholly without interruption until it was merged in Hopkins Academy after its incorporation in the year 1816.

Under date April 25, 1665, about a year after the agreement of Mr. Davenport and Mr. Goodwin concerning the distribution of Gov. Hopkins's estate it was "Voted by the Towne that they would give 20 pound pr Annum for 3 yeares towards the maintenance of a Schoole master to teach children and to be as a helpe to m^r russell as occasion may require."

This is the earliest record of the kind. The first teacher employed probably was Mr. Caleb Watson. Graduated at Harvard in 1661. He was a native of Roxbury. He was in Hadley in January, 1667, and probably came in 1666 and continued until 1673, when he and Mr. Russell were no longer in full harmony. March 31, 1668, he took the freeman's oath in court at Northampton. In 1674 he undertook the school in Hartford and continued to teach it until 1705 when a vote was passed " that he be no longer school master to this town."

(Bacon's Address, p. 64.)

About 1674–1680, John Younglove was the school master, from Ipswich, was a preacher first at Quaboag, (Brookfield) and after he left Hadley at Suffield. Salary £30 and use of house and land.

In 1682-1683. Samuel Russell, son of Rev. John Russell, Harvard 1681. Was minister at Branford, Conn.

1685. Samuel Partrigg of Hadley, three months. Was Colonel, Representative in 1685-1686, judge of Probate and one of his majesty's council, the most important man in the western part of the Province after the death of Major Pynchon in 1703.

1686-87. Warham Mather, H. C. 1685. Son of Rev. Eleazar Mather of Northampton. Was judge of Probate at New Haven.

1688-89. John Younglove again. 6 months.

1689-90. Thomas Swan, H. C. 1689. From Roxbury. He was Register of Probate in Middlesex. 6 months.

1693-94. John Morse, H. C. 1692. From Dedham. Was minister at Newtown, L. I. He kept school near a year.

1694-95. Salmon Treat, H. C. 1694. Son of James T. of Weathesfield. Was minister at Preston, Conn. Kept a year. Wages £39.

1695-96. Joseph Smith. Son of Lieut. Philip Smith of Hadley. Was minister at Upper Middletown. Kept three quarters, at the rate of £38.

1696-97. John Hubbard, H. C. 1695. Son of John H. of Boston. Was minister of Jamaica, L. I. Kept one year at £30 as money.

1698-99. Joseph Smith again, one year or more.

1700-1. Samuel Melyen, H. C. 1696. Son of Jacob M. of Boston. Was minister at Elizabethtown, N. J. Kept one year, £38.

1701-2. Mr. Woodbridge. Either Ephraim or Samuel. Both graduated at H. C. 1701. Both were ministers. 1 year, £38.

1702-3. Nathaniel Chauncey, Yale College 1702. First graduate of Yale. The only member of the class. Son of Rev. Nathaniel C. of Hatfield. Minister at Durham, Conn. 3 months.

1703-4. Samuel Ruggles, H. C. 1702. From Roxbury. Was minister at Billerica. Kept 8 months, at the rate of £40.

1705-6. Samuel Mighill, H. C. 1704. Son of Rev. Thos. M. of Scituate. A teacher in Mass. and Conn. Died in South Hadley 1769. 1¼ year, at £40.

1706-7. Jonathan Marsh, H. C. 1705. Son of Jonathan M. of Hadley. Was minister at Windsor, Conn. 1 year, £30 as money.

1707-8. John Partrigg, H. C. 1705. Son of Col. Samuel P. of Hatfield. Died 1717. 1 year, £40.

1708-9. Aaron Porter, H. C. 1708. Son of Samuel Porter of Hadley. Was minister at Medford. Kept 6 months, at the rate of £40.

1709-10. Rev. Daniel Boardman, Y. C. 1709. Son of Daniel Boardman of Weathersfield. Was minister of New Milford, Conn. Kept 8 months at the rate of £26⅔ as money.

1710–11. John James. A native of England, Honorary degree at H. C. in 1710. He had previously been minister at Derby, Conn. 6 months, at the rate of £26⅔ as money.

1711–12. Elisha Williams, H. C. 1711. Son of Rev. Wm. W. of Hatfield. Was president of Yale College from 1725 to 1739. 11 months at the rate of £26⅔ as money.

1712–13? Thomas Berry, H. C. 1712. Was a physician. Lived at Ipswich. 6 months at the rate of £30 in money.

1713–14. Stephen Williams, H. C. 1713. Son of Rev. John W. of Deerfield. Was minister at Long Meadow. 1¼ year at the rate of £34 in money.

1714–15. Ebenezer Gay, H. C. 1714. From Dedham. Was minister at Hingham. 9 months at the rate of £26.

1715–16. Rev. Nathaniel Mather, Y. C. 1715. Son of Rev. Samuel M. of Windsor, Conn. Minister at ———— Kept 4 months.

1716–18. "Mr. Chauncey's Son." If he was the son of Rev. Isaac Chauncey of Hadley he was only 16 to 18 years old. 1⅔ years at the rate £36.

1718–19. Rev. Stephen Steele, Y. C. 1718. Son of James Steele of Hartford. Was minister of Tolland, Conn. 1 year £40.

1719–20. Solomon Williams, H. C. 1719. Son of Rev. William W. of Hatfield. Was minister at Lebanon, Conn. 1 year, £40.

1720–21. Hezekiah Kilburn, Y. C. 1720. He was born at Weathersfield and resided there. 1 year £40.

1721–23. Rev. Daniel Dwight, Y. C. 1721. Son of Nathaniel D. of Northampton. Episcopal minister at Charlestown, S. C. 1¼ years at £40 a year.

1723–24. Benjamin Dickinson, H. C. 1723. Son of Nathaniel D. of Hatfield. A preacher many years. Lived in Hadley. 1 year, £40.

1724–25. Israel Chauncey, H. C. 1724. Son of Rev. Isaac Chauncey of Hadley. He was an able preacher, but became deranged, and was burned to death in a small building near his father's, Nov., 1736. Kept ¾ year at the rate of £40.

(This roll is copied from Mr. Judd's History of Hadley, pp. 66–67. The fruit of painful, patient research.)

In March, 1743, Josiah Pierce, H. C. 1735, a native of Woburn, began to keep the Grammar School. He was to instruct in reading, writing, arithmetic, Latin and Greek. He kept 12 years to 1755 and again 6 years, from 1760 to 1766. His pay was £27½ in N. E. currency, or $91, and he had the use of 25 acres of meadow land.

Mr. Pierce for a long period was town clerk as well as teacher. He sometimes preached though he was probably never ordained.

Mr. Pierce began to teach school in Hadley as early as Jan., 1741. He had 29 scholars on the 23rd and on the 29th day of that month. From entries in his diary, kept in an interleaved almanac each year, it appears that the school was frequently not in session, from one day to one or more weeks at a time, on account of storms, town meetings, fasts, company, want of wood, master's absence on a journey, or to take care of his farm, when no help could be had. Under date Nov. 19, 1742, occurs this entry:

This day being the day before Thanksgiving I keep school all day, as I have heretofore, willing to attend; if parents will let their children attend; but they, the most of them, letting their children play about the streets rather y^u send them to school, I determine not to attend ye school in ye afternoon of such day hereafter.

No mention is made of regular vacations. The school week was six days. The school day more than six hours. The number of scholars varied from 5 to 30. Average attendance, 25 or less, rather than more. He notes that he taught Latin and Greek. Sometimes he mentions Arithmetic as taught to sundry pupils gratis. June 8, 1743. "No school because no scholars sent."

From the Book of Treasurer's accounts No. 1 these facts are gathered. p. 14.

1760, (date illegible). Agreed with m^r Pierce to keep the school one year, to give him the improvement of ye school lands in Hadley 3 acres excepted for which he is to have O L D T and give him £205 as Salary, the year begins Sept. 10

In his own diary is this entry:

Sept. 8. I enter the school at Hadley.

And this in another place:

1760, Sept. 8. I entered the school again at Hadley this day, Sal. to be as when I left it, vizt, £205 O. T. that is £27.6.8 L. M. per ann. and the use of all the school land in Great meadow and Hockanum to be accounted £50 O. T. I e £6 13s. 4d. l. m. per ann.

     27 6 8 p^r ann.
      6 6 8 p^r quarter
      2 5·6 p^r month
     11 4 p^r week

Here is given the Covenant of Josiah Pierce and the school committee:

Feb. 28, 1742-3. The school committee consisting of Eleazar Porter, Westwood Cook, John Smith, Saml Dickinson and Job Marsh made a covenant with Josiah Pierce. This covenant bound Josiah Pierce "to settle in the work and business of keeping a Grammar and English School in said Hadley first Precinct viz instructing in Reading, Writing and Arithmetic and in the Latin and Greek tongues so far as is requisite for admission into Harvard and Yale Colleges, for so long a time as sd Pierce Shall be able to discharge sd work and business faithfully."

His salary was to be £115 in bills of public credit whose equivalent was £27—6—8 lawful money, payable annually, and the use of all the school land in the Great Meadow, Hockanum Field and Northampton meadow, 25 acres in all, to be accounted £6-13s.-4d. lawful money, per ann.

This covenant continued in force until May 7, 1755, when it terminated at the desire of Mr. Pierce. The committee at this date were Eleazar Porter, Moses Cook, Joseph Eastman, Moses Marsh, Enos Nash.

See the original covenant in the Judd collection with J. R. Trumbull, Northampton.

In Sept. 8, 1760, Mr. Pierce entered the school again at Hadley on the same terms as before, and continued in service six years. Judd. Diary of Josiah Pierce, Sept. 8, 1760.

From this covenant it is clear that the committee understood that a Grammar school must be maintained and that a Grammar school was one in which enough Latin and Greek must be taught to meet the requirement to enter Harvard or Yale Colleges. It is also plain that the committee were responsible to the teacher for his annual salary. More than one-sixth of this was received as the use of land. How the rest was paid does not appear.

We can look into the school master's mind a little through such entries as these:

May 26, 1744. I begin to instruct Mr. F— in Latin and he breaks off like a F—l.

May 7, 1855. I give up the school at Hadley. I am to improve the lands as heretofore this year.

Dec. 9, 1755. I enter in ye school at Hadley till Mr. Strong is well who is sick.

Jan. 26, 1756. I keep the Hopkins School this day and no longer. 33s.

Dec. 28. I opened a school at my own house.

During the time between 1755 and 1760 he taught at South Hadley and at Northampton for terms of three or six months, four weeks to the month, days of absence to be made up. In the list of his pupils in South Hadley appear the names of persons who became leading citizens. Boys only seem to have been his pupils. The same is true largely if not wholly of the Hopkins School until its incorporation in 1816 as Hopkins Academy.

Oct. 27, 1766. Mr. Pierce began to teach school in Amherst, and taught six months a year or more, for 32 shillings, or $5.33 a month and board.

Winter evenings he kept a ciphering school, a few weeks at one shilling an evening. In the cold months 30 to 40 were in his day school in Amherst, in the warm months 15 to 30. His family resided in Hadley, as was the case when he taught in Northampton and South Hadley. He preached in vacant pulpits occasionally, gratis, or at 18 or 20 shillings a Sabbath. March 29, 1629, he dismissed the school for the want of wood.

(Judd. Hist. Hadley, p. 421.)

After Mr. Pierce retired, Mr. Strong was his successor. How long is not known. Mr. Pierce taught for him a short time while he was sick. From this time on the list is incomplete.

Mr. Oliver Warner charges the school committee for the board of Mr. Whitney, Aug. 3, 1772 to April 13th, 1775, deducting for absence 11 days at New Haven, 4 days at Brimfield, 2 weeks at Cambridge. Mr. Whitney, no doubt, was the school master during this time. Old acct. book, p. 20.

1779. From Sept. 15 to March 15, 1780, Rev. Sewel Chapin kept school.

1780. From Dec., 1780 to Dec. 25, 1786, Moses Hubbard, H. C. 1765 Honorary A. B., Y. C., A. M. also, married Mabel, daughter of Samuel Hopkins, D. D.

1786. From Dec. 25, to Nov. 10, 1791, Mr. Enos Cook, Y. C. 1785, son of Joseph, son of Noah, son of Westwood, son of Aaron.

1791. Dec. 15, to July 8, 1792, Mr. Heman Ball.

1792. July 23, to Oct., two m. and one week, Ebenezer White.

1792. Oct. 1, to Apr. 6, 1793, Mr. Jasper Bentley.

1793. Apr. 6, to Oct. 9, Mr. Ebenezer White, except 1 m. and 8 days absent, being in the whole 4 months and 25 days at £3 per month, 14-9-8.

1793. Oct. 8, to April 1, 1794, Mr. John Smith.

1794. May 5, to Sept. 5, Mr. Samuel Grimes.

1794. Sept. 15, to April 5, 1795, Mr. John Smith.

1794. Rev. Gardiner Kellogg, Y. C. 1791. Kept school 2 weeks, ending Apr. 1, apparently.

1795. Apr. 27, to Oct. 6, 5 mos. in all, Ebenezer White.

1795. Nov. 23, to ye 15 April, 1796, Rev. John Gurley, Y. C. 1773. 1796 from Apr. 25, to Sept. 9.

1796–1797. Nov. to March 8, Mr. Fanning Tracy, Y. C. 1796, also from March 9 to June 9 and two months ending Aug. 9, 1797. After Mr. Tracy, 2 mos., 17 days, dates not noted, Mr. Joseph Bridgman.

1798. Jan. 18 to July 1, and to Oct. 12, 2 mos., 25 days and from Oct. 8, 1798 to 1799, May 1, Mr. John Dickinson.

1799. May 1 to Sept. 1, and 3 mos., 23 days to Dec. 24, Mr. James Woodward.

1801. 7 mos. to April 30, Giles C. Kellogg, Y. C. 1800.

1803. 6 mos. ending Apr. 5, 1803 Rev. Bela Kellogg, W. C. 1800.

1803. Mr. Taylor.

No record is found of teachers of the Grammar school between 1803 and 1816. But it is remembered by one who was during this period a member of the school, Dea. Simeon Dickinson of Northampton, that Rev. Mr. Gray was teacher for a time. Dr. Rogers taught for a season and Mr. Chester, Y. C. 1804, afterwards distinguished as Rev. John Chester, D. D.

It appears that these teachers with few exceptions, were young men, recent graduates of College. Many of them afterwards distinguished. Their terms of service were short for the most part. Very few of them made teaching their life work. Hence the quality of their work, though excellent, would not be what it might have been, had it been their permanent choice.

CHAPTER VIII.

SCHOOL AFFAIRS FROM 1755-1816.

After the troubles concerning the school estate were settled in 1688 and the School Committee established and confirmed in their care and management of the property, all went on quietly until about the middle of the 18th century.

The period between 1750-70 was one when warm interest was felt concerning the Hopkins school. Some controversy arose concerning it. The committee were charged with neglect of duty in that the Grammar school was practically such no longer. English scholars were suffered to come in, in such numbers, that the master could not give due attention to Grammar scholars. During this period there was a scheme to set up a college with the Hopkins fund as a basis. A Grammar school was started in Hatfield for scholars that did not get their dues at the Hopkins school in Hadley.

This vote of the town of Hadley shows that interest concerning education was alive in the minds of the people.

TOWN VOTES SEPT. 30, 1754.

At a legal meeting of the inhabitants of the Town of Hadley holden at the meeting-house in the first Precinct in said Hadley.

Voted. The Town is willing that the estate given for the support of a Grammar School in the Town of Hadley, be employed (in conjunction with other estates that may be obtained by subscription) for the support of an Academy in the Town of Hadley; the Grammar School being always maintained by the same, for the benefit of the said Town of Hadley.

A true copy from the Book of votes in the Town of Hadley, extracted Oct. 12th, 1754, by Josiah Pierce, Clark for sd. Town of Hadley.

Jan. 1, 1759. I. Williams, of Hatfield, wrote to Eleazar Porter of the school committee, complaining that the design of the donor of the school estate was not furthered as it ought to be by the trustees, that so many English scholars were sent to the school that the master had not time to attend properly to Grammar scholars and giving it to be understood that if the trustees or committee did not heed the warning and change their course, measures were in contemplation to remove them from office, for having failed in duty.

A letter of I. Williams without date or address, written probably about this time, goes to show that a lively interest was felt in the school question, to what end the school estate should be managed, and what right and interest the town had in it. He argues strongly and at much length that the trust was not with the Town, but with the trustees, for the ends indicated by the original donors. A Grammar school was set up in Hatfield about 1754. About this time, too, occurred the movement for a college in Hampshire county. See the letters in the Judd collection with J. R. Trumbull.

July, 1766, (day of the month torn out.) Samuel Cooke of Cambridge, wrote a letter to Rev. Samuel Hopkins of Hadley, claiming very strongly that the school estate belonged to Hadley solely and exclusively.

This letter seems to have been intended as an answer to the views of Mr. Williams and those in sympathy with him and opposed to the scheme they were anxious to carry out,—to establish a college and perhaps use the Hopkins estate in aid of the enterprise. He complains of the disposition and effort to send English scholars from the school.—(Judd papers with J. R. Trumbull.)

Letters of *Israel Williams concerning these matters are preserved in the collections of the Mass. Historical Society in Boston.

This controversy died away. The committee were not disturbed. The school was continued, it may be, with some interruptions. No complete list of teachers can be found. A very few persons are living who remember the Hopkins Grammar School as pupils in it during the earlier years of the present century. At this time, as before, it was understood to be a Grammar school taught by a master able to teach the tongues and fit young men for college, though those who sought such instruction were few. By far the larger number were taught only the common English branches.

---

*Israel Williams was evidently an educated man, friend of education and positive clear convictions and able to express them strongly.

CHAPTER IX.

INCORPORATION OF HOPKINS ACADEMY.

At this time and onward there is reason to think that in the minds of the committee and other friends of education the feeling was growing, that something more and better than had been realized was to be desired. This desire found expression in a movement to secure from the General Court of Massachusetts, an act of incorporation under which the Hopkins Donation School should become Hopkins Academy.

The earliest record of this feeling and movement is found in the doings of a town meeting held Jan. 1, 1816, when this vote was passed:

Jan. 1, 1816. In a town meeting held this day it was voted that the town will unite with the Committee of the Hadley Donation School in petitioning the Legislature for the establishment of an academy in this town.

The committee themselves presented such a petition, as appears from the act of incorporation herewith given.

Whereas it appears by the petition of Seth Smith and others, the Committee of the Donation School in the town of Hadley, that a fund heretofore given for the support of said School by the Honorable Edward Hopkins, may be more conveniently and advantageously directed to the furtherance of the benevolent objects of the donor by establishing a body politic for the management of the same; Therefore

Sec. 1. Be it enacted by the Senate and House of Representatives in General Court assembled, and by the authority of the same, that there be, and hereby is established an Academy in the town of Hadley and County of Hampshire upon the foundation of the Hopkins Donation School, to be known and called hereafter by the name of Hopkins Academy and that Seth Smith, William Porter, William Dickinson, Jacob Smith and Moses Porter, the Committee of the Donation School aforesaid be, and they are hereby incorporated into a body politic by the name of the Trustees of Hopkins Academy; and they and their successors shall be and continue a body politic by the same name forever.

Sec. 2. Be it enacted, That all the lands and monies heretofore given or subscribed to the Committee aforesaid for the use of the said school, or which shall hereafter be given, granted and assigned to the Trustees aforesaid for the use of the said Academy, shall be confirmed to the said Trustees and their successors in that trust forever for the uses designated by the Donors; and they the said Trustees and their successors shall be further capable of having, holding and taking, in fee simple by gift, grant devise or otherwise, any lands, tenements or other estate real or personal, provided the annual income of the same shall not exceed five thousand dollars; and that the rents and profits thereof shall be applied in such a manner as that the designs of the donors may be effectually promoted.

Sec. 3. Be it further enacted, That the said Trustees shall have power from time to time as they shall determine, to elect such officers of the said Academy as they shall judge necessary and convenient, and fix the term of their respective offices; to remove any Trustee from the Corporation, when in their opinion he shall be incapable through age or otherwise of discharging the duties of his office; to fill all vacancies by electing such persons for Trustees as they shall judge best; to determine the times and places of their meetings, the manner of notifying the said Trustees, and the method of electing or removing them; to ascertain the powers and duties of their several officers, to elect preceptors and instructors of the said Academy, and determine the duties and tenures of their offices; to ordain reasonable rules, orders and bye-laws not repugnant to the laws of this Commonwealth, with reasonable penalties, for the good government of the said Academy, and to ascertain the qualifications of students, requisite to their admission and the same rules, orders or bye-laws at their pleasure to repeal.

Sec. 4. Be it further enacted, That the Trustees of the said Academy may have one common seal, which they may change at pleasure and that all the deeds signed and delivered by their Treasurer or Secretary, by their order, and sealed with their seal, shall, when made in their name, be considered as their deed, and as such to be duly executed and valid in law; and that the Trustees aforesaid may sue and be sued in all actions, real, personal or mixed and prosecute and defend the same to final judgment and execution.

Sec. 5. Be it further enacted, That the number of said Trustees and their successors, shall not at any one time be more than nine, nor less than five, and a majority of the whole number for the time being, shall constitute a quorum for transacting business, and a majority of members present at a legal meeting shall decide all questions proper to come before the Trustees.

Sec. 6. Be it further enacted, That Seth Smith be, and he hereby is authorized to fix the time and place of holding the first meeting of the said Trustees, and to notify them thereof.

Approved by the Governor Feb. 14, 1816.
CALEB STRONG was Governor at this time.

An act in addition to an act entitled " An Act to incorporate the Trustees of Hopkins Academy."

Sec. 1. Be it enacted by the Senate and House of Representatives, in General court assembled and by the authority of the same, That the number of the Trustees of Hopkins Academy and their successors, shall not at any one time be more than fifteen, nor less than five; and a majority of the whole for the time being, shall constitute a quorum for transacting business; and a majority of the members present at a legal meeting, shall decide all questions proper to come before the Trustees.

Sec. 2. Be it further enacted, That the fifth section of the Act entitled "An Act to incorporate the Trustees of Hopkins Academy" be and the same is hereby repealed.

June 9, 1821.

The Trustees thus incorporated held their first meeting June 4th, 1817, at the house of Dr. Wm. Porter, chose Rev. Dan Huntington and Rev. John Woodbridge as two additional trustees and adjourned to the sixth of the same month at the house of Dea. Seth Smith. On Friday, June 6th, the Trustees met and chose Rev. Joseph Lyman, D. D. and Isaac C. Bates, Esq. as two additional Trustees, making the whole number nine, and adjourned to meet on the eleventh at the house of Rev. John Woodbridge.

June 11th. The Board met and chose the Rev. Dan Huntington Secretary of the Board, the Rev. Joseph Lyman, D. D., President and Wm. Porter, Esq., Treasurer. Isaac C. Bates, Esq., Rev. Dan Huntington and Moses Porter, Esq. were appointed a committee to frame Bye-laws for the regulation of Hopkins Academy, and Rev. John Woodbridge, William Porter, Esq. and Dea. Jacob Smith were appointed a committee to procure an instructor of the Academy.

June 30. The Board met as adjourned. The committee appointed to prepare bye-laws, reported as follows:

1st. The officers of the Board of Trustees shall consist of a President, a Secretary, a Treasurer and a Prudential Committee of three persons, which shall be elected by ballot at the annual meeting of the Board, to be holden on Tuesday, fifteen days before the first Wednesday of December 10 o'clock, A. M.

2nd. The President shall be empowered, upon application of three or more, Trustees, to call a special meeting of the Board, or when in his opinion it shall be necessary, giving seasonable notice of the time and place of meeting, and in case of the absence or inability of the President the same powers are entrusted with the Prudential Committee.

3rd. The Treasurer shall give adequate bonds, with sufficient securities to the Prudential Committee, for the faithful discharge of his duty.

4th. All orders on the Treasurer for the payment of money shall be drawn under direction of the Prudential Committee.

5th. The Prudential Committee shall provide sufficient instructors for said Academy, who shall be continued or removed at the discretion of the Trustees, and the general concerns of the Institution shall be under the Superintendence of Said Committee.

6. The Instructors shall be persons of good moral character, of competent learning and abilities, firmly established in the faith of the Christian Religion, the doctrine and duties of which they shall inculcate, as well by example as precept.

They shall instruct their pupils whether males or female, in the several arts and sciences, which may be necessary or proper to an accomplished education of either.

The Preceptor shall open and close the school each day with prayer. He shall be authorized to adopt such rules for the internal government of said Academy under the revision of the Prudential Committee, as shall be found necessary, nor contravening those established by the Trustees.

[He shall also keep and at the end of each term render to the Treasurer, a catalogue of the students, specifying, respectively the time of their entering and leaving the school.]

7th. Youth of both sexes, who can read decently, in a common English book without spelling and write a joined hand and are of good moral character shall be entitled to admission.

[8th. Males studying the Greek and Latin languages are exempt from the expense of tuition.

9th. Tuition by the term, shall be two dollars, one-half payable in advance, the residue at the expiration of six weeks from the time of admission.]

10th. All the students [shall uniformly attend upon the public worship of the Sabbath] shall be in subjection to the authority and government of the Institution; shall be punctual and seasonable in their attendance upon its exercises; orderly and studious in their habits; decent in their apparel and deportment; and shall in all things conform to the rules and regulations which are or may be prescribed for their direction and government.

11th. All damages shall be estimated by the Preceptor and repaid by those who occasion them.

12th. Punishments shall be either private or public admonition, and degradation to be inflicted at the discretion of the Preceptor, and for more aggravated offences suspension or expulsion to be inflicted by the Preceptor, with the concurrence of the Prudential Committee.

[13th. There shall be four terms in each year and four vacations consisting of two weeks each. The terms shall respectively commence on the first Wednesdays of December, March, June and September. And at the end of each term there shall be a public examination of the students.]

14th. Each meeting of the Board of Trustees shall be opened with prayer by the President or some person nominated by him.

15th. Any alteration or amendment of the bye laws shall be proposed at a previous meeting.

Voted to accept the above as the Constitution of Hopkins Academy.

[Aug. 30, 1819. The 8th and 9th articles of the Bye laws were so far altered as that the price of tuition shall, in future, be two dollars and fifty cents, as well for Latin and Greek, as English scholars and in case any student shall at the same time attend to more branches than two, the tuition shall be increased at the rate of fifty cents for each additional branch of study, excepting in the French language, the terms of tuition in which will vary according to the number of scholars, and be subject to the order of the Prudential Committee, provided, however, that in case any Latin and Greek scholar shall attend to any other branch of study, the Latin and Greek shall be deemed but one branch; and provided also, that all charity scholars who may be placed in the Academy by any Education Society, or by the Prudential Committee, as such, shall be exempted from all expense for tuition.

Sept. 6, 1821. It was voted that as a standing rule, there shall be a regular meeting of the Trustees, for the transaction of business, at the close of each quarter, when the publick examination is had.

Dec. 5, 1825. Voted that the annual meeting of the Board be held each year on Monday next preceding the Wednesday which commences the winter quarter, at 11 o'clock A. M.

Voted that it be the official duty of the preceptor to furnish the Treasurer, at least three weeks previous to the expiration of such quarter, a list of the names of the students, their place of residence, and the sums due from them severally to the Treasury.

Voted that in future the number of officers be enlarged by the choice of a vice-president.

Nov. 9, 1839. It was voted that members of colleges be not admitted as members of the Academy from this time.

Jan. 23, 1852. It was voted that the By-laws be so altered as to allow the Preceptor of the Academy liberty to punish the younger scholars as is customary in common schools.

Feb. 17, 1852. Voted that the 12th article which relates to the punishment of scholars be erased.]*

BY-LAWS OF HOPKINS ACADEMY AS REVISED AND AMENDED MAY 5, 1889.

ARTICLE 1st. The officers of the Board of Trustees shall consist of a president, a vice-president, a secretary, a treasurer, a prudential committee of three persons and an auditor of accounts, which officers shall be elected by ballot at the annual meeting of the Board to be holden on the last day of the Fall term in each year.

ART. 2d. The Prudential Committee shall be empowered, upon the application of three or more trustees, to call a special meeting of the Board, or when, in their opinion it shall be necessary, giving seasonable notice of the time and place of meeting.

ART. 3d. The Treasurer shall give adequate bonds, with sufficient securities to the Prudential Committee for the faithful discharge of his duty.

ART. 4th. All orders on the Treasurer for the payment of money shall be

---

*Articles in brackets subsequently repealed.

drawn under the direction of the Prudential Committee and be signed by not less than two of them.

ART. 5th. The Prudential Committee shall provide sufficient instructors for said Academy, who shall be continued or removed at the discretion of the Trustees, and the general concerns of the institution shall be under the superintendence of said committee.

ART. 6th. The instructors shall be persons of good moral character, of competent learning and abilities, firmly established in the faith of the Christian religion, the doctrines and duties of which they shall inculcate by example as well as by precept. They shall faithfully instruct all their pupils in all the branches of the course of study as prescribed by the Prudential Committee, with the view to prepare young men and women for admission to college, or other higher institutions of learning or for the conduct of life.

The Principal shall open the school each day with prayer. He is authorized to adopt such rules for the internal government of said Academy under the revision of the Prudential Committee as shall be found necessary, not contravening those established by the Trustees.

The Principal shall return to the secretary, at the end of each term, the names of all scholars to be entered on the records.

ART. 7th. Pupils of good character, who have completed the study of Geography, Grammar, Arithmetic and the History of the United States and the rudimentary branches as taught in the Grammar Schools of the town, on examination or on certificate satisfactory to the Prudential Committee, shall be admitted to membership in the school with all its privileges, free of tuition, if they belong to town. Pupils from out of town shall be entitled to membership on payment of tuition at rates established by the Prudential Committee. In special cases pupils whose needs are not met in other schools, may be admitted to membership for the winter term, on the approval of the Prudential Committee, provided they can be taught to advantage in existing classes.

ART. 8th. All students shall be in subjection to the authority and government of the institution, shall be punctual and seasonable in their attendance upon its exercises, orderly and studious in their habits, decent in their apparel and deportment and shall in all things conform to the rules and regulations which are or may be prescribed for their direction or Government.

ART. 9th. All damages shall be estimated by the principal and repaired by those who occasion them.

ART. 10th. Each meeting of the Board of Trustees shall be opened with prayer by the president or some person nominated by him.

ART. 11th. Any alteration or amendment of these by-laws shall be proposed at a previous meeting.

ART. 12th. All by-laws or parts of by-laws inconsistent with the forgoing are hereby repealed.

SCHOOL HOUSES.

The committee in trust with the Hopkins Fund seem never to have built a school house for their use until after the act incorporating Hopkins Academy in 1816. Nathaniel Ward, who died in 1664, gave a piece of his homelot on the street with his house for the use of the school. A part of this building was used for a school house for many years. After 1688 a room was hired for the school. In 1710 the Ward house was said to be "ready to fall down." It had probably ceased to be used for school purposes.

July 13, 1698 the town voted to build a school house 25 by 18 feet and 7 feet between joints, to be set in "middle of the town." This was the first school house built in Hadley. It stood in the broad street.

The Hopkins school, says Mr. Judd, was apparently the only public school in the old parish of Hadley, for more than a century, except a school for boys and girls voted in 1760 for that year. It was the common or town school. The master, with rare exceptions, was a man of collegiate education and he instructed some in Greek and Latin, but most, only in reading, writing and arithmetic. When Hadley had 99 families in 1695, there was but one town school. There still survives one man who remembers attending the Hopkins school kept in the house in the middle of the street early in this century.*

Following the act of incorporation came the erection of the Academy building. No votes of the Trustees are on record looking to the choice and purchase of the site or the contract for building. The name of the builder is not preserved. The lot, 63 feet front, 53 feet deep, containing thirteen rods of land, was part of the homestead of Mr. Chester Gaylord and was bought of him for the sum of fifty dollars. The building fronted south on the street known as Middle Lane and later as Academy Lane and Russell street. It was a plain brick structure painted, three stories high, having its entrance close to the sidewalk with no yard in front, and only a narrow space on the other sides. April 7, 1817, the town voted that the Trustees be permitted to enclose a part of this middle lane in front of their building for a yard under the direction of the selectmen not exceeding fourteen feet in width. The ground floor was divided equally into two school rooms, one on either side of the hall, running through the building from south to north.

---

*Dea. Simeon Dickinson who died May, 1890, aged 95.

The second story had five apartments. A small one over the entrance at the south was sometimes used for a library. The other rooms were repositories for chemical and philosophical apparatus and recitation rooms as they were needed.

The whole of the third story was known as the Academy Hall, which was thought to be fine and attractive. Its eastern end was occupied by a stage raised about four feet above the floor. This Hall was used for rhetorical exercises every Wednesday afternoon, quarterly examinations and for exhibitions and public lectures and sometimes for preaching services on Sunday. The congregation of the Russell church worshiped in it for several months during the erection of their church building, when they had Rev. Dr. Allen, ex-president of Bowdoin College, as their preacher, and likewise Rev. H. B. Smith, D. D., Prof. at Amherst College and afterwards at Union Theol. Sem. He was known to say, " In that hall I spread my wings." These apartments were severely plain and poorly equipped and furnished for the work to be done in them, according to the standards of to-day. But notwithstanding these limitations, good work was done and benign results wrought in the development of character in the young people, who resorted hither for instruction and training, of which not a few living witnesses are left, though the departed are now the majority.

Means for building were obtained in part by voluntary subscriptions. Some ninety persons became subscribers for this object in sums varying from fifty cents to eighty dollars. A very small fraction of these subscriptions was paid in money, but more in labor, in building material and supplies of one kind or other.

Windsor Smith, a merchant of that time, subscribed forty dollars in two installments, one of twenty-five and one of fifteen dollars, and twenty-five dollars of this amount was paid in two installments each, of ten gallons of rum, at seven shillings and sixpence a gallon, without which those walls could not have risen. It is possible that liquor in still larger quantity was deemed needful to this work, but hidden from notice among charges for " sundries." In the treasurer's accounts under date May 7, 1817, these charges are found, " 33 galls. rum at 6s., 9d. bbl. 7s, $38.29, 1 qt. mug, 1 1½ lbs. sugar .31."

The accounts for building were audited Nov. 28, 1817 and the whole expenses of the Academy so far as then finished, found to be $4954.90. This sum is much larger than the amount subscribed. The costs of building beyond this, were paid from the treasury of the institution by degrees from time to time. The treasurer's accounts lead to this inference.

Before the opening of the school a service of dedication was held Dec. 9, 1817.

The prayer of dedication was offered in Academy Hall by Rev. Joseph Lyman, D. D., of Hatfield, President of the Board of Trustees. Divine service appropriate to the occasion was attended at the meeting house at 2 o'clock P. M. A sermon was preached by Rev. John Woodbridge, from Deut. vi: 7, "And thou shalt teach them diligently unto thy children." The Trustees voted that the thanks of the board be given to Rev. Mr. Woodbridge for his sermon and that a copy be requested for publication.

Dec. 10, 1817, the day following the dedication, the school was opened under Rev. Dan Huntington as preceptor and Giles C. Kellogg, Esq. and Miss Sophia Mosely, assistants. The first catalogue published in 1818, has the name of Miss Sally Williston of Easthampton, as preceptress, from which it would appear that although Miss Mosely had been engaged, she did not serve that year, but was employed the year succeeding. For the second year Mr. Huntington's salary was five hundred dollars. Mr. Kellogg had twenty dollars a month and board with promise of more if the condition of the funds would warrant an increase. Miss Mosely was to have twelve dollars a month and board.

CHAPTER X.

HOPKINS ACADEMY IN COURT. TOWN OF HADLEY *VS.* TRUSTEES OF HOPKINS ACADEMY.

Under this Charter and Constitution Hopkins Academy entered upon its career of usefulness, having a large number of pupils from out of town as well as from within, employing a principal and one or more assistants. This course of prosperity continued without hindrance or molestation until 1831, when at the annual town meeting held April 4th, adjourned from March 28th, of that year, it was voted that a committee of three be appointed for investigating the subject of the Hopkins Fund to report at the May meeting.

Voted that the Hon. Chas. P. Phelps, Giles C. Kellogg and Col. Ephraim Smith be the committee.

At a meeting held May 11th, the committee above named to ascertain whether the Funds of the Hopkins School have been appropriated by the Trustees of Hopkins Academy for the benefit of the Town of Hadley, conformably to the intentions of the donors, reported that in their judgment, after perusing the documents bearing on the question, that the Town would be better satisfied with the opinion of men learned in the law, than with their own. They, therefore, had consulted Messrs. Billings and Clark who, after examination of the documents referred to, give their opinion of the interesting question presented to them and the argument by which it is supported, which the committee now present for the consideration of the town. This report was accepted and filed.

It was further voted at the same meeting that a committee of three be appointed with full power to take all such measures as may be necessary to obtain an adjudication or judicial decision of the question "Have the Trustees of Hopkins Academy, in Hadley, applied the income and proceeds of the Hopkins School Fund (so-called) and of the funds and estates heretofore contributed thereunto by the Town of

Hadley or any of the inhabitants thereof and which have fallen under the control and management of the said Trustees in all respects conformably to the intentions of the donors, in order solely that if by such decision any misappropriation of said income and proceeds shall appear to have been made by the said Trustees, they may hereafter apply the same in conformity to such decision.

Voted that the committee appointed at the last meeting, to whom the subject of the application of the Funds was then referred, be the committee for procuring the decision.

At a meeting of the Trustees of Hopkins Academy, Aug. 16, 1831, the following proposition was then made, seconded and adopted :

Whereas the Town of Hadley has directed a suit to be commenced against the Trustees of Hopkins Academy.

Voted that the Prudential Committee be, and are hereby authorized to procure good counsel and adopt all other suitable measures which may be necessary for a defence in the case.

The case was heard in the Supreme Court, Sept. term, 1833, and the report of the case and the decision reached are given below.

THE INHABITANTS OF HADLEY *VERSUS* THE TRUSTEES OF HOPKINS ACADEMY.

In 1657, Edward Hopkins, of England devised estate, real and personal, to certain individuals, in full assurance of their trust and faithfulness in disposing of the same according to the true intent and purpose of the testator, namely, " to give some encouragement to those foreign plantations (New England) in breeding of hopeful youth in a way of learning both at the Grammar School and College for the public service of the country in future times."

In 1664 the Trustees executed an instrument under seal, by which they order that " the property be equally divided between the towns of New Haven and Hadley to be in each of those towns respectively managed and improved towards the erecting and maintaining of a grammar school in each of them and the management thereof to be in the hands of our assigns, which are for that at New Haven, &c., and for that at Hadley J. R. &c. These we constitute to be our Trustees for the ordering of said estate and carrying on the work, wherein it is to be employed, in their town, hereby committing to them and investing them with full power to act in the same, in all respects as ourselves, both in managing the trust themselves and in choosing successors from time to time &c. who shall have full power to pursue and put in execution the pious end and intentions of the worthy donor, yet reserving to ourselves while we live, the full power of a negative vote, for the hindering anything that may cross that end." In 1664 another testator devised land " to the town of Hadley, for promoting and advancement of a school for learning." In the same year another testator devised " to the town of Hadley " certain real estate " to be improved towards the maintaining of a school ever." In 1666 the town passed the following vote " The town have granted to and for the use of a grammar school in this town of Hadley, and to be and remain perpetually to and for the use of said school" certain lands specified in the vote. In 1669 one of the surviving trustees made a proposal to the town of Hadley, that he should appoint three persons, to be submitted to the town and to be approved of by them, and that the town should appoint two and that these five with himself whilst he lived, should have the sole disposal and management of the estate in all respects, for the end to which it was bequeathed; and that the same five persons with himself whilst he lived, should have the sole management of all other estate given by any donor, or which might be given while they survived, to the town of Hadley, for the promoting of literature or learning; that these Trustees should have power to perpetuate the Board by filling their own vacancies; and that the school should be called the Hopkins school. The town approved of three persons named by the Trustees and appointed two themselves, and voted that " the committee thus chosen should jointly and together have the full ordering and disposal of the estate given by the Trustees of Hopkins to the town of Hadley, or any other estate or estates that were or might be given, either by the town itself or by any other donor, for the use, benefit and maintenance and promoting a grammar school to and for the use and in the town of Hadley." In 1675 another testator devised land to the town of Hadley, "committing it to the care, disposing and ordering of S. S. &c. [naming the persons constituting the Hopkins school committee] to be by them disposed of (in case they quietly keep and remain in their committeeship for Hopkins school) unto Hopkins School for Hadley; but if they be put out or disturbed in that committeeship, then to be disposed of as they see meet, for the good of the town." It was held that the legal estate in the property given by Hopkins, did not, by his will and the instrument made by his Trustees in 1664, vest in the town of Hadley; that the devise was not made for the purpose of founding a common town school for the exclusive benefit of the inhabitants of that town, but was designed for the encouragement of all persons in that (then) newly settled part of the country, who should desire to avail themselves of the benefit of a grammar school adapted to instruct and qualify pupils for the university; that a long continued usage of admitting pupils from other towns than Hadley, to participate in the benefits of the Hopkins school, was of weight in establishing such construction of the devise; and that all the other donations above mentioned were to be held upon the same trusts and be appropriated to the same purposes as the principal one from Hopkins.

It is probable that in 1666 the county courts and the President and Council of New England had jurisdiction over trusts of the kind above described.

BILL IN EQUITY.

The bill alleges, that in 1657, Edward Hopkins, Esquire, a resident in the Kingdom of Great Britain, by his last will bequeathed and devised as follows: "And the residue of my estate there (New England) I do hereby give and bequeath to my Father Theophilus Eaton, Esquire, Mr. John Davenport, Mr. John Cullick and Mr. William Goodwin, in full assurance of their trust and faithfulness in disposing of it, according to the true intent and purpose of me, the said Edward Hopkins, which is to give some encouragement in those foreign plantations for the breeding up of hopeful youth in a way of learning, both at the grammar school and college, for the public service of the country in future times. My further mind and will is, that within six months after the decease of my wife, five hundred pounds be made over into New England, according to the advice of my loving friends Major Robert Thompson and Mr. Francis Willoughby; and conveyed into the hands of the Trustees before mentioned, in further prosecution of the aforesaid public ends, which in the simplicity of my heart are for the upholding and promoting of the Kingdom of the Lord Jesus Christ in those parts of the earth:" That in 1664, Davenport and Goodwin being the only surviving Trustees, by an instrument under their hands and seals, after reciting the trusts and powers given to them in the will, proceed to execute the trust and dispose of the property confided to them in manner following: "We therefore, the said John Davenport and William Goodwin, being the only survivors of the said Trustees, for answering the trusts committed to us by the last will and testament of our worthy honored friend, do order and dispose of said estate as follows, &c. (disposing of a portion of the property confided to them, and then proceeding:) we do further order and appoint, that the rest of Mr. Hopkins his estate, both that which is in New England and £500, which is to come from Old England when it shall become due to us after Mrs. Hopkins her decease, be all of it equally divided between the towns of New Haven and Hadley, to be in each of those towns respectively managed and improved towards the erecting and maintaining of a Grammar School in each of them."

That in 1664 John Barnard, in his last will, devised "unto the town of Hadley for promoting and advancement of a school for learning, twelve acres, one rood and nine poles of meadow land, perpetually to be and remain to the use aforesaid, lying within the lands of the township of Hadley, six acres two roods and twenty-nine poles lying in the meadow called Hockanum; another parcel in the meadow called the Great Meadow, containing five acres, two roods, twenty poles;" and that in a codicil he devised as follows: "To the use and towards the maintenance of a school, I give perpetually my piece of land lying in the Forlorn; as also my piece of land that lies in Hockanum; and also that land I have given to a school; if there be not a school in Hadley at the decease of my wife, then the land to be improved by four of the poorest men in town till there be a school set up."

That in 1664, Nathaniel Ward devised as follows: Item, to the town of Hadley, I give, after the decease of my wife, my now dwelling house, with about five roods or an acre and a half of land on which it standeth, and my lot of five acres, more or less, in north meadow, and my lot in Hockanum containing nine acres, more or less; to be improved towards the maintaining of a school ever."

That in 1666 the town of Hadley passed the following vote: "The town have granted to and for the use of a grammar school in this town of Hadley, and to be and remain perpetually to and for the use of said school, the two little meadows next beyond the brook commonly called the mill brook, and as much land to be laid to the same as the committee, chosen by the town, shall, in their discretion, see meet and needful, provided, withal, it be left to the judgment of the said committee, that so much of the second meadow shall be excepted from the said grant as that there may be a feasible and convenient passage for cattle to their feed."

That in 1669, by agreement between Goodwin and the town of Hadley, five persons were chosen, partly by Goodwin and partly by the town, as a joint committee, "who together with Goodwin while he lived, and after his decease should jointly and together have the ordering and full dispose of the estate or estates given by Mr. Davenport and Mr. Goodwin (as trustees as aforesaid to Mr. Hopkins) to this town of Hadley, or any other estate or estates that ever may be given, either by the town itself, or any other donor or donors for the use, benefit and maintenance and promoting a grammar school to and for the use and in the town of Hadley." That it was also agreed that the committee should have power to fill vacancies in their number occasioned by death.

That in 1675, Henry Clark devised as follows: "My nine acre lot in Hockanum in the town of Hadley, and two acres and a half of my lot in the lower end of Great Meadow in Hadley, on the other side of the lot, I give to the town of Hadley, committing it to the care of Lieut. Samuel Smith, Ensign Cook, Dea. Tilton and Mr. John Russell, junior, to be by them disposed of (in case they quietly keep and remain in their committeeship for Hopkins School) unto Hopkins school for Hadley; but if they be put out of or disturbed in that committeeship, then to be otherwise disposed of as they or the survivors of them see meet for the good of the town."

That the committee above described and their successors continued to have the management of the property and to appropriate its annual income agreeably to the uses and for the purposes above mentioned, until 1816, when the committee, in concurrence with the town of Hadley, petitioned the legislature for an act of incorporation; and an act was accordingly passed, entitled, "an Act to incorporate the trustees of Hopkins Academy." That the trustees of the academy succeeded to and accepted of the trust above described; and that in and by the act of incorporation, all the lands and moneys, which had been heretofore given or subscribed to the committee before mentioned, for the use of the school, are confirmed to the trustees of the academy and their successors forever, for the uses designated by the donors."

That the plaintiffs hoped the trustees would have managed the property and appropriated the annual income, thereof, to and for the uses designated by the donors, and according to the agreement between Goodwin and the town of Hadley, for the use and benefit and maintenance and promoting a

Grammar School, to and for the use of the town and its inhabitants, but that they refuse, and have for a long time refused to administer the trust, according to the directions of the donors, and to appropriate the annual avails of the property to and for the exclusive use and benefit of the plaintiffs, and have appropriated the same, as well to the use and benefit of others, as of the plaintiffs, and sometimes to the exclusion of the plaintiffs.

The bill then prays for disclosure and relief.

The defendants in their answer, admit that Hopkins, Barnard, Ward and Clark made the several devises, and that the town of Hadley made the grant set forth in the bill.

They admit, that in 1664, Davenport and Goodwin, for the execution of the trust created by the will of Hopkins, made an instrument, containing the clause recited in the bill, but they allege that after that clause, the instrument proceeded as follows, "And the management, thereof, be in the hands of our assigns, which are for that at New Haven at present, (and so to continue, unless some other way be by us agreed on) the town court of New Haven, consisting of the magistrates and deputies and the officers of the church at New Haven, and for that at Hadley, John Russell, junior, pastor of the church of Christ at Hadley, Lieut. Samuel Smith, Andrew Bacon and Peter Tilton, these we, the said John Davenport and William Goodwin, do appoint and constitute to be our trustees, for the ordering of the estate and carrying on the work, wherein it is to be employed, each in their several towns respectively; hereby committing to them and investing them with full power to act in the same, in their several towns respectively; in all respects, as ourselves, both in managing the trust themselves and in choosing successors from time to time, as they shall see meet, who, or the major part of whom, (or in case at any time the rest of the trustees being taken away before others be chosen, any of whom) may and shall have full power to pursue and put in execution the pious end and intendment of the worthy donor; yet reserving to ourselves while we live, the full power of a negative vote for the hindering anything that may cross that end." The defendants further say, that the agreement made in 1669, between Goodwin and the town, was as follows: "Mr. Goodwin proposeth as that wherein he is willing to concur, viz. as to the ordering of the estate distributed and given by Mr. Davenport and himself (as trustees of Mr. Hopkins) to the town of Hadley, donors of the said estate, both for the present and the future, he, the said Goodwin hath chosen three persons or will choose them, to have power in the premises; he is willing also that the town should make choice of two more able and pious men, which five persons, together with himself, shall have the sole and full dispose and management of the estate above expressed, in all respects, for the end to which it is bequeathed. 2. As also the said five persons together with himself while he lives, to have the sole dispose and management of all other estate or estates given by any donor, or that may be while they survive, to the town of Hadley, for the promotion of literature or learning.

3. These five persons to continue, abide and remain in the work above expressed, till death or other providence of God remove any of them, and

the survivors to choose to themselves the full number aforesaid. 4. Mr. Goodwin desires the name of the school may be called Hopkins school, which communication being so made to the town of Hadley on March 20, 1669, the town, on the 29th of the same March *voted*, that Mr. Goodwin be sent to by the town, to know the persons he will make choice of as respects the premises. He returns, that he has chosen Mr. John Russell, pastor of the church at Hadley, Lieut. Samuel Smith and Aaron Cook; and the said town voted their approbation of Mr. Goodwin's choice. The town also voted Nathaniel Dickinson and Peter Tilton to join with the persons before mentioned, as a joint committee, who, together with Mr. Goodwin, while he lives, and after his decease, shall jointly and together have the ordering and full dispose of the estate or estates given by Mr. Davenport and Mr. Goodwin (as trustees as aforesaid to Mr. Hopkins) to the town of Hadley, or any other estate or estates that are or may be given, either by the town itself, or any other donor or donors, for the use, benefit and maintenance and promoting a grammar school to and for the use and in the town of Hadley; as also jointly and together to do, act and conclude, finish and execute, anything respecting the premises, faithfully and according to their best discretion. Voted also by the town, that as to the five persons, before expressed, if any decease or be otherwise disabled by the providence of God, the rest surviving shall have the sole choice of any other in the room and place of those surceasing, to the full number of five persons, provided they be known discreet, pious, faithful persons. And the town directed Mr. Clark and Peter Tilton to present the premises to the court to be recorded." They further state, that in 1671, the town granted a piece of land near the corn mill, for the erecting a dwelling house upon the same for a miller, which grant had this provision viz., that whatever land or estate with said house and mill etc. that hath been given by the town of Hadley or any other, for the maintaining a grammar school there, be ordered, managed and disposed by the present school committee in being, and after them by their successors whom they shall choose, provided they be still pious, discreet, faithful men; otherwise the said grant to be void and invalid to the end and purposes aforesaid."

They further state that at a county court held at Springfield, in September, 1682, an order was passed accepting and allowing a return from the committee of the Hopkins School, and taking notice that John Russell, Aaron Cook, Philip Smith and Samuel Partridge constitute the committee and approving of them all, and desiring their further management and carrying on of the affairs of the school, from time to time, which the court would be always ready to promote and encourage as need might require.

They further state, that while the care of the school was thus lawfully in the hands and under the oversight of a committee with full powers to manage the same without the intervention of the town, yet about August 23, 1686, the town voted, "to take into their own hands to manage, order and dispose to the use of a school in the town of Hadley, all the estates of houses and lands bequeathed and given by any donor or donors, in their last wills and testaments, to the town of Hadley, or to a school in said town, as the legacy of Nathaniel Ward, John Barnard and Henry Clark;" which interference on the part of the town, induced the committee of Hopkins school to apply to the County Court held at Springfield, in September, 1686, being a court having jurisdiction of the premises, whereupon the following order was passed viz: "The declining estate of Hopkins School in Hadley being presented to this court by the Rev. Mr. John Russell, Aaron Cook, Joseph Kellogg and Samuel Porter, the committee of said school, for that some of Hadley do disturb or obstruct the management of the estate of said school, therefore this court do order and declare that the whole donations to a school there, from the charitable donors, be all employed and improved for and towards the maintenance of the Grammar school in Hadley; it appearing that the intent of Mr. Henry Clark, in what he gave to a school, was, that it should go and be employed to the said school called Hopkins school. Also the like doth appear as to goodman Ward's gift. And goodman Barnard's gift may as well be taken for that school as any other. Wherefore this court order that all said gifts and others, with the land given by Hadley town, be all accordingly improved by the aforesaid committee." They further state that upon application duly made to the President and Council of his (then) majesty's territory and dominion of New England in America, upon the concerns of the Hopkins school and the friends thereof, it was, on December 8, 1686, ordered by the President and Council, that the Committee for the Hopkins school be and remain the "Feoffees of the grammar school in said town, and that Mr. Partridge be and hereby is dismissed from any further service in that matter, and that the said committee make report of the present estate of Mr. Hopkins and other donations to said school, which, (having been orderly annexed to the grammar school and hereby confirmed to that service) unto the next county court of Hampshire, who are hereby empowered to supply the place of Mr. Partridge with some other meet person in Hadley, and that the said court do find out and order some method for the payment of Boltwood's expenses upon the mill, that the mill, farm and other lands given to the scoool, may return to that public use, the president and council hereby declaring it to be beyond the power of the town of Hadley, or any other to divert any of the lands or estate, or the said mill stream or privileges thereof (which are legally determined to this said grammar school) to any other use whatsoever; the president and council judging the particular gifts in that town a good foundation for a grammar school, both for themselves and the *whole county**; and that the grammar school can be no otherwise interpreted, but to be a school holden by a master capable to instruct children and fit them for the university. Council House, Boston, Dec. 6, 1686."

They further state that at a county court held at Northampton on June 8th, 1687, an order was made (which is set out at length in the answer) reciting the proceedings of the President and Council, and of the county court held at Springfield in September, 1686, and that the court held at Northampton approves of the same, and concluding as follows: "It is therefore hereby ordered, that those persons of Hadley who have any ways meddled or intrenched upon the school estate thereof, which ought to be managed by

*Or country.

John Russell, Aaron Cook, Joseph Kellogg and Samuel Porter, the feoffees of said school (to whom this court of sessions, according to orders, have now by consent and choice of the rest of the committee added Chiliab Smith of Hadley, to make up the number of five feoffees) do deliver up all the estate they have entered on, forthwith, into the hands and ordering of the feoffees, on penalty of all damage that may come to themselves by neglect thereof." And the defendants therefore allege, that as, from their obvious nature, the donations were, and by the judgment of the President and Council, and of the court held at Northampton, they were adjudged to be "a good foundation for a grammar school, both for themselves and *the whole county*" [or country] and as it was further adjudged, "that a grammar school can be no otherwise interpreted but to be a school holden by a master capable to instruct children and fit them for the university," the plaintiffs should not now be allowed to claim that the committee, or those who have succeeded them in the trust in question, should apply the trust fund exclusively to the use of the inhabitants of Hadley.

The defendants admit that an act of the Legislature was passed on June 14, 1816 (St. 1815 C. 104) to incorporate the Trustees of Hopkins Academy, by which it is provided, that there shall be established an academy in the town of Hadley upon the foundation of Hopkins donation school, and that the committee of the school be incorporated into a body politic by the name of the Trustees of Hopkins Academy; and that all the lands and moneys heretofore given or subscribed to the committee for the use of the school, or which shall be hereafter given, granted and assigned to the Trustees for the use of the academy shall be confirmed to the Trustees, and their successors in that trust, forever, for the uses designated by the donors, and that they shall be further capable of taking and holding estate, real or personal, provided the annual income of the same shall not exceed $5000 and that the rents and profits thereof shall be applied in such a manner as that the designs of the donors may be more effectually promoted. And the defendants advise that this act was procured upon the petition of the committee of the donation school acting in concurrence with the town, pursuant to a vote of January 1, 1816, "that the town will unite with the committee of the donation school in petitioning the legislature for the establishment of an academy in this town." And the defendants represent that the town, in thus uniting with the committee, intended that all the funds in the hands of the committee should be hereafter applied to maintaining an academy in the town, upon the footing and system of other academies in New England; and that in consequence of the town,s concurrence with the committee in obtaining the act of incorporation, donations had been made by the legislature and by individuals, for the general purposes of an academy, and it would be a fraud upon such donors, if the town should now withdraw all the funds of the donation school and appropriate them to the exclusive use of the inhabitants of Hadley.

They further allege, that the Trustees of Hopkins Academy established a grammar school in Hadley, and have from time to time furnished the best instruction their ability permitted, in Latin, Greek, Astronomy, Ancient and Modern History, Logic, Ancient and Modern Geography, Natural, Moral and Intellectual Philosophy, Rhetoric, Geometry, Chemistry, Arithmetic, Composition, Reading, Declamation, and such other studies as are usually taught in academies; that to this school every person in Hadley of proper age and qualifications to receive benefit from the school could be admitted and none such have ever been refused; that the Trustees have supposed it to be their duty to have at all times, a master capable to instruct our children and fit them for our university or some of our colleges; that the expense of such instruction has at all times more than exhausted the whole annual income of the funds in the hands of the Trustees, and the balance of the expenses has been assessed on the scholars as tuition fees; that it is true the school has been resorted to by youth from other towns, but this has not only been in no way detrimental, but, on the contrary has been highly beneficial, inasmuch as the excess of expenses of instruction over the income of these funds, instead of being assessed wholly upon the scholars who are inhabitants of Hadley, has been apportioned among all the scholars, while the opportunities for instruction have been in no degree lessened.

In an amended bill the plaintiffs allege that no record is to be found of any such judgment of the President and Council of New England, as is stated in the answer of the defendants, but that from writings which have been preserved, it appears that there was a controversy between the town of Hadley and the committee above mentioned, upon the point whether the town had a right to take into their hands and management the property mentioned in the original bill, and appropriate the proceeds to the support of a common school in Hadley, but then the point whether the committee were bound to administer the funds and appropriate the avails for the support of a grammar school for the exclusive use of the town, was not drawn in question, nor was the town heard thereon; that the declaration of the President and Council, that the donations were a good foundation for a grammar school for the whole county, was extrajudicial and not authorized by the issue before them; that at the time of the several donations mentioned in the original bill, the town of Hadley embraced the territory which now constitutes, besides the present town of Hadley, the towns of Amherst, South Hadley, Granby, Hatfield, Williamsburg and Whately, and that some individuals in these towns might have claimed that the donations were to be appropriated for the common benefit of all these towns, and that under such impressions students from these towns might have occasionally attended the school; that the town of Hadley has by no act whatever recognized the right of the committee or Trustees to admit into the school or academy students from any other place than Hadley, and that as the plaintiffs believe, prior to the act of incorporation, no students, except from the towns above mentioned, ever attended the school under the claim of right; that the plaintiffs voted to concur with the committee in an application to the legislature for an act of incorporation in the belief that the funds could be better managed by a corporation than by a committee, but without any intention of surrendering their right to the exclusive use and benefit thereof and that the act was cautiously framed with a view to secure the exclusive right of the town.

In their answer to the amended bill the defendants state that there cannot be found at Boston any record of the judgment of the President and Council, and the reason is, because there is a loss of the public records of the General Court, and also of the council records, during the period from May, 1686, to 1689, when the affairs of the province were managed by a President and Council; but that full transcripts of records of the proceedings stated in their former answer, are found in an ancient book purporting to be records of the county court of pleas and sessions holden at Northampton for Hampshire, for June 1687, and also in an ancient book of records kept by the donation committee, purporting to contain an account of the various donations for the school, and of the judgments of the President and Council, and of the county courts of Hampshire respecting the same; that they have no knowledge that some of the inhabitants of the other towns formerly constituting a part of Hadley claimed a common right in those funds any further than appears from their previous answer; that in admitting students they have not confined themselves to the limits of Hampshire, in its former extent but have adopted as their guide the will of Edward Hopkins, which expresses the object of his donation, in the manner before stated; and that the question of the school being a public school for others than those residing in Hadley, must have been in controversy between the town and the committee before the President and Council, at the time of making the adjudication declaring it a public school, as set forth in the former answer. The plaintiffs filed a general replication.

Sept. 23. At the hearing the defendants read several depositions and introduced a book of records of the county court reciting the proceedings of the President and Council, and containing the adjudication of the county court thereon, as set forth in the pleadings; also a certificate of the Secretary of the Commonwealth, that there are no records of the proceedings of the Council from May, 1686 to 1689.

Billings & Forbes argued in support of the bill in regard to the jurisdiction of the President and Council, they referred to the ancient charters, &c. 52, 90, 93; and to the point that the proceedings of the President and Council were not conclusive against the plaintiffs, Smith v. Sherwood 4 Connect R. 277. 1. Stark Evid. (Metcalf's Edit.) 198: Foster v. Jackson Hob. 53, Bul. N. P. 233. Spooner v. Davis, 7 Pick. 147 and authorities there cited.

Bates & Dewey for the defendants, cited in regard to the powers of the Council and of the county courts, 1. Belknap. Hist. N. Hamp. 184 et seq.; 1 Chalmers' annals 417; Ancient Charters &c. 52, 92, 93, 94; 4 Dana,s Abr. 243 6 Dana,s Abr. 400, 401, 402; and as to the effect of usage on interpretation of ancient grants attorney General v. Parker 3. Att. 577.

The opinion of the court was afterwards drawn up by Shaw, C. J.

In order to understand the true grounds of controversy in the present case, it may be useful, before coming to a direct consideration of the point in controversy, to consider what the question is, and to distinguish it from others which may be considered as connected with it.

In the first place, no question is made of the legal title of the defendants, to the real and personal property held by them and it is very clear that no such question could be made in a court of equity. Questions of legal title are to be tried elsewhere. We are not called upon to consider an obvious difficulty, which might have presented itself, before the act of incorporation, in establishing a legal seizure in the donation committee, not being a corporation, and having no capacity to take and hold real estate in succession. Probably, however, they must have been considered at least as in actual possession by taking the rents, and such possession would have been considered as sufficient against all the world except those who could have set up a better title.

It is a rule in Equity that a gift of real or personal estate, either *inter vivos* or by will, to promote education is a charity. It is also considered as a settled rule that such a gift to a charitable use is to receive a most liberal construction; and if the Trustees pervert the fund to other uses, or even if they refuse to accept or execute the trusts, the charity itself shall not fail, nor will the property revert to the donor. But it will be competent for a court of Chancery to direct in the former case that, the Trusts shall be executed, and in the latter that new Trustees shall be appointed, in whom the legal estate shall vest, to be holden in trust for the purposes of the charity. It is quite clear, therefore, that, even if the donation committee, prior to the act of incorporation, had met with a technical difficulty in maintaining their legal title, no forfeiture and no reversionary interest therein, could have been claimed by the heirs of the donors, could they still have been traced, and therefore, as the lands and estate must still have been holden for the purposes of the trust, it would have been very immaterial, whether the legal estate should be considered as vested in the particular individuals composing the donation committee or not. That technical difficulty, however, was removed by the act of incorporation, passed with the consent and indeed upon the application of the committee, whereby they were made capable in law of taking and holding the legal estate in succession. Another question which has been alluded to may be considered, for the purpose of being laid out of the case. It was stated in the argument for the plaintiffs, that the defendants, by introducing the higher branches of science into the Academy, have changed the character of the institution from that of a school, to that of a college, whereby the inhabitants of Hadley are deprived of the benefits intended to be conferred upon them by the establishment of a grammar school. This complaint at first seemed plausible, but we think it has no place in the present inquiry. It was not set forth in the bill as a breach of trust; it was advanced only in argument, and that argument was founded upon a statement in the defendants, answer, of the studies pursued at the Academy. But as a distinct complaint of a breach of trust, it has not been made in the bill, nor have the defendants had opportunity to answer to it. The point might have some influence as an argument upon the other question which is afterward to be considered, if it could be shown that such a school as the present is, was not the grammar school contemplated by the donor. For instance if it was shown *aliunde*, that the school was intended exclusively for the inhabitants of Hadley, it might perhaps be argued that the inhabitants had no need of an institution of so high a character, and therefore, that such an institution was not intended. But till that question is settled, the argument bears with the same force the other way. If the donors, by a grammar school, contemplated an institution of higher character than is ordinarily required for the children of a single town, then it could not be intended by the donors, that the benefits of such a school should be confined to the children of the inhabitants of Hadley. It can therefore have no weight, as an argument on that question.

But the real question raised and discussed in the present case is whether the funds placed under the control of the defendants, for the support of a school, are to be so administered, as to confine the benefit of them exclusively to the inhabitants of the town of Hadley.

By the terms of the act of incorporation St. 1815, 104, 12, all lands and moneys given to the committee for the use of said school, shall be confirmed to the Trustees of Hopkins Academy, and their successors in said trust forever, *for the uses designated by the donors.* The same trusts therefore, under which the committee held the funds, prior to the act of incorporation, are those under which the defendants as Trustees of the academy are still to hold them and appropriate them, so that the question in this respect is the same as if there had been no act of incorporation.

Two sources of evidence are relied upon by the defendants, to show that they have heretofore rightly administered these funds, as a trust for a public school, not confining the benefits of them to the town of Hadley, but communicating them equally to the youth of other towns who may desire the benefits of them.

1. The terms under which the grants were originally made, the will of Edward Hopkins and the appointment made under it by his surviving executors Davenport and Goodwin.

2. Certain judicial proceedings, which are alleged to have taken place before the county court for the county of Hampshire, and before the President and Council of New England, about the year 1686, in which this very question was raised and determined against the claim and pretensions of the town of Hadley.

And they insist that these grounds are strengthened by an immemorial usage, acted upon by the Trustees of the school called the committee of the donation school, and acquiesced in by the inhabitants of Hadley, not to exclude but to admit pupils from other towns seeking the benefit of the school in fitting for college.

These grounds are denied by the plaintiffs, who insist that the construction of the original instruments by which the donation was made, will lead to a contrary conclusion; that the judicial proceedings were not well proved, or if they were, that the court had no jurisdiction; and that there has been no usage to admit pupils from other towns so general or so notorious, as to raise an implication that it was acquiesced in by the inhabitants of Hadley.

To trace the foundation of this school, we are carried back through an interval of nearly two centuries. The clause in the will of Edward Hopkins the liberal benefactor of New England, recited in the bill and admitted in the answer is to this effect, "And the residue of my estate there," &c. (as before, p. 241.)

This is a devise to the Trustees, by which the real and personal property became vested in them, on the trusts designated, indicating certain objects to be accomplished and intrusting them with full power to specify those objects and execute the purposes intended by the will, according to their discretion and their views of his known wishes, and his true intent and purpose." In 1664, Davenport and Goodwin, the two surviving Trustees, proceeded to execute the trust and power reposed in them by an appointment of the particular uses of this property by an instrument under their hands and seals (vid. ante. p. 241, 244).

Had this instrument contained only that provision, which is extracted and set forth in the bill, directing that the property shall be equally divided between New Haven and Hadley, to be in each of those towns managed and improved towards the erecting of a grammar school in each of those towns, taking the views that we have derived from later experiences, by which we consider towns, in all respects, as strict corporations, there would have been ground for contending that the gift and appointment was to the town of Hadley, in its corporate capacity. But in that case, it would have been open to contend, that the legal estate was to Hadley, as a corporation capable of taking and holding property for the use of a school. But the subsequent provision, appointing Trustees and vesting the legal estate in them, expressly negatives this hypothesis, and shows that the legal estate was not vested in the town, nor does it appear that the town have claimed to be the holders of the legal estate, since the attempt to take the management of it into their own hands in 1686. Besides at the period of these conveyances, towns in Massachusetts were not considered so fully corporations as they have since been, but their corporate powers have been increased from time to time by particular legislative enactments. But it is believed, that the name by which a township or settlement was designated, was as often used to express the idea of place, as to describe the body of inhabitants or settlers, in their municipal corporate capacity. When therefore the phraseology is, that the money shall be equally divided between Hadley and New Haven, and then in the same instrument Trustees are appointed to hold and manage it, it seems to import nothing more than to direct that it shall be apportioned equally to the institutions to be established at the two places respectively. We must therefore resort to other considerations to determine the question in controversy.

In doing this, it is necessary to look carefully at both instruments, the devise to the Trustees, and the appointment and settlement by them, and to consider both in reference to the state and condition of the colony at that time. The purpose of the pious donor was, as he modestly expressed it " to give some encouragement, in these foreign plantations, for the breeding up of hopeful youth in a way of learning, both at the grammar school and college, for the public service of the country in future times." This looks not only to great and useful objects, but to public objects. The establishment of the grammar school is coupled immediately with that of the college, which although it must be established in some place, and so is local in its existence, yet is necessarily public and general in its purposes. The end contemplated was the public service of the country in future times. It was to breed up hopeful youth in a way of learning. These expressions seem inconsistent with the purpose of establishing a local school for teaching the humblest rudiments of education to the children of both sexes, who usually resort to such a school. If it be said that these expressions are adapted to that part of the provision, which points to the encouragement to be given to the college, the answer is obvious, that both are included in precisely the same terms. It seems much more like having regard to a course of liberal education and the fitting of men with that degree of learning which might qualify them for public service as professional men especially for the service of the church. In that view the two leading objects are perfectly consistent and calculated to advance each other, supposing a grammar school designs to fit young men for college, and the college to enable them to complete a liberal education, preparatory to public or professional life. He afterwards with much solemnity and earnestness speaks of the aforesaid *public ends*. This looks like a design to found a local school, confined in its benefits to the children of a single settlement.

And we are of opinion, that the original trustees of Mr. Hopkins, who were specially charged with the execution of the liberal and beneficent designs of the donor, understood it in the same way, by the instrument which they executed.

After performing that duty which consisted in providing for the college, they proceed to execute their powers in regard to the school. They direct the property to be divided equally between the towns of New, Haven and Hadley, to be *in* each of the towns managed and improved towards maintaining a grammar school in each of them, and they direct in whose hands the management thereof shall be, and as to Hadley this management is committed to four trustees specially named, with power to appoint successors and fill vacancies, and their powers are to extend both to "the ordering of said estate, and carrying on the work wherein it is to be employed" with full power to pursue and put in execution this pious end and intendment of the worthy donor, that is, to be trustees of the estate, and directors or managers for the establishment, maintenance and regulation of the school. This object was further secured, as far as it was in their power to secure it, by reserving to themselves, whilst they lived, the full power of a negative vote, for the hindering of anything that might cross that end. In this appointment, the trustees of Mr. Hopkins seem to have done little more in the execution of their powers, than to apportion the amount of property to be appropriated to this school, fix the place where it should be established, designate the persons who should hold the property and manage the school, and provide for perpetuating them. But as to the great object to be kept in view, in administering this trust, they referred to the objects expressed by the donor. In considering those objects, we can perceive nothing which looks like a restraint upon the permanent board of trustees, obliging them to consider the trust as intended exclusively for the benefit of the inhabitants of Hadley. It is incumbent on the plaintiffs to show that they are exclusively entitled to the benefits of this trust, and if that is not shown, they must fail in establishing this claim. There is nothing, either in the original will, or in the appointment under it, to indicate that such an exclusive right was intended; but on the contrary, we think it more consistent with the avowed intention of the testator, to conclude that it was designed for the encouragement of all those, in that newly settled part of the country, who were desirous of availing themselves of the benefit of a grammar school, to qualify them for the university. The mere circumstance of being fixed in Hadley, has no tendency to show, that any other exclusive or peculiar benefit was intended than that which arises incidentally to any place, from having a public school in its immediate vicinity.

Nor can we perceive that the trusts and purposes of this appointment are varied by the proposal subsequently made to the town by Mr. Goodwin, one of the surviving trustees, in 1669, to which the town acceded.

Whether the property had been actually placed in the possession or under the control of the trustees named in the deed of appointment, does not distinctly appear; nor does it appear what occasion there was for any new arrangement. One purpose, perhaps, may be safely conjectured, that of connecting two or three other donations, made for the support of a school, and one by the town itself, with that of Mr. Hopkins, so as to place the whole under one administration and appropriate the whole to one object. The proposal made by Mr. Goodwin was substantially this: that he should appoint three persons, to be submitted to the town and be approved by them, that the town should appoint two, and that these five, with himself while he lived, should have the sole disposal, and management of the estate in all respects, *for the end* to which it was bequeathed; and the same five persons, with himself whilst he lived, were to have the sole management of all other estate given by any donor, or which might be given while they survived, to the town of Hadley, for the promotion of literature or learning. These trustees were appointed for their lives, with power to perpetuate the board by filling their own vacancies. And Mr. Goodwin modestly requested that it might be called the Hopkins school. This proposal being submitted to the town, they voted to send to Mr. Goodwin to know the persons he would make choice of, and he names three, two of whom appear to be the same, who had been named in the deed of appointment. These are approved by the town, who elect two on their part conformably to the proposal, one of whom, Mr. Tilton, appears to be the same with one named in the deed of appointment. These acts, done in pursuance of Mr. Goodwin's proposal seem to be a distinct acquiescence and concurrence in that proposal. But some reliance and indeed the principal reliance seems to be placed by the plaintiffs, upon the terms of the vote passed on that occasion by the town. It was in substance that the committee thus chosen should jointly and together have the ordering and full disposal of the estate given by Mr. Davenport and Mr. Goodwin as trustees of Mr. Hopkins, *to the town of Hadley*, or any other estate or estates that were or might be given either by the town itself, or any other donor or donors, for the use, benefit and maintenance and promoting a grammar school, *to and for the use* and *in the town* of Hadley.

They also state, that the trustees shall supply vacancies, in their own body, by the choice of other persons, so that they be known, discreet, pious, faithful persons, and they direct two persons named to present the premises to the court to be recorded.

It appears to us, that these proceedings did not in any degree change the nature of the trusts upon which the property was to be held; it merely changed, in a slight degree, the organization of the board of trustees, so as to give the town an effectual agency in its constitution, by which they had the exclusive nomination and appointment of two, and a negative upon Mr. Goodwin's nomination of the other three. It substantially placed the control of the whole under the agency of the appointees of the town. The town might, therefore, well consent that their own and the other small donations for the like object, should be under the same government.

They chose to speak of the property given by Mr. Goodwin and Mr. Davenport, under Mr. Hopkins's will, as property given to the town of Hadley. If they meant given to the town in its corporate capacity, we have already shown that it was not so given, but to trustees to establish a school in Hadley. And the other clause, *to and for the use of the town* of Hadley, is so introduced, as to leave it doubtful, whether it was intended to intimate their views of the purpose, to which the funds were to be appropriated, or to be descriptive of the other estate, which might be given by the town itself, or by any other donor. But what renders it quite certain that it was not intended to declare any other or different trust, from that already declared by Goodwin and Davenport, is this; that Mr. Goodwin's proposal was, that the committee should hold the property, in all respects, for the end to which it was bequeathed by Mr. Hopkins; and that the town intended to accede to this proposal, and not to change or qualify it, or make a new one, is manifest from this, that they did not submit this vote of theirs to Mr. Goodwin, for his concurrence, as they would, if they had proposed a change or modification of his proposal; but on the contrary, they directed the proceedings to be presented to the court, probably the county court, to be recorded, as a complete and settled arrangement. Besides, when it is considered that how peculiarly a grammar school, permanently fixed in any town, enures practically to the use of such town, and when by this arrangement the school was permanently established in Hadley, and was placed under the control and management of a board of trustees, in the appointment of whom the town had a direct participation, and who, by the mode of perpetuation, might generally be expected to be inhabitants of that town, it was not very wide from the truth to describe it as a school to be for the use of, as well as established in the town of Hadley. But there are no words of exclusion or limitation and no intimation that the beneficial use was to be confined exclusively to the inhabitants of Hadley. We think, therefore, that there is nothing in these proceedings, which was intended to vary, or, if so intended, which could legally vary the trusts, upon which the property in question was conveyed to, and vested in the committee thus appointed.

In regard to the other donations set forth in the bill, it appears to us that they clearly follow the principal one derived from Hopkins.

The devises by Barnard and Ward were both made in 1664, the same year that the deed of appointment was made by the trustees of Hopkins and the object being the same, the establishment of a grammar school, the intent to give it the same distinction might be presumed. But it does not stand on this presumption.

By the vote of the town in 1669, it was decided by the town, that all the estate which had been given, or might be given for the same purpose, should be held and managed by the same committee; which is in effect a declaration, that they shall be held upon the same trusts, and appropriated to the same purposes. And even if it were a question of legal title, it is to be recollected that in transactions of this antiquity, a conveyance by vote, by a corporation, is held sufficient to convey an estate, and pass the fee. *A fortiori*, is it good as the manifestation of a trust.

That portion of this estate appropriated by the town itself, was thus done in 1666, before the above agreement. It was not strictly a grant, because there was no grantee. It was rather an appropriation, then made, and vested in the committee by the subsequent vote of 1669, subject to the same trust. So much are charities of this sort favored, that when the grantee in trust for education, is not in *esse*, as in the case of a grant to a body not yet incorporated, but afterwards a corporation or board of trustees is created, chancery will uphold the trust and carry the object into effect, by directing the necessary conveyances, and settling the proper trusts.

Here the town did voluntarily and by its own act, all that was necessary to give the grant effect, by designating the grantees and vesting the estate in them by vote.

The grant of Henry Clark was after the vote of 1669, to wit, in 1675. But it is to be observed that, although by the terms of Henry Clark,s will, he gives the estate to the town of Hadley, yet it is under this limitation; committing the same to the care, disposing and ordering of Lieut. Samuel Smith, etc. (naming the Hopkins committee) to be by them disposed of, to Hopkins school, for Hadley, with an express condition, that if they are disturbed in their committeeship, it shall be otherwise disposed of, as they shall see meet for the good of the town.

It might be difficult to put a legal construction upon this devise, so as to determine whether the fee vested in the committee or the town. But as already shown, that question is not now before the Court. One thing is perfectly clear, that is, that the trust of this devise was for Hopkins School, whatever were the purposes of that school, the same were those of this gift. It must clearly, therefore, follow the same trusts, which had been already declared as those upon which this school was founded by Hopkins, and those who were entrusted by him with the power of giving a specific form to his declared purpose of promoting a public grammar school.

The second principal ground on which the respondents rely, to show that these funds were not held exclusively for the benefit of the inhabitants of Hadley, is, the acts and adjudication of the county court and of the president and council of his Majesty,s territory and dominion of New England, which are set out in the answer.

Two objections are taken to these proceedings, by the plaintiffs in this case; one is, that they are not duly authenticated; and the other is, that neither the county court nor the president and council, had any jurisdiction of the subject matter, and that their proceedings, therefore, ought not to be considered as having any legal effect. We have not thought it necessary to examine either of these questions very strictly, for reasons which will be sufficiently manifest. These transactions connect themselves with one of the most remarkable periods in the history of Massachusetts. The proceedings, so far as we have evidence of them, were before the president and council of New England, in the autumn of 1686, very shortly before the arrival of Governor Andros. We have a certificate from the secretary,s office stating that there are no records of the proceedings of the council from May, 1686 to 1689. It will not be difficult for those who are conversant with the history of that disturbed period, to account for the entire absence of these records. The commission of Governor Dudley as first president, was received on the 15th of May, 1686, and he was superseded by the arrival of Sir Edmund Andros in December of the same year. By him and his council all the affairs of the colony were managed until 1689, when he was arrested, and forcibly put out of the government. It was the manifest policy of those who thus forcibly superseded him, and who were in truth the champions of the chartered rights of the colonies, to leave as few traces as possible, of the arbitrary and, as they believed, tyrannical proceedings of this president and his council. Still it was a government *de facto*, and as such, acts done within its jurisdiction would probably be binding. From the imperfect view which alone can now be obtained of those proceedings, it cannot be certainly determined how the case of this school was brought before the president and council. The county court, under the colonial government, had an extensive and, perhaps, not very strictly defined jurisdiction. Ancient charters, etc., 91, And it is expressly ordained that all persons " betrusted to receive or improve " any gift or legacy " given and bequeathed to the college, schools of learning or any other public use, shall be liable from time to time to give account of their disposal and management thereof to the county court of that shire where they dwell and where such estate shall be, and to appoint feoffees of trust to settle and manage the same according to the wills of the donors.'' Ancient charters etc., 52.

Under the charter, the general court was deemed and declared to be the chief civil power in this commonwealth, with authority to act in all affairs according to such power, both in matters of council, making of laws, and matters of *judicature*. Ancient Charters, etc., 88.

By an ordinance in 1654, in consequence of the general court being so much oppressed with the weight of business, it was ordered that causes properly cognizable by the county court, should not be transferred to the general court, but that difficult cases might be presented by inferior courts for its opinion. Ancient Charters, etc., 92.

After the dissolution of the Colony Charter in 1685, and the establishment of the royal government, it was provided in the King's commission, first to Dudley and afterwards to Andros, which commissions, together with the royal instructions constituted the basis of that government, that all former ordinances should remain in force, and that the president and council should have and exercise the same powers which had formerly been exercised by the government under the colony charter. From this general view, it would seem that the jurisdiction both of the county court and of the president and council, was amply sufficient to embrace a case like this.

It appears that the county court did in fact, exercise a superintending authority over cases of this kind, because there is a record showing that as early as 1682 the committee of the Hopkins school presented a report of their proceedings to the county court, which was accepted and allowed. The court also take notice who are trustees, and confirm and approve of them and desire and expect their further management in carrying on the affairs of said school, which the court will be always ready to promote and encourage as need may require.

It is also to be recollected that upon the final adjustment of this trust, by the proposal of Mr. Goodwin and the votes of the town in 1669, the town ordered the proceedings to pe presented to the county to be recorded, thereby recognizing their jurisdiction of trusts of this kind and confirming the conclusion that it was a public trust. But the judicial proceedings relied upon, commenced at a later period. It appears that in August 1686, the town of Hadley passed a vote to take into their own hands to manage, order and dispose to the use of a school, etc., all estates bequeathed etc., as the legacies of Ward, Barnard and Clark. It is to be remarked, that by this vote, they did not seem to claim the property of Hopkins, except in general terms. In consequence of this vote in September of the same year, proceedings were commenced in the county court at Springfield, by the committee, who presented the declining state of the school in Hadley, for that some of Hadley do disturb or obstruct the management of the estate of said school. Upon this the court passed an order that all the gifts to that object should be improved by that committee.

It does not appear how proceedings were instituted before the president and council, whether by reference from the county court, or by an original application. A decision, however, seems to have been made, December 6, 1686, which was afterwards laid before the county court and by that court fully adopted and affirmed. But we do not think it necessary to refer to these proceedings at large. We have looked into them only so far as to see that they do not militate against the opinions which we have formed upon the effect of the original grants and the trusts upon which they were made. On the contrary, the effect of the decisions, both of the county court and of the president and council, was, that the committee be and remain feoffees of the school, judging the particular gifts in that town a good foundation for a grammar school, both for themselves and for the whole *county*, and that a grammar school can be no otherwise interpreted, but to be a school holden by a master capable to instruct children and fit them for the university. This adjudication was adopted and measures taken to carry it into effect by the county court. We should not be surprised to find, if the early manuscript could be obtained, that the word written *county* was *country*, it being more consonant with the true nature of the trust, contemplated by Hopkins, and because the term " country " was then generally adopted to express the public or the whole community. But in either form it negatives the claim of the town of Hadley to the exclusive benefit of these funds. Had these adjudications been the other way, or had the claim of the respondents rested solely upon them it would have been necessary to examine with a more rigid scrutiny, both the authority of the documents in which these proceedings are now found, and the jurisdiction of the courts over the subject matter, and over the particular question of the trusts, on which the donations were made, all these points being controlled by the plaintiffs. But as we have already stated we have only looked into them so far, as to see that they do not militate against the decision to which we have now come upon other grounds. As the case of the defendants does not rest solely or principally upon those adjudications, as their case is established independently of them, it would not vary the result if the objections made to their authority and sufficiency by the plaintiffs should be fully sustained.

3. The last ground upon which the defendants rely, is the usage and practice of the trustees or donation committee from 1686 to the present time.

Usage in ancient transactions is a good contemporaneous construction of a doubtful grant.

In looking at the evidence adduced upon this point, nothing is found in the records of the trustees to show whether they did or did not confine the benefits of this grammar school to children of the inhabitants of Hadley. The evidence, therefore, must rest upon living memory, which extends back fifty or sixty years; and by this it appears most satisfactorily, that in point of fact, although practically it has enured principally to the use of the inhabitants, yet it has not been confined to them, but many boys from other towns have been fitted for college there; and those who have been longest conversant with the actual management of the school as trustees testify that they have always considered it as a school the benefits of which have not been confined, and of right were not to be confined, exclusively to children of the inhabitants of Hadley.

Perhaps some of the minor questions in this case may have been passed over without notice. We have endeavored to consider the general question upon its merits, and upon the broadest principles; and upon the whole, are of the opinion that the inhabitants of the town of Hadley are not exclusively entitled to the benefits of these ancient donations, that the defendants in their mode of administering them, and extending the benefit of them to children of other towns, have not been guilty of the breach of trust charged in the bill, and therefore, that the suit must be dismissed.

This decision was received with acquiescence. The good work of the Academy went on for many years with great prosperity, Meanwhile changes were taking place and the Academy, as it had existed here and elsewhere, was losing its importance in general estimation. The larger towns were supporting High schools for themselves, and large schools liberally endowed, like Williston Seminary at Easthampton, became the resort of young men fitting for college, so that the patronage of Hopkins Academy was coming more and more to be derived from within the town. Fewer and fewer pupils came from abroad, so that the question was becoming importunate whether the Academy Fund could not be made more largely beneficial to the people of the town. Mingled with this there was something of the feeling which had shown itself in former years, that the town as such had rights in the fund, not so fully enjoyed as they might and should be.

Hence the question came up for consideration. Communications were exchanged between the town and the trustees of the academy extending over a period of more than ten years. The matter was discussed in town meetings and meetings of the trustees, until, at length, these negotiations issued in the existing arrangement which has continued nearly twenty-five years with a good measure of satisfaction to all concerned.

The account of these doings is given in the succeeding chapter.

High School Building, Built in 1865.

CHAPTER XI.

DOINGS OF THE TOWN AND THE TRUSTEES IN CONFERENCE, WITH REFERENCE TO MAKING THE SCHOOL FREE TO HADLEY.

As has been noted the decision of the Supreme Judicial Court was received with acquiescence. Agitation ceased and all went on with quiet prosperity, though with steadily decreasing numbers, until the year 1851. About this time a change began in the system of public school instruction. Graded schools were coming to take the place of the district school as it had been hitherto. The subject was brought prominently to notice in the report of the Secretary of the State Board of Education. The school committee of the town in their annual report that year suggested as possible some change in the schools of the town, looking to their partial gradation, and outlining a plan for such a work. It was urged that it was a good time to take the first steps in this direction. A committee of inquiry was recommended to give thought to this matter and report at a future meeting. A committee of three was chosen " to examine and print the report of the School Committee if they think proper, and report at some future meeting." Samuel Nash, Esq., Dr. F. Bonney and P. S. Williams, Esq. were the committee chosen.

At this meeting adjourned to April 9, 1851, this committee reported and was authorized to carry into effect the subject of their report, viz. : " to confer with the gentlemen who have the care of the Hopkins School Fund, ascertain their views respecting it, whether in their opinion anything could be done to make the advantages arising from that fund free to all the inhabitants of the town, and such other information as they may be able to obtain, and report thereon."

This Committee in obeying their instructions conferred with the trustees of Hopkins Academy, and made inquiry at such other sources as were open to them concerning the fund in question, its origin, the sources whence it was derived, the form under which it existed, its amount, principal and income, the uses to which it was given, with something of its history from the beginning.

This committee thus instructed entered into correspondence with the Trustees of Hopkins Academy as follows herewith.

At a special meeting of the Trustees of Hopkins Academy, Feb. 3, 1852, the following paper having been received by the Secretary was submitted for consideration.

HADLEY, Jan. 23, 1852.

Rev. John Woodbridge, D. D., Dea. Jacob Smith, Rev. Dan Huntington, Rev. Joseph W. Curtis, Moses Porter, Esq., Mr. James B. Porter, Mr. Dudley Smith, Dea. Simeon Dickinson, Rev. Warren H. Beaman, Rev. Rowland Ayres and Dea. C. P. Hitchcock, Trustees of Hopkins Academy.

GENTLEMEN:

By a vote of the inhabitants of our town of Hadley, passed at a legal meeting held on the 9th day of April last, the undersigned were appointed a Committee to carry into effect some recommendations of a previous Committee in their report to the town on the aforesaid 9th of April.

That report recommended that a committee be appointed and instructed to confer with the gentlemen who have the care of the Hopkins School Fund, ascertain their views respecting it, whether in their opinion anything can be done to make the advantages arising from the fund free to all the inhabitants of the town, and such other information as they may be able to obtain and report thereon."

In pursuance of the objects of our appointment, we would most respectfully request of the Trustees answers to the following questions, together with such other information as you may think proper to communicate.

1st. Will the Trustees consent to the appropriation of the funds under their care to the establishment and maintenance of one or more *free High Schools* in Hadley, in connection with such aid from the town as may be necessary?

2nd. In what do the funds under the care of the Board consist and what is their present estimated value?

3rd. What is the present annual income of said fund?

4th. What part of the fund at the present time arises from the bequest of Edward Hopkins of England?

5th. What are the rights and privileges of the inhabitants of the town resulting from this fund?

The first inquiry is proposed in the belief that a majority of the legal voters of the town desire to some extent the introduction of the sytem of gradation of schools, so highly recommended by the friends of education, and so successfully adopted in various places. Answers to the four remaining inquiries would doubtless correct some erroneous opinions and furnish reliable information upon a subject regarded by many as of much importance, and one in which they are in some measure interested.

With respect,

SAMUEL NASH,
FRANKLIN BONNEY, } Committee.
P. S. WILLIAMS,

After some discussion in reference to the contents of the above communication it was voted:

1st. That the Trustees cannot consistently apply the funds committed to their trust to the establishment and support of High Schools.

2d. For answer to the second, third, fourth and fifth questions in the above communication, the committee of the town be referred to the records of the corporation, including the Treasurer's accounts, and requested themselves to convey the information thus obtained to the town.

It was also voted:

That an answer to the communication from the town be prepared by the President and Secretary, in accordance with the above votes, and upon its approval by the Prudential Committee be handed over to the Committee of the town.

At a meeting of the trustees held March 9, 1852, to take into consideration a second communication addressed to them by the Committee of the Town in reference to applying the funds of the Academy to the promotion of a High School.

In reference to a proposed "arrangement" the following particulars were contained in the above named communication—submitted to the consideration of the Trustees:

"1st, Would you be willing to open the doors of the Academy to scholars in the town who have attained to a certain point in education, provided the town raise and appropriate some adequate sum to be added to the Hopkins Fund, by the way of either general or individual tuition.

2nd. That the school be under the joint government of the Trustees and a committee appointed by the town, which committee shall be so far inferior in number to the board of Trustees, that the latter may control in all matters of vital importance.

3rd. That the Trustees be not disturbed in the financial management of the Fund, there being merely a union of the income derived from it with the sum raised by the town.

4th. That if the Trustees feel that the school must be left open to the public, they be allowed still to come in, as at present, by paying a specified tuition.

Have not the Trustees a right to require a certain point of attainment in scholars from abroad before they be admitted to the advantages of the school?

In reference to the above particulars, contained in the letter of the Town Committee, the Trustees voted in reference to the query under the head of No. 1, to give an affirmative answer provided, however, that in place of the phraseology "to be added to the Hopkins Fund" be substituted "be paid annually to the Treasurer of Hopkins Academy."

Voted in reference to No. 2 that inasmuch as the Board of Trust of Hopkins Academy was incorporated with express reference to the establishment and support of an academy and required by the very terms of their charter to adopt and enforce proper regulations for the government of the same, the Trustees feel in doubt as to the possibility, under our present charter, of delegating the government of the school in whole or in part to other hands.

The third particular was passed over as not demanding a formal notice.

Voted in reference to No. 4, that notwithstanding whatever accommodation might be afforded town scholars on account of an appropriation from the Town to the income of the Academy, there would be no impropriety in charging tuition for scholars from abroad. As for fixing upon a standard of qualifications for admission to the Academy the Trustees are expressly authorized to do this by the 2nd Section of their Charter.

The Secretary was instructed to transmit a copy of the above votes after its approval by the Prudential Committee, to the Committee of the Town. The Committee of the Town having then conferred with the Trustees and made such further enquiry as they would, made extended report to the town at the annual meeting, March 29th, 1852. This report gave some account of the fund, its origin, history, disposition, the controversies concerning it and their decision. It labored to show that the town of Hadley as such had rights in the fund, from whose full enjoyment it had been and still was kept. The only action recommended for the town to take was to invite the trustees to unite with the town in a petition to the Legislature to amend the charter incorporating the Trustees of Hopkins Academy. The existing state of things was held to be an evil, whose remedy might be secured in one of four ways.

1. Mutual agreement between the town and Trustees.

2. By both parties uniting in a petition to the Legislature for an amendment to the Charter so that the Trustees should be required to make report yearly of all their affairs to the town.

3. The town might make such petition ex-parte.

4. A possible remedy might be found in the Supreme Court as having power in equity to hear and determine all suits and proceedings for enforcing and regulating the execution of trusts.

By vote this report was accepted and ordered to be printed, and a copy supplied to each family in the town. It was further voted that whereas there are funds under the care of the Trustees of Hopkins Academy worth some $15,000, the principal part, if not the whole, of which was originally given either by the town itself or individuals in it, for the promotion of learning here. And whereas no public report is now made of the condition and improvement of the funds in which the town are believed to have rights and privileges; therefore voted that the committee on the Academy fund be a committee to request in behalf of the town the aforesaid Trustees, to make an annual report to the town, in town meeting, of the condition, receipts and disbursements of the fund, together with any changes in the board of Trustees. Also to invite the said Trustees to unite with the town in a petition to the legislature, so to amend the charter of the Academy as to require such report, together with such amendment of the charter with reference to applying the funds to a free High School or schools as such Committee and the Trustees may agree upon. Voted that in case the Trustees assent, then the aforesaid committee is authorized and instructed in behalf of the town, to make such petition for such amendment or amendments of said charter.

Voted that the Committee on the Academy Fund take into consideration the subject of establishing a free High School in Hadley and report at a future meeting.

As the outcome of this action of the town there was further correspondence between the Town Committee and the Trustees.

At a special meeting of the Trustees, held Jan. 25, 1853, the following communication was received and submitted for consideration:

To the Trustees of Hopkins Academy,—Gentlemen:

The accompanying preamble and votes were passed at our last annual town meeting, and the undersigned were appointed the committee therein named. (Votes just quoted). Should you give an affirmative answer to the proposition of the town, we shall most cheerfully coöperate with you in any measure authorized by these votes of the town. An answer as early as convenient is respectfully requested.

SAMUEL NASH,
P. S. WILLIAMS, } Committee.
F. BONNEY,

Hadley, Jan. 3, 1853.

The subject was considered and further consideration deferred to another meeting held Feb. 1, 1853, when it was voted that it is not expedient for the trustees to comply with vote of the town to make an annual report to the town of the condition of the funds of Hopkins Academy, etc., also that it is not expedient to petition the legislature so to amend the charter of the Academy as to require such report.

Voted, that the portion of the vote of the town in the words following, "together with such other amendments of the charter with reference to applying the funds to a free High School or schools, as such Committee and the Trustees may agree upon," be referred to a committee to confer with the Committee of the Town and enquire into the expediency of such a change and report at a future meeting. Voted, that Rev. R. Ayres, Rev. W. H. Beaman and Rev. J. W. Curtis be said committee.

March 9th, 1853. The Committee above named presented their report which was accepted and the question of its adoption deferred to the next meeting of the Trustees, to be held April 13, 1853.

In consequence of a recent vote of the town in reference to the Academy, (see town votes) it was deemed inexpedient to have any further action on the report of the committee which was accepted at the last meeting.

ORDER PRESENTED TO THE TOWN BY PARSONS WEST, ESQ.

At a town meeting, April 4, 1853, adjourned from March 28, the town passed this vote following:

It is ordered by the town that the sum of six hundred dollars be raised, for the purpose of establishing and maintaining a free High School; provided the trustees of the Academy will appropriate the funds of the Academy or a portion of them, for this object, and give the use of their Academy building for the school.

That the General School Committee, together with the Trustees, be authorized to procure teachers, decide upon qualifications of scholars for admission into the school, and adopt proper measures to establish said school the present season.

Nothing in this vote shall be construed so as to authorize the committee above named to draw upon the treasury for more than six hundred dollars, and if the whole of this sum is not wanted for the school: it shall remain in said treasury.

COMMUNICATION FROM THE TRUSTEES OF HOPKINS ACADEMY TO THE TOWN.

To Samuel Nash, P. S. Williams and F. Bonney, committee of the town of Hadley. Gentlemen:

At an adjourned meeting of the Trustees of Hopkins Academy, holden the 13 instant, the Board took into consideration the vote passed at the last town meeting, making an appropriation upon certain conditions, to aid the object of constituting the Academy a free High School, and in reference to said vote came to the following result, a copy of which is hereby transmitted to you by direction of the Trustees.

The Trustees approve of the vote of the town and concur therein with the following provisos:

1st. That the responsibility for employing teachers for the Academy devolve upon the Trustees with the concurrence of the general school committee.

2nd. That the Trustees consider themselves pledged to the plan proposed for no more than one year, and that the town by their vote are bound for no longer period.

3rd. That there be equal opportunity with that which is now afforded for advancement on the part of pupils in the superior departments of literature and science and that it be the duty of the Trustees to furnish instruction to those engaged in the higher branches of learning.

4th. That the doors of the Academy shall be opened as now to students from abroad, paying the regular tuition fees demanded by the Trustees, and possessing the same qualifications required of students from the town.

5th. That in deciding on questions of discipline, in relation to students from the town, the general school committee shall have a concurrent voice with the Trustees.

6th. That by the adoption of the town's vote no alteration is understood to be effected or attempted in the organization of the Academy. The only difference is the payment of six hundred dollars by the town, on account of which, qualified students from the town shall be entitled to the benefits of the school without any charge for tuition and to the other privileges customarily enjoyed in the seminary, and the general school committee be authorized in connection with the Trustees, to decide on their qualifications, and take a general supervision of their conduct as specified in proviso No. 5.

JOSEPH W. CURTIS, Sec. of Trustees of Hopkins Academy.
Hadley, April 14, 1853.

At a town meeting held May 2nd, 1853, the town having received the above communication from the Trustees of Hopkins Academy voted that the foregoing provisos of the Trustees of Hopkins Academy be accepted with two conditions:

1st. That the General School committee include this among the other public schools in their report to the town.

2nd. That the Trustees be requested either by themselves or through the General School Committee to make an annual report to the town of the condition, receipts and expenditures of the school fund under their care.

Voted that the Town Clerk be authorized to transmit a copy of the foregoing votes to the Trustees of Hopkins Academy.

At a town meeting held May 18, 1853, the town received the following communication from the Trustees of Hopkins Academy:

The following vote was passed at a legal meeting of the Trustees of Hopkins Academy, May 9, 1853, in reference to a vote of the town passed at their meeting May 2, 1853, making request of the Trustees of the Academy that they annually report either by themselves or through the General School Committee to the town, the condition, receipts and expenditures of the school fund under their care.

Voted that the Trustees deem it inexpedient to make an annual report to the town, but that their books are open now, as they ever have been, to the inspection of any person in the town. A true copy of the votes of the Trustees.

J. W. CURTIS, Sec. of the Trustees of Hopkins Academy.

At the same meeting of the Trustees it was further voted that C. P. Hitchcock, J. W. Curtis and Geo. Dickinson be a committee to carry into effect on the part of the Trustees the plan for converting the Academy into a free High School, as set forth in their provisos adopted April 13, 1853, provided the way is opened for this plan to be carried out.

At the town meeting before mentioned it was voted by the town, that in passing the resolve requesting the Trustees to make an annual report, the town did not expect that any action of the Trustees upon that resolve would affect the general plan of the High School.

Voted that the town in their votes of May 2d, did not intend to insist on compliance with their request for an annual report from the Trustees, as a condition essential to the consummation of the plan of union.

It is easy to read in this vote the feeling that the vital question for the town was the enjoyment of the school privileges thus brought within reach and that it would not be wise to risk their loss by insisting on a point of so much less consequence. It is the expression of the desire to cultivate good feeling and good understanding between the town and the Trustees.

Under the plan thus agreed upon the school was conducted for the year. It was proposed as an experiment and might last longer or not according as the working of the plan pleased the parties to it.

The committee appointed by the Trustees and the school committee of the town worked together in harmony in examining pupils for membership in the school, which they enjoyed free of tuition. The experiment was in a good degree a success, and the prospect fair that some such arrangement might be permanent. But inasmuch as it was limited by its terms to one year, further negotiation must ensue. Its progress and result are now to be noted.

At the annual town meeting March 27, 1854, it was voted to raise the sum of nine hundred and one dollars, for a high school, six hundred of which are to be expended in connection with the school at the Academy, and three hundred and one dollars to be expended at the north part of the town, all of which shall be expended under the direction of the general school committee.

At the same meeting adjourned to April 7, it was voted that a committee of three be chosen to confer with the Trustees of the Academy and if after consultation they are of the opinion that it is illegal or inexpedient to continue the High School on the present plan, then the committee are instructed to request the Trustees to unite with the town in petitioning the next Legislature to pass an act authorizing the town and the Trustees to unite in sustaining a free High School, and if the Trustees will unite in such petition the committee of the town request them to join in the adoption of some plan for sustaining a free High School which plan shall be submitted to the town at the annual meeting in November next.

Voted that the superintending school committee be the above committee.

Franklin Bonney, P. Smith Williams, and Samuel Nash were chosen school committee at the annual meeting March 27, 1854. This was the committee named above.

May 2, 1854. The Trustees received the following communication from the committee of the town:

HADLEY, April 21, 1854.

GENTLEMEN OF THE TRUSTEES:

At the annual March meeting the town passed the following vote: Voted to raise the sum of nine hundred and one dollars for a High School, six hundred of which are to be expended in connection with the school at the Academy and three hundred and one dollars to be expended at the north part of the town, all of which shall be expended under the direction of the general school committee. In order to carry out the wishes of the town in this respect we wish to propose the following questions:

Are you willing to appropriate the necessary portion of the income of the Hopkins fund to carry on the free High School, for the ensuing year in connection with the town, upon a plan similar to the one acted upon during the past year?

If so will you please to take the necessary preliminary steps as soon as may suit your convenience. Respectfully yours, &c.,

FRANKLIN BONNEY,
P. S. WILLIAMS,   } Gen. School Committee.
SAMUEL NASH,

In reference to the above communication the following vote was passed by the Trustees and ordered to be presented to the committee of the town by the Secretary:

Voted that the Trustees are willing to unite with the town school committee in carrying on a High School on the same plan as last year the provisos of the Trustees passed last year to remain still in force. The following named persons were chosen as committee to unite with the town in carrying into effect the plan of the free High School:

    Rev. R. Ayres,
    Dea. C. P. Hitchcock,
    Dea. Geo. Dickinson.

May 16, 1854. Information was communicated to the Trustees that the committee of the town decline executing on their part the plan of the High School, in consequence of the supposed illegality of such a measure, legal authority having been consulted.

At a meeting of the trustees held Oct. 6, 1854, the following communication from the school committee of the town was read for consideration.

Hadley, Sept. 23d, 1854.

To the Trustees of Hopkins Academy,—Gentlemen:

At a meeting held March 27, 1854, the town passed the following votes: Voted that a committee of three be chosen to confer with the trustees of the Academy, and if after consultation they are of the opinion that it is illegal or inexpedient to continue the High School on the present plan, then the committee are instructed to request the trustees to unite with the town in petitioning the next legislature to pass an act authorizing the town and the trustees to unite in sustaining a high school, and if the trustees will unite in such petition, the committee of the town request them to join in the adoption of some plan for sustaining a Free High School, which plan shall be submitted to the town at the annual meeting in November next.

Voted that the superintending school committee be the above committee.

In accordance with the provisions of the above votes, we would respectfully address you upon the subject therein considered. The question having early come up in committee upon the legality of pursuing the same plan of operations as was carried on last year, it was deemed advisable to consult counsel upon the matter. The answer obtained was that the plan was illegal. It was consequently not entered upon. This being the fact, it seems desirable to come at once to the action predicated on the above fact being ascertained.

1st. We would, therefore, respectfully request you to unite with the town in petitioning the next legislature to legalize some plan, which may be agreed upon between the parties, for the joint maintenance of a Free High School, by the trustees and the town.

2d. If you should not deem it proper to accede to the above request, would you be willing that the town should make such petition for the attainment of the same object?

Should either proposition meet with your approval, will you be good enough to appoint a committee of conference, whose duty it shall be to meet the town's committee, that they together may discuss the merits of some plan which shall form the basis upon which action can be taken. Your earliest convenient action upon the above is desirable on account of the limited time. Very respectfully yours &c.

Franklin Bonney, } Committee
P. S. Williams,   } of the
Samuel Nash,   } Town.

A true copy, F. Bonney.

After sometime spent in conferring together on the subject of the above communication, the Trustees voted to defer the consideration of it to another meeting.

Oct. 10, 1854. The consideration of the matter was still further postponed until Oct. 16th, when the following letter in the form of an answer to the communication from the committee of the town was adopted:

Hadley, Oct. 10, 1854.

To Messrs. Franklin Bonney, P. S. Williams and Samuel Nash,

Gentlemen:

Your communication dated the 23d ult., to the trustees of Hopkins Academy has been received by the trustees and the proposals it contains have been fully and amply considered. We quote your own words. See the questions 1 and 2, as contained in the copy of the letter of the committee.

With respect to the second of these questions we regard it as a virtual repetition in another form of the first, inasmuch as consent requested in the last instance would involve the same obligations on our part with the appointment of a special committee by us to coöperate with the town for the purpose expressed.

Our answer, therefore, is general, meeting at once both the questions.

We feel constrained to say, gentlemen, that we do not deem it expedient to accede to your proposals and must, therefore, with a due sense of our responsibilities decline the coöperation which you solicit. Our principle reasons for this decision may be expressed in a few words.

1. We are well satisfied with the charter as it is, being the result of combined legislative and judicial wisdom and a vast improvement on any plan of a free school before existing on the basis of the Hopkins fund. For nearly forty years the Academy has been, upon the whole, a great blessing to the town, and it has been, moreover, a source of rich instruction to not a few, whose influence is now felt in all parts of our land, and in the remote regions of the earth. We are not willing to hazard the abrogation or material modification of a charter, the effects of which have been so widely beneficial, nor do we think that the alleged advantages of a single year's experiment under peculiar circumstances, have been sufficient to justify such an attempt.

2. We believe that the objects contemplated in your communication, can be better secured by such a corporation as the charter has established, than by the concurrent authoritative agency of the trustees and a school committee of the town, chosen annually for the purpose. Committees and towns may fluctuate. But a charter remains the same in its principles and provisions.

3. The design of many of the donors to the Academy will be defeated if its management in whole or in part be taken from the hands of the trustees.

4. The slightest invasion, by legislative enactments or in any other way, of chartered rights and obligations, is dangerous as a precedent and in its natural consequences, to the entire interests for which a charter is given and the justification of it involves a principle which if extensively carried out, would destroy all confidence in the most sacred legal securities.

5. The town has no more exclusive right to the funds of Hopkins Academy than to those of any other literary institution, and can, therefore, claim no just authority to appropriate them for its own exclusive benefit. This

point has been long since settled in law, and by the decisions of the highest judicial tribunals.

6. It will probably be admitted that the trustees, as individuals, are as well qualified as any school committee appointed by the town could be, to manage the funds of the institution for the public benefit and to determine their appropriation. Will it be contended that the trustees are not as much the friends of the town and the cause of education as the generality of their townsmen and neighbors? They cannot then see any reason that their good will and fidelity should be distrusted merely on account of their peculiar relation to the Academy as the constituted guardians of its interests. If unreasonable prejudices do exist they cannot with propriety be quieted by concessions to unreasonable demands.

7. The price of tuition here is extremely low, compared with that of most institutions of a similar character and in proportion to the increase of our income there may be expected a diminution of charges for the benefits of instruction in all the higher branches of learning. What more can be asked? If the town, as such, cannot vote money for the common good of the Academy, individuals can easily bind themselves to secure such a result, by their personal subscriptions and contributions. Nor is it absolutely certain that the town may not obtain leave of the legislature to raise money for the payment of the tuition of children here under the present organization. At all events, the trustees believe, whatever may have been done in other places, that it is best, on the whole for all concerned, that the charter of our Academy should remain unmolested, and that one important departure from the original principles of the incorporation might hereafter be pleaded as an apology for other and more essential deviations, subversive of the entire object for which the Seminary was founded. The first step in a wrong direction is most scrupulously to be avoided and naturally leads as by a kind of necessity to wider and wider aberrations from the course of wisdom and duty.

For these among other reasons the trustees decline any action favorable to the wishes of the committee on the subject propounded in their letter for consideration. If the trustees have in any instance transcended their constitutional powers, they would not on this account repeat the offence, much less ask a repeal or essential alteration of their charter.

It was voted to adopt the above letter as the answer of the board to the communication from the committee of the town, and the secretary was instructed to forward accordingly, and copy of the same.

The vote of Rev. Rowland Ayres is here recorded by his request as having been in opposition to the vote of a majority of the trustees, to give a negative answer to the communication from the general school committee.

At this date all attempts at negotiation ceased between the town and the trustees until March, 1860.

It is clear from this record that the vote of the trustees to return such answer to the committee of the town was not unanimous. There were other dissentients than the one whose dissent was by request made matter of record. There was a feeling in the minority, that the answer hardly did full justice to the other party, and that rather than dispose of the question so summarily and finally, it was better to keep it open for further conference, in the hope that some result in which all could concur and rest content, might be reached. But that this might be, there was need of time. With it came change such as is now to be recorded.

The school still went on with its good work. The matter was no longer agitated until, in course of Providence, occasion which none had looked for arose.

On the morning of Feb. 18, 1860, the Academy building and all its contents were destroyed by fire. No insurance. The school, however, was not discontinued. Two rooms in the house of Lucius Crain were engaged, where the school was kept, until a room for the purpose was made ready under the First church building, the next autumn.

Feb. 18, 1860, the Trustees voted to instruct the Prudential Committee to make such an arrangement for the continuance of the school in consideration of the burning of the Academy Building on the morning of this day, as they may deem advisable.

At a meeting of the Trustees March 26, 1860, Mr. S. C. Wilder, chairman of a committee appointed by the town for that purpose, presented the following proposition:

"At a legal meeting of the inhabitants of the town of Hadley, held in the Town Hall in said Hadley, the 26th day of March, 1860. Voted, whereas, in the Providence of God, the Academy building has been destroyed by fire and thereby a favorable opportunity presented to the town for an effort to make available to all the inhabitants of the town the benefits of the school fund, which was given by the town and by benevolent individuals, for the promotion and advancement of learning; therefore voted: that the town will erect a building suitable for the accommodation of a Free High School, provided the trustees will enter into an arrangement and agreement with the town, that they will appropriate the annual income of the Fund to aid in support of such school."

At this meeting a committee of ten, one from each school district, was appointed to confer with the trustees of Hopkins Academy in relation to the use of the income of their fund to support a High school or schools and to form some plan both of schools and buildings to be submitted to the town for their action at an adjourned meeting.

This committee was:

From Dist. No. 1, S. C. Wilder,   Dist. No. 6, R. M. Montague,
" " 2, O. E. Bonney,   " 7, Stephen Johnson,
" " 3, Rodney Smith,   " 8, Benjamin Adams,
" " 4, Wm. S. Shipman,   " 9, Edmund Smith,
" " 5, Chas. Lamson,   " 10, Parsons West.

On receiving from the town an official communication informing the trustees of this action it was voted "that the trustees of Hopkins Academy look with favor upon the vote of the town passed this day, March 26, indicating their wish to secure more fully the benefits of the Hopkins Fund and they will respectfully consider any definite proposition presented by the committee of the town for the attainment of that object."

Voted that the trustees meet the committee of the town on Friday evening, March 30th, at 6 o'clock at the house of Lucius Crain.

At this meeting on invitation the town's committee, through S. C. Wilder, their chairman, laid before the trustees two separate propositions either of which it was considered would be satisfactory to the town, provided they should meet the approval of the trustees.

The prudential committee was appointed a committee to consider the propositions of the town, and to prepare a statement of the views of the trustees to be presented to their board on Monday afternoon immediately after the close of the school. At this meeting it was voted not to seek legal advice at present.

At the meeting of the trustees April 2, 1860, the prudential committee made report on the subject committed to their consideration at the previous meeting. The proposition drawn up by them to be presented to the committee of the town consisted of ten articles, and after discussion and some slight modifications by the board, was acted upon and accepted. The vote on Article 1st, was as follows:

AYES.	NAYS.
Dea. C. P. Hitchcock,	Capt. E. Smith,
Rev. R. Ayres,	Rev. Tuxbury,
J. R. Davenport,	J. B. Porter, Esq.
Rev. W. H. Beaman,	
F. Bonney.	

The succeeding articles were adopted unanimously. Voted to present this document as a proposition of the trustees to the town, to the committee of the town.

This proposition had reference to a communication of the committee of the town here given, as follows:

April 6, the trustees met the committee of the town in conference and after full discussion this plan submitted by the trustees was, with some slight modifications, adopted as the joint action of the two to be submitted to the town on Tuesday next (April 10) at the adjourned town meeting.

This proposition had reference to a communication of the committee of the town here given, as follows:

To the Trustees of the Hopkins Fund, Messrs:

In accordance with the vote of the town passed at its annual town meeting, March 26, 1860, and to secure the privileges therein referred to, we would respectfully present to your honorable body the following propositions as a *plan* of *union* or *agreement* between the trustees of the Hopkins Fund and the town of Hadley, whereby the wishes of said town, as expressed in their vote, may be successfully carried out.

1. The town shall furnish a building with its necessary appendages, conveniences and furniture suitable for a high school.
2. The town shall appropriate two hundred dollars, at the outset, or from time to time as need may require, for the purchase of maps, charts, globes, philosophical and chemical apparatus etc. for the use of the school, provided the trustees of the Hopkins Fund shall appropriate from the income of said fund a like sum for the same purpose.
3. The trustees of the Hopkins Fund shall maintain a High school in this building, which school shall be free to the whole town.
4. The High school shall comprise the higher English and classical departments which shall be of a grade equal to the best academies.
5. The terms of admission to said school shall be uniform, and shall be prescribed by the trustees of the Hopkins Fund and yet made acceptable to the school committee of the town as now constituted.
6. Scholars admitted to this school from other towns shall pay in advance, such rates of tuition as those having the supervision of it may demand; but in no case shall such tuition be less than that charged by the trustees of Hopkins Academy at the present time.
7. There shall be such a prescribed course of studies in said High School as shall usually require three years to complete and these studies shall be determined by the trustees of the Hopkins Fund.
8. Every pupil who shall have completed the full course of study prescribed and whose general deportment, during his or her connection with the school, shall have been worthy of commendation, shall receive a diploma certifying to that effect, which diploma shall be signed by the principal of the school and by the President of the board of trustees.
9. Under the above requirements and limitations the trustees of the Hopkins Fund shall have the sole supervision of the said High school.

All of which is respectfully submitted,

S. C. Wilder, Chairman Town Committee.

Hadley, March 29, 1860.

Just what action was had on this paper in the board of trustees is not clear. This plan of union, however, in its essential features was accepted by the trustees, embodied in the report of the committee to the town and by the town accepted and adopted.

The proposition of the trustees in answer to the foregoing from the town committee is as follows:

To S. C. WILDER, ESQ., CHAIRMAN OF COMMITTEE OF THE TOWN OF HADLEY.

Sir:—The trustees of Hopkins Acadmy recognizing the Providence of God in the loss by fire of the Academy building regard the present as a very important and critical time in the history of their affairs. They wish to understand and meet the demands of the town in the best possible manner, and so that the fund may be more widely useful than it has been heretofore, especially to the town. We wish, if possible, to enter into such arrangement with the town as shall make the Academy a permanent blessing to all future generations, the ornament and pride of the town.

If their fund can be relieved of expense for other purposes. the trustees believe its income adequate to the support of a school of a high order free to all the children of Hadley, of suitable age and qualifications, and are willing that the whole of said income be devoted to this use on certain conditions accepted by both parties. To this end the trustees do not deem it necessary to surrender their charter, nor at present at least, seek its modification. They prefer still to be known as the trustees of Hopkins Academy and use their rights and powers as such, and to have the school, which their fund supports, known as Hopkins Academy and under their own oversight and control. But though such be the legal technical designation and character of the school, they wish it to be to all practical intents and purpose, a high school of no common order. Holding these views it is obvious that the plan No. 2, submitted by your committee is without objection to the trustees of Hopkins Academy, and they are ready to adopt it with certain modifications, which they hope and believe will be approved by the committee and the town. The trustees would, therefore, submit for consideration the following

PLAN OF UNION.

1. The town shall build and furnish and keep in repair a neat and commodious house for the proposed school, after a plan and upon a site to be agreed upon by the trustees and a committee chosen by the town. In case a site near that lately destroyed be chosen, the trustees will give so much of the material of the old building as may be useful in the construction of the new one.

2. The town shall support an intermediate school in said building, to be wholly under its own control for scholars of attainments insufficient to enter the Academy, but pupils duly qualified elsewhere may enter the Academy without passing through said intermediate school.

3. The town shall appropriate one hundred dollars, at the outset, for the purchase of maps, charts, globes, philosophical and chemical apparatus etc..

for the use of the Academy. The trustees of the Hopkins fund engaging to appropriate a like sum for the same purpose.

4. The trustees of Hopkins Academy shall maintain in this building a school embracing the higher English and classical departments of a rank corresponding to that of the best academies, and free to all the children duly qualified in the town, said school to be the best that the net income of the fund will afford.

5. The terms of admission to said school shall be uniform and be prescribed by the trustees of Hopkins Academy, but made acceptable to the school committee of the town, as at present constituted, provided, however, that scholars of proper age may enter the *classical* department without examination and provided also that scholars 15 years of age and upwards may be admitted without examination on petition of the school committee of the town, at the discretion of the trustees.

6. Scholars not of this town shall pay in advance on their admission, such rates of tuition as the trustees may fix, but in no case shall they be admitted at lower rates than those now charged.

7. There shall be a prescribed course of study in said school, such as ordinarily to require three years to complete it, to be regulated by the trustees so as to meet the approbation of the present school committee of the town.

8. Every pupil who shall have completed the full course of study prescribed and whose general deportment during his or her connection with the school shall have been worthy of commendation, shall receive a diploma certifying to that effect, which diploma shall be signed by the principal of the school and by the President of the board of trustees.

9. Under the condititions and limitations above specified, the trustees of Hopkins Academy will pay the whole expense of instruction, and that only, in said school and have its entire oversight and control.

10. Either party shall be at liberty to withdraw from the above arrangements when its own interests shall seem so to require and either party violating the terms of the engagement the other may consider it to have expired by its own limitations.

The trustees at a meeting held April 2, accepted this plan of union and on the sixth of the same month, in a meeting of the trustees and the committee of the town, after full discussion, it was adopted, with some slight modifications, as the joint action of the two, to be submitted to the town at the adjourned meeting April 10. This meeting of the town voted to accept and adopt the report of this committee, and appoint a committee of ten, one from each school district, with power to act under the first article of the general plan for establishing a high school. In case said committee cannot agree with the trustees in locating said building, then said committee shall be empowered to refer the question for final adjustment to a disinterested reference, chosen from out of town and report their action to the town at some future meeting. The names of the committee are these that follow: Dist. No. 1, Eleazar Porter; 2, Oliver E. Bonney; 3, Rodney Smith; 4, Wm. S. Shipman; 5, L. N. Granger; 6, Levi Stockbridge; 7, Stephen Johnson; 8, Benjamin Adams; 9, Edmund Smith; 10, Parsons West. Voted that the above committee also submit a plan for a building and a site for a High school at North Hadley.

April 10, 1860. In presenting this plan to the town the committee use these words by way of preface:

" In all their deliberations among themselves and in their various meetings with the Trustees, an earnest desire to secure to the town the amplest literary privileges within their power has been abundantly manifested and as much harmony of feeling and action has prevailed as was consistent with a full discussion of the propositions coming under their consideration, and in all their consultations with one another and with the Trustees unanimous results have usually been achieved."*   See report on file with Town Clerk.

April 13, 1860. At a meeting of the Trustees a communication was received from the committee of the town empowered to consult with the Trustees with reference to a site for the school building, stating that a sub-committee consisting of Eleazer Porter, Esq., Levi Stockbridge, Esq., and Gen. Parsons West, was ready to meet the Trustees for the purpose indicated. It was voted that the Prudential Committee be appointed a sub-committee to meet them in behalf of the Trustees.

Voted that the Trustees have a strong preference for a site contiguous to that occupied by the old building.

April 19th, 1860. The Prudential Committee made a verbal report with regard to their interview with the committee of the town having in charge the selection of a site for the contemplated Academy building. A proposition was received from the committee of the town asking the Trustees to accept for a site the land now occupied by Mr. John Pierce, on Middle street.

After a discussion of this communication the following action was taken:

Voted that the Trustees do not deem it advisable to accede to the proposition of the committee of the town for a site, but that all things considered, they believe it for the best interests of all concerned, that the house to be

---

*NOTE.—In the proposition presented to the town occurs this addition to Art. 2, as found above: "The town shall also provide a suitable building and therein support a high school in the north part of the town for at least two terms of eleven weeks each, every year, and all the money appropriated to the ten district schools shall be divided hereafter equally among said schools."

built should be located upon a site which can be procured, upon the land of Mr. George Gaylord, near the site of the old building. And the Trustees sincerely hope that the town will see fit to accept of the location proposed.

April 26, 1860. The following communication was presented by the committee of the town:

"TO THE TRUSTEES OF HOPKINS ACADEMY:

At a meeting of the committee of the town in regard to a site for a High School house, held at the Town Hall in Hadley, April 23, 1860.

Voted not to accept the proposition of the Trustees of Hopkins Academy for a site for a High School house.

*Voted, that owing to a difference of opinion between the committee of the town and the Trustees of Hopkins Academy, we in compliance with the vote of the town respectfully ask said Trustees to submit the question of the location of the High School house to disinterested arbitrators from out of town, to be agreed upon by the Trustees and the town committee.

WM. S. SHIPMAN, Secretary."

After a full discussion of the proposition of the committee of the town it was moved and seconded that the proposition of the town to decide the question of a locality for a High School building by a reference of the question to disinterested arbitrators from out of town be accepted. A vote upon the above motion was taken by yeas and nays, with the following result:

YEAS.	NAYS.
Rev. W. H. Beaman,	Capt. Elijah Smith,
Rev. R. Ayres,	Dea. C. P. Hitchcock,
Dea. Simeon Dickinson,	James B. Porter, Esq.,
Mr. J. R. Davenport,	Dea. George Dickinson,
F. Bonney.	Rev. F. Tuxbury.

The committee of the town in their report presented May 7, 1860, close with these words: "At this point all further action was stayed. Your committee, feeling that they had no power to proceed in the premises, concluded to refer the whole subject to the town for their consideration, hoping that they in their wisdom will devise some plan whereby this difference between them and the Trustees may be compromised in a way that shall give the town the advantage of this great boon which has come almost within their grasp." It was voted that the report of the committee of the town in regard to a site for a High School house was read and voted to be accepted and placed on file and the committee was discharged from all further duties."

At this point attempt at futher negotiation ended.

Aug. 3, 1860. The Trustees voted to instruct the Prudential Committee to inquire into the expediency of fitting up the room in the rear of the First church or some other room for the use of the school. Aug. 6, voted to instruct the Prudential Committee to fit up the room back of the vestry of the First church for a school-room. The Parish Committee propose that if the Trustees do this and insure the church against fire for the year they will charge nothing for the use of the building. It is understood that the committee are to purchase desks and chairs, which shall answer for a part of the furniture of the new building which may be hereafter erected. In the school-room thus fitted up the school was kept, reduced to such numbers as the capacity of the room would accommodate. The number of classes was reduced to ten so that one teacher might do the work of instruction without assistance. All scholars were to enter some of these classes, their fitness to be ascertained by an examination by the Trustees.

At this period, between Feb. 18, 1860, and Jan. 18, 1861, several votes were passed at different meetings with reference to obtaining a site and plan for a new building and securing funds for its erection, with no result.

July 30, 1861. It was voted that it is expedient to secure another room in connection with the present one and employ an additional teacher. Voted that the Prudential Committee be instructed to provide two rooms for the accommodation of two teachers the coming year.

In Sept., 1861, an agreement was signed by the Prudential Committee and the Parish Committee of the First Religious Society concerning the use of the school-rooms provided as aforesaid, for a term of years not exceeding four, at an annual rent of $125.00.

At the annual meeting of the Trustees, Nov. 17, 1862, Rev. R. Ayres, Levi Stockbridge, Theodore G. Huntington, were chosen a committee to enquire if the benefits of the Hopkins Fund cannot be more widely diffused in its relation to the town.

This committee presented their report in writing to the board at a meeting held March 30, 1863, as follows:

The committee for enquiring into the expediency of extending the benefits of the Academy more widely would report that it is, in their view, meet and desirable to make to the town of Hadley at its annual meeting held this day, the overture following:

HADLEY, March 30, 1863.

The Trustees of Hopkins Academy moved by the desire to elevate the character of the school under their care, and extend its benefits to a larger number than at present, hereby make to the town of Hadley the following proposition, namely, in consideration of a sum of money not to exceed three hundred dollars, to be paid by the town to said Trustees to aid in paying the expense of necessary instruction, and a further sum not to exceed one hundred dollars for the purpose of seating the north school-room, now occupied by said Trustees, uniformly with the south room, the seats to remain the property of the town. They will open the school with all its advantages, free of charge for tuition, to such scholars from the town of Hadley as shall sustain examination according to the standard of admission hereinafter named. The number to be admitted must be limited by the present accommodations of the school-rooms, &c.

It is proposed to offer such qualified scholars the advantages of a thorough *course of English instruction* to be completed ordinarily in three years. Such pupils will be entitled likewise to a course of classical study and instruction sufficient to qualify young men for admission to college.

Students from abroad are to be admitted to the same privileges by the payment of tuition.

The standard of admission for the present, subject to such modifications as experience may dictate, shall be the following:

Some knowledge of the English language in its elementary sounds and characters; ability to read with tolerable facility in Sargent's Fourth Reader and to spell the words in Sargent's Speller; mental Arithmetic and written Arithmetic to percentage, in Robinson's or an equivalent; Colton and Fitch's School Geography.

The Trustees make this offer for a single year and yet they make it in good faith, hoping that some such arrangement may be permanent and mutually satisfactory. The understanding in making this proposal is that the school shall be under the care of the present principal, and the Trustees engage to secure for the year or part of it, as may be found necessary, such assistance as shall be acceptable to the General School Committee of the town. They will likewise encourage in said committee the most watchful scrutiny of the school, receive from them hints for its improvement, and study to make it in all respects worthy of their approbation and that of the citizenship of the town. R. AYRES, Vice-Pres. of the Board of Trustees.

F. BONNEY, Secretary.

At the town meeting of this date, March 30, 1863, under article eleventh of the warrant to see what action, if any, the town will take with reference to a proposition of the Trustees of Hopkins Academy inviting the town to unite with them in maintaining a free High School for the year ensuing. Voted to accept the proposition made by the Trustees of Hopkins Academy to the town.

March 31st, 1863. The Trustees voted to choose a committee of three to make arrangements with the general school committee of the town for the examination of persons applying for admission to the High School and other matters appertaining thereto. The town having accepted the proposition made by the Trustees, J. R. Davenport, Levi Stockbridge and F. Bonney were chosen.

April 8, 1864. It was voted that the Trustees accept the proposition of the town to continue the same arrangements respecting the High School as was in action last year. The committee of last year was reappointed to co-operate with the General Committee of the town in carrying out the agreement.

Nov. 20, 1864. A committee of the Trustees was appointed to consider the necessities of the school the coming season with reference to furnishing a room for the increasing number of scholars. This committee reported verbally, Nov. 30, and a vote was taken that an examination be held at the opening of the winter term, for such as present themselves, those attaining the highest rank to be admitted first and so on by rank as vacancies occur according to the accommodations of the school-rooms.

Voted that no person shall be considered to have passed examinations who has not answered correctly fifty per cent. of the questions given him.

Feb. 24, 1865. It was voted that the Trustees propose to the town that if the town will provide and furnish a suitable building, and keep it in repair, they will sustain a High School free of expense to the town for such scholars as may be able to pass successfully such an examination as is usually required for admission to similar schools in other towns.

March 6, 1865. The Trustees voted to assume the expenses of the High School under the expectation that a building would be in readiness for occupation by the commencement of the winter term.

At the annual meeting held March 6, 1865, under the article 14th of the warrant "To see if the town will accept of a proposition made by the Trustees of Hopkins Academy* by which they propose and agree to sustain a High School, free of expense to the inhabitants of the town of Hadley, provided that the town will build, furnish and keep in repair a suitable building, and act anything thereon."

Art. 15. To see if the town will continue the existing arrangement with the Trustees of Hopkins Academy for maintaining a free High School.

Voted to accept the following proposition of the Trustees of Hopkins Academy. [See above.]

Voted to build a building for a High School the ensuing year.

Voted that the town appropriate the sum of twelve thousand dollars to build a building for a High School.

*This vote of the Trustees passed Feb. 24, 1865. See record.

At this meeting a committee of five was appointed to procure a plan for and superintend the erection of the building for a High School, and likewise procure a site, and empowered to purchase, grade, and otherwise prepare and properly fit up a site for the High School building, at an expense not exceeding two thousand dollars.

This committee nominated by a committee of five appointed for the purpose by the moderator, P. S. Williams, consisted of P. S. Williams, John A. Morton, L. N. Granger, Dr. F. Bonney and F. Edson.

The committee found difficulty in the choice of a site acceptable to all. But they carefully estimated the number of families and the number of scholars in each of the several districts to be more particularly accommodated by the building and the amount of travel to be performed by those scholars. They were unanimous in the conclusion that the most central location would be some place on or near the four corners, near the town hall. Of several lots examined, the committee chose the homestead of William Blake and made a verbal contract for the same. But before the deed could be executed, a town meeting was called for May 4th, " to see if the town will reconsider the vote whereby they authorized their committee to locate the High School building and act anything thereon." It was voted that this meeting instruct the committee to locate the High School building on Kellogg's corner, with one acre of land, provided a sum above two thousand dollars sufficient to furnish the site be raised by subscription, within ten days, if a sufficient sum be not raised within the specified time to secure the location on Kellogg's corner, then to locate the High School building on the east end of the lot of Geo. H. Gaylord's home-lot, one acre to be presented to the town for that purpose free of all cost.

At a town meeting held May 19th, voted to rescind the vote whereby the town voted at a town meeting held May the 4th, 1865, to locate the High School building on Kellogg's corner or on the land of George Gaylord.

Voted that the committee be instructed to locate the High School building on the corner of Wm. Blake's home-lot.

At a town meeting held June 2nd, 1865.

Voted not to change the location of the High School building from the corner of Wm. Blake's home lot to the east end of Geo. Gaylord's home lot.

As a result of the action of the town, individuals offered to buy the homestead of Edward Stebbins and give a part of the land to the town to enlarge and beautify the lot and make it more convenient·

March 5, 1866. Voted that the High School committee purchase the remainder of the Stebbins homestead and dispose of the buildings and so much of the land as is not necessary for the High School house lot.

At this date negotiations between the Town and trustees were suspended. The vexed question of site being in such wise solved, the building committee before named proceeded to contract for the erection of a school building upon the spot chosen.

The plan of the building was drawn by Architect Wm. F. Pratt of Northampton, who superintended the work of erection. The contractor was Lauriston Ware, whose bid was $11,750. In dimensions the main building was 76 by 36 feet with two transverse wings, 30 by 12 feet. Height of the lower story 13 feet, of the upper story 15 feet. The lower story was divided into two rooms, separated by a hall, for the use of the town, one for a Grammar and one for an Intermediate school. The upper story was used by the Trustees for their school. The main school-room is the full size of the second floor. In the west wing is a recitation-room, and a room for apparatus, etc.

This building, thus provided and furnished, was ready for occupancy early in December, 1865. In these quarters the school has since then found a home and done its work. The cost to the town of the building and its furnishing and appointments, as shown by the report of the building committee at the town meeting March 5, 1866, was $15,882.30. A large sum, they say, and of necessity, since the building itself is large and erected at a time of greatly enhanced cost of material and labor, by reason of an inflated currancy, an evil incident to a long and costly civil war.

Under the plan indicated by the foregoing action of the town of Hadley and the Trustees respectively, Hopkins Academy began its career as a school with all its advantages *free*, for the first time in its history, to all scholars in the town, who on examination should be able to gain admission. Since that date a new class has been admitted each succeeding year, of varying numbers, with a three year's course of study open to them, extended later to four years, with the still further advantage of post-graduate study when desired.

CHAPTER XII.

THE PERIOD OF THE SCHOOL'S GREATEST PROSPERITY.

During the decade from 1830 to 1840 Hopkins Academy attained its greatest growth. At this time numbers were larger than before or since. Probably the corps of instruction was never better. Enthusiasm in study was the reigning spirit, inspired by earnest teachers and furthered by the attrition of bright minds brought together from many places.

Rev. E. Russell, D.D., writing of the school as it was in 1831, says. "The scholars to me were always very pleasant and agreeable. Their industry was untiring and with scarcely an exception successful and satisfactory." Of one pupil he writes, "He was always modest, prompt, accurate, thorough. It made and left its impression on the whole school."

The religious influence of the school at this period was decided and strong. Many young people began the Christian life in connection with the school who have since done eminent service in the line of the designs and wishes of Gov. Hopkins. All pupils were required to attend church regularly every Sunday. A weekly Bible lesson was a general exercise in which all had part. This was sometimes conducted so as to be of inestimable worth. Teachers and pupils met together at the Academy for prayer and religious conference. All who would took part in these exercises, and some of the older pupils did so. In seasons of more than usual interest there was sometimes preaching in the Academy.

Many young people who came to this school from other towns received inspiration and impulse towards all that is best in living, which was never lost. An influence went out through these and reached other young people, who never enjoyed these advantages, kindling hope and stimulating high endeavor.

In the year 1835, the price of board, including room-rent and washing was $1.50 a week. Price of tuition $3.00 to $3.50 a quarter. Although this is a low rate of tuition it was in many cases nearly or quite prohibitory. Not a few of the young people of Hadley, though the desire was strong, could not enter the Academy, and more entered for only a short time, perhaps one quarter or even a half. The cost of tuition for a family of average size for a series of years was felt as no light burden. When this barrier was removed later and the school was open to all alike, there was occasion for joy, that abides to this day.

The school was inexpensive as compared with the present. Rates of tuition were low. The same is true of board and incidental expenses.

The question has interest, whence the Academy derived its patronage? Something in the way of answer may be learned from catalogues of the institution published at different times. The first of these bearing date Feb., 1818, has the names of 99 students. Of these five were from other states than Massachusetts. One from N. Y., one from Conn., one from N. H., two from Vt., seventeen from Hampshire Co. out of Hadley, eight from Mass. out of Hampshire Co., the remainder, 65 from Hadley.

On the catalogue of Aug., 1818, are found the names of 141 pupils. Of this number, thirteen were from out of Massachusetts, nine from Vt., one from Conn., two from N. Y., one from Georgia, sixty from other towns in Massachusetts, 73 in all; sixty-eight, or less than half that number from Hadley.

On the catalogue of Feb., 1819, are 118 names, thirteen from out of Mass., five from Vt., two from N. H., four from Conn., two from N. Y., eighteen out of Hampshire Co. in Mass., sixty-one out of Hadley, the rest, fifty-eight, from Hadley.

The catalogue for the year ending Nov. 17, 1835, shows the whole number of pupils to have been 271, gentlemen 150, ladies 121. Of these twenty-one were from out of Massachusetts, from nine different states, one from Canada and one from the island of Ceylon, 51 from Mass. out of Hampshire Co., 76 from Hampshire Co. out of Hadley, 123 from Hadley, 148 from out of Hadley. These 148 all paid tuition and board as well, and it seems hard to see how their coming hither to enjoy these advantages should not enhance their value to the dwellers in the town and be in other respects promotive of their wellbeing. It was not far from this time, however, that a different feeling prevailed, finding expression in a suit at law in the supreme court.

For the year ending Nov. 21, 1837, whole number of pupils 286, gentlemen 154, ladies 132; winter term 111, spring 131, summer 84, fall 109; in the languages 57. From out of Mass. 27, N. H. four, Vt. one, Conn. nine, N. Y. six, Del. one, Ohio one, Ga. one, Va. one, Fla. one, Ala. two, ten different states. Fifty-one from Mass. out of Hampshire Co., 54 from Hampshire Co. out of Hadley, 154 from Hadley. From this time on numbers gradually grew less so that at the beginning of the fall term in 1842 there were but twenty-seven pupils. There was soon rapid increase, however, though the decline in numbers was permanent from this time on.

During this period a definite course of study was prescribed only for students who proposed to enter college. These must of course take the studies required in order for admission to the higher institutions.

For other pupils the range of elective studies was wide. The attempt to teach so many branches must have had in some instances, the result of superficial mental discipline and attainment. So much was attempted that too little was done to best purpose. Too few sought to teach too many pupils, too many things to be sure of the best work from teacher or pupil. Both did what they could under such limitations. The spirit that reigned in both was excellent. The best results were fruits of character whose worth is beyond estimation. These teachers had noble ideals with which they failed not to inspire appreciative, sympathetic, responsive pupils, such as many of them were, as is plain from the record they have made.

The same spirit in good degree has prevailed since this period and there is assured hope that it will continue and grow, as it should. But the pupils of the time under notice were many of them mature in years, gaining such education as they could, with difficulty and costly sacrifice, and hence they were stimulated to make the most of their opportunities and of themselves.

CHAPTER XIII.

TRUSTEES OF HOPKINS ACADEMY. ROLL OF TEACHERS. ROLL OF HONOR.

TRUSTEES OF HOPKINS ACADEMY FROM ITS INCORPORATION TO THE PRESENT TIME.

Original members who applied to the General Court for an act of incorporation, and are named in the charter.

Seth Smith, 1796, died June 30, 1828.
William Porter, 1796, died Nov. 6, 1847.
Jacob Smith, 1804, died Apr. 5, 1852.
William Dickinson, 1812, died March 15, 1849.
Moses Porter, 1815, died May 22, 1854.

	ELECTED.	RETIRED.
Rev. Dan Huntington,	June 4, 1817	died 1864.
Rev. John Woodbridge, D.D.,	" "	Feb. 22, 1831
Rev. Joseph Lyman, D. D., of Hatfield, President.	June 6, 1818	died 1826
Hon. Isaac C. Bates of Northampton,	June 6, 1817	Nov. 20, 1828
Rev. Vinson Gould, of Southampton,	Sept. 6, 1821	Feb. 23, 1836
Rev. Nathan Perkins, of Amherst, President.	Sept. 6, 1821	Nov. 17, 1835
Hon. Jonathan H. Lyman, of Northampton,		retirement not recorded.
Hon. Joseph Strong, Esq., of South Hadley,		Nov. 20, 1828
Rev. Henry Lord, of Williamsburg,	May 17, 1825	May 21, 1834
Dea. Nathaniel Coolidge, Jr.,	May 17, 1825	died 1835
Rev. Jared B. Waterbury, D.D. of Hatfield,	Feb. 19, 1828	Aug. 16, 1831

	ELECTED.	RETIRED.
Rev. Horace B. Chapin, of South Amherst,	Nov. 20, 1828	retirement not recorded
Rev. Ichabod S. Spencer, D.D. of Northampton,	Nov. 20, 1828	Aug. 19, 1834
Maj. Sylvester Smith,	Nov. 20, 1828	declined service.
Rev. Levi Pratt, Hatfield,	Aug. 17, 1830	May 21, 1834
Dea. Elisha Dickinson,	Aug. 17, 1830	declined service.
Rev. John Brown, D. D., President, from Nov. 17, 1835 to March, 1839.	Nov. 23, 1831	died in 1839
Capt. Elijah Smith,	May 21, 1834	June, 1861
Mr. James B. Porter, Elected again May 19, 1835.	May 21, 1834	
Rev. Joseph Penney, D. D., of Northampton,	Aug. 19, 1834	Feb. 23, 1836
Rev. John Todd, D. D., of Northampton,	Aug. 19, 1834	retirement not recorded.
Mr. James B. Porter, Treasurer from 1835-1862.	May 19, 1835	Nov. 16, 1868
Mr. Dudley Smith,	May 29, 1835	May 27, 1858
Rev. Joseph D. Condit, of South Hadley,	Nov. 17, 1835	died Sept. 13, 1847.
Rev. Wm. Tyler, of South Hadley Canal,	Nov. 22, 1836	Nov. 21, 1842
Rev. John Ferguson, Whately,	Nov. 20, 1838	retirement not recorded.
Rev. David L. Hunn of North Hadley, President from Nov., '39-'41.	Aug. 20, 1839	retirement not recorded.
Rev. Joseph W. Curtis,	Nov. 19, 1839	died 1857
Rev. Francis Danforth,	Feb. 18, 1840	retirement not recorded.
Dea. Chas. P. Hitchcock,	Nov. 16, 1841	declined service.
Dea. Simeon Dickinson,	Nov. 16, 1841	Dec. 14, 1864
Rev. John Woodbridge, President Nov. 20, 1842 to Nov. 22, 1859.	Feb. 18, 1842	Nov. 22, 1859
Rev. Warren H. Beaman, of North Hadley, Pres. Nov. 22, '59 to Dec. 1, '65.	Aug. 12, 1845	Nov. 20, 1873
Capt. Oliver Warner,	Nov. 18, 1845	died June 6, 1850
Rev. Rowland Ayres, President since Dec. 1, 1865.	Feb. 15, 1848	
Dea. Chas. P. Hitchcock,	Feb. 20, 1849	died 1867
Mr. William P. Dickinson,	Aug. 17, 1852	March 7, 1863
Dea. George Dickinson,	Aug. 17, 1882	died Aug., 1889
Rev. Franklin Tuxbury,	Nov. 19, 1857	March 7, 1863

	ELECTED.	RETIRED.
Mr. Jesse R. Davenport,	Nov. 19, 1857	Nov. 16, 1868
Franklin Bonney, M. D.,	Nov. 19, 1857	
Hon. Levi Stockbridge,	April 1, 1862	
Mr. Theodore G. Huntington,	April 1, 1862	Dec. 16, 1877
Eleazar Porter, Esq.,	April 1, 1862	died April, 1886
Treasurer from 1862-1878.		
Mr. Horace Cook,	April 1, 1862	
Rev. E. S. Dwight, D. D.,	Nov. 22, 1864	
P. S. Williams, Esq.,	Nov. 22, 1864	April 15, 1870
L. N. Granger,	Prior to 1865	1876
Record of election failed to be made,		
John C. Hammond, Esq.,	Nov. 15, 1870	
S. C. Wilder, Esq.,	Nov. 15, 1870	died 1873
Charles E. Lamson,	Nov. 15, 1870	died March 17, 1879
John A. Morton,	Nov. 15, 1870	Nov. 27, 1878
Rev. James M. Bell,	Nov. 20, 1873	retirement not recorded.
Oliver E. Smith,	Nov. 20, 1873	May 5, 1883
Mr. Wm. P. Porter,	Nov. 17, 1876	
Treasurer since Nov. 22, 1878.		
Mr. John N. Pierce,	Nov. 17, 1877	
Mr. Charles Cook,	Nov. 17, 1877	
Dea. Rodney Smith.	Nov. 17, 1877	died Feb. 2, 1890.
Rev. John W. Lane,	Sept. 2, 1878	
Dea. Baxter E. Bardwell,	Nov. 20, 1885	
Rev. John S. Bayne,	Nov. 23, 1888	

Of the sixty-three names in this list, sixteen only have been chosen from out of town. Since the election of Rev. John Ferguson, Nov. 20, 1838, no one has been chosen out of Hadley.

PRESENT BOARD OF TRUSTEES.

Rev. Rowland Ayres, D.D.,	1848
Franklin Bonney, M. D.,	1857
Horace Cook, Esq.,	1862
Rev. E. S. Dwight, D. D.,	1864
John C. Hammond, Esq.,	1870
William P. Porter, Esq.,	1876
Dea. John N. Pierce,	1877
Charles Cook, Esq.,	1877
Rev. John W. Lane,	1878
Dea. Baxter E. Bardwell,	1885
Rev. John S. Bayne,	1888

OFFICERS OF THE BOARD.

Rev. Rowland Ayres, D. D., *President.*
Rev. E. S. Dwight, D. D., *Vice-President.*
Franklin Bonney, M. D., *Secretary.*
William P. Porter, Esq., *Treasurer.*
Charles Cook, Esq., *Auditor.*
Rev. R. Ayres, D. D., F. Bonney, M. D., J. C. Hammond, Esq., *Prudential Committee.*

ROLL OF TEACHERS IN HOPKINS ACADEMY.

The history of the school is made up largely of the names, work, and record of its teachers. This list of honored names is here given.

PRINCIPALS.

	CAME.	WENT.
Rev. Dan Huntington, Y.C. 1794,	Dec. 17, 1817	1820
Rev. Worthington Smith, D. D., W. C. 1816, Pres. U. Vt. and Trustee.	Dec., 1820	Feb., 1822
Oliver S. Taylor, M.D., died March, '85, aged 100.	Feb. 22, 1822	May, 1826
Rev. John A. Nash, A.C., 1824	May, 1826	Nov., 1827
George Nichols, Y. C., 1824, Rector of Hopkins Grammar Sch., New Haven, taught, Springfield, d. '41, salary $600.	1827	1829
Timothy Dwight, A.C. 1827, tutor,	1829	1830
Rev. Ezekiel Russell, D.D., A.C. '29, tutor, minister N. Adams, Springfield Olivet church, and Holbrook, Mass.	March, 1830	Sept., 1831
Rev. Lewis Sabin, D.D. A.C. '31, Trustee, minister, Templeton, died 1873.	1831	Aug., 1835
Rev. Amos S. Cheesebrough, D.D., Y.C., member Corporation Y. C., minister, Chester and Glastonbury, Conn., and elsewhere.	1835	1836
Rev. Jesse G.D. Stearns, A.C. '36, tutor, minister, Billerica, and elsewhere, died 1882.	1836	1837
Rev. Mortimer Blake, D. D., A.C. 1835, died 1884.	1837	1839
John P. Sanderson, A.C. 1839,	1839	Jan., 1840
Cyrus Holmes, could not have been employed more than a few weeks. Paid to Jan. 20, $48.50.	1840	

	CAME.	WENT.
Rev. Horace Hutchinson, A.C. '39. From the Treasurer's account it is inferred that Mr. H. was in charge of the school one quarter, ending May 19.	1840	May 19, 1840
Miss Almira Henshaw, in charge one quarter, ending Aug. 18, inferred from books of Treasurer.	1840	Aug. 18, 1840
O. Fisher, Y.C. 1836,	1840 or '41	May 19, 1841
Isaac Witherell, 3 quarters,	Sept., 1841	May, '42,
Miss Mindwell Woodbridge had charge one quarter, ending in August, with very few pupils.	1842	Aug., 1842
Rev. Addison Ballard, D.D., W.C. 1842, tutor; Morris Prof. Rhetoric, Latin and Math., Ohio Univ.; Prof. Latin and Astron., Marietta; Prof. Christian Greek and Latin, and Prof. Mor. Phil. and Rhet., LaFayette Coll.	1842	1843
Rev. Henry B. Hosford, W. C., tutor, minister, Sunderland, Prof. Int. Mor. Phil. and Rhet., Western Reserve Coll.	1843	1844
Rev. Henry K. Edson, A.C. '44, Principal Denmark Academy, Prof. in Iowa College.	1844	1849
Rev. Henry Lobdell, M.D., A. C. 1849, missionary to Mosul, Turkey.	1849, one quarter 1849	
Marshall Henshaw, D.D., LL.D., A. C. '45, tutor, principal Pinkerton Acad., Derry,N.H., Dummer Acad., Byfield, and Williston Sem., Prof. Math. Rutgers Coll., lecturer, Nat. Phil., A. C.	1849	1850
Rev. Lucius D. Chapin, A.C. '51, Prof. Mor. and Intell. Phil., Univ. Mich., Chanc. and Prof. Ment. Philosophy, Ingh. Univ. One quarter.	1850	1851
Rev. Wm. F. Avery, A.C. '50, minister Huntington and Lanesboro, one quarter.	1851,	1851
Rev. C. V. Spear, A. C. '46, minister at Sudbury, Prin. Maplewood Institute, Founder of Spear Library, Prof. at Oberlin, College, O.	1851	1852
Augustus H. Buck, A.C. '49, Prof. Greek and German, Boston Univ.	1852	1853
Reuben M. Benjamin, LL.D., A.C. '53, tutor, Judge county court, Ill., Prof. Law and Real property, Ill. Wesl. U.	1853	1854

	CAME.	WENT.
Jesse R. Davenport, A. C. '51, Prin. Am. Acad., Prin. High Schools, Oxford and Woonsocket, R. I.	1854	1867
Charles A. Chandler, A. C. '66, Editor *Boston Herald*.	1867	1869
Rev. Herbert J. Cook, A.C. '69, minister Coldwater, Mich., and Dayton, O.	1869	1869
Geo. H. White, A.C. '70, instructor A.C., Prof. Preparatory Department O. C.	1870	1873
Walter G. Mitchell, W.C. '70, principal High School, Winsted, Conn.	1873	Jan., 1874
W. W. Mitchell, W. C. '39, Prin. High Schools Northampton and Chicopee, Mass. House Rep. 1882.	1874	1878
Edward Ayres, A. C. '78, teacher Lake Forest Acad., Ill., instructor in Latin A.C., principal High School, Orange, principal High School and Supt. of schools, Warren, Mass., Supt. of schools, La Fayette, Ind.	1878	1880
George Sherman, A. C. '79, Prin. High School, Winchester, N. H.	1880	1881
Edmund P. Barker, A.C. '76, Prin. Acad. Dudley, Prin. High Sch., Swampscott.	1881	1883
William Orr, Jr., A. C. '83, Prin. Smith Acad., Hatfield, teacher of Science Springfield High School.	1883	1885
Edward A. Baker, A.C. '84,	1883, part of one term	
Francis J. Heavens, A.C. '84, principal High School Enfield, Ct., Brookfield, Mass., principal High Sch. and Supt. of schools, Wallingford, Conn.	1883	one term, 1884
Francis L. Palmer, A. C. '85, Theol. student,	1885	1886
Nathaniel F. Wilcox, W. C.	1886	1887
Daniel W. Rogers, A. C. '87,	1887	1887
Elmer Case, B. U. '84,	1888	
ASSISTANT TEACHERS.		
Giles C. Kellogg, Esq., Y. C. 1800, taught at intervals afterwards, as late as 1831.	1817	1826
Miss Sally Williston, preceptress,	1817	1818
Miss Sophia Mosely, preceptress,	1818	1819

	CAME.	WENT.
Miss Sarah Whitney, preceptress, m. Henry Marsh.	1820	1821
Miss Mary W. Fiske, preceptress,	1821	1822
Miss Elizabeth P. Huntington, taught smaller children,	1821	
Miss Mary Ann Little, taught smaller children, m. Rev. Worthington Smith, D.D.	1821	
Miss Eliza Merrill,	1822	1822
Miss Strong,	1823	1823
Miss Dolly Blair, m. Geo. Nichols,	1824	1829
Charles L. Strong, A. C. '26,	1827	1827
Miss Emily H. Williams, preceptress,	1829	1830
Rev. Wm. F. Nelson, A. C. '29, Prof. Theol. Richmond Coll., Prof. Bibl. Lit. West. Bapt. Theol. Inst., Covington, Pres. Minn. Central Univ.	1829	1829
Miss Mary Dwight, preceptress,	1829	1830
Miss Louisa S. Billings, preceptress, m. Rev. Ezekiel Russell, D.D.	1830	1835
Aaron B. Hall, A. B.,	1830	1831
Miss Louisa Packard,	1831	1831
Arnold Hannum,	1831	1831
Wm. Zephaniah Stewart, LL.D., A. C. '33, Judge Supreme Court, Ind.	1832	1832
Rev. E. W. Bullard, minister Royalston,	1832	1833
Rev. Adiel Harvey, A. C. '32,	1832	1833
Miss Mary W. Billings, m. Rev. Rob't O. Dwight, missionary to India.	1832	1832
Miss Abigail Clark,	1832	1832
Miss Lucy Ann Brown,	1833	1833
Rev. Amos Bullard, A. C. '33, tutor, minister, Barre, Mass.	1833	1833
Miss Lucretia Porter,	1834	1834
Miss Proctor,	1834	1834
Miss Thankful Murdock, preceptress,	1835	1838
Chauncey Howard, A. C. '35, lawyer,	1834	1835
Rev. S. W. Banister, A. C. '35,	1835	1835
Rev. Mortimer Blake, D.D., later Prin.,	1835	1835
Rev. David Caldwell, A. C. '37,	1835	1835
Rev. Roswell D. Hitchcock, D.D., LL.D., A. C. '36, tutor, Trustee, Prof. Nat. and Rev. Religion, Bowdoin College, Pres. and Prof. Eccl. Hist., Union Theol. Sem.	1835	1835

	CAME.	WENT.
Rev. Chas. C. Corss, A. C. '30,	1834	1834
Rev. Samuel Hopkins Emery, A. C. '34, minister Taunton,	1834	1834
Miss Mary D. Smith,	1835	1835
Miss Abigail Clark, assistant pupil,	1835	1835
Rev. Austin Isham, Y. C. '36,	1836	1836
Lycortas L. Bruer, M. D., A. C. '36,	1836	1836
Rev. Jesse K. Bragg, A. C. '38,	1836	1836
Horace T. Blake, A. C. '38,	1836	1836
Rev. David Andrews, A. C. '36,	1836	1836
Miss Mary Hooker,	1836	1837
Miss Sarah P. Coolidge, preceptress,	1837	1837
Rev. Samuel A. Taylor, A. C. '37,	1837	1837
Rev. Asa Mann, A. C. '38, minister, Hardwick and Exeter, N. H.	1837	
James O. Pratt,	1837	1837
Rev. Chas. Lord, A. C. '38, minister at Whately and Buckland.	1837	1837
Miss Sarah A. Smith,	1837	1837
Miss Lucy B. Gaylord, assistant pupil,		1839
Miss Mary A. Crossett, " "		1839
Watson Loud, M.D., teacher Chirography,	1837	1839
Miss Hannah B. Church, preceptress,	1838	1839
Rev. Henry Seymour, A.C. '38, minister Deerfield, Hawley.	1838	1838
Jonathan B. Marshall, A. C. '38,	1838	1838
Chas. E. Washburn, M.D., A.C. '38, tutor,	1838	1838
Miss Mary A. Reed,	1838	1838
Miss Mary Clark, preceptress,	1839	
Rev. Horace Hutchinson, A. C. '39,	1839	1840
John P. Sanderson, A. C. '39,	1839	1839
Rev. Alden B. Robbins, D.D., A.C. '39, minister, one of the " Iowa Band."	1839	1839
James A. Taylor, A. C. '39,	1839	1839
Miss Jane A. Cook, assistant pupil,	1839	1839
Miss Emily Pomeroy, assistant pupil, m. Rev. David Eastman.	1839	1839
Rev. Elijah H. Bonney, A.C. '39, minister Pawlet, Vt.,; Vernon Centre, N.Y.; Lenox, N. Y., and Clarkson, N. Y.	1840	1840
Miss Almira Henshaw,	1840	1841

	CAME.	WENT.
Miss Mindwell Woodbridge,	1841	1841
Rev. Henry B. Hosford, W.C. '43,	1842	1843
Miss Train, sister of Hon. Chas R. Train, Attorney General of Mass.	1843	1843
Rev. Theron H. Hawks, D.D., W.C., '44, minister West Springfield, Inst. Un. Theol. Seminary, trustee Western Reserve, Trustee Marietta.	1843	1844
Miss Louisa A. Hosford,	1843	1844
Miss Harriet A. Hinsdale, preceptress, m. Rev. Henry L. Hubbell, D.D.	1844	1846
Rev. Chas. V. Spear, A.C. '46,	1844	1844
Jos. P. Dowse, A. C. '46,	1845	1845
Rev. Chas. N. Williams, W. C.,	1846	1846
Miss Rebecca M. Woodbridge, m. Judge E. S. Willliams.	1846	1846
Miss Joanna Stanwood, m. Rev. Francis V. Tenney.	1846	1849
Hanson L. Read, A.C. '48,	1848	1848
Miss Susan A. Woodbridge,	1848	1848
Rev. John A. Seymour, A.C. '49,	1849	1849
Rev. Henry Lobdell, M.D., missionary, A. B. C. F. M., to Mosul, Turkey, acting principal.	1849	1849
Mrs. Francis J. Henshaw preceptress,	1849	1850
Miss Miranda Smith,	*1850	1850
Mr. Augustus Whitaker,	1850	1850
Horace M. Smith,	1850	1850
J. Edwin Whitaker, B. U.,	1849	1850
L. M. Morton, teacher of penmanship,	1850	1850
Hon. John E. Sanford, A. C. '51, tutor, Trustee, Speaker Mass. House Rep.	1850	one term, 1851
L. C. Chapin, M.D., Y.C. '52, tutor,	1850	one term, 1851
John Smith, A. C. '49,	1851	one term, 1851
Anton Ruppaner, M. D., teacher French and Music.	1851	1852
Miss Abby C. Mayhew, m. Rev. David Temple Packard,	1851	1852
George E. Dudley, A. C. '52,	1852	one term, 1852
John F. Buerger, teacher Music, French and German,	1852	1853
Mrs. C. L. Buck,	1852	1852

	CAME.	WENT.
Miss Abby P. Smith,	1852	1854
Rev. Geo. N. Webber, D.D., A. C. '52, tutor, Prof. Int. and Mor. Phil., Middlebury, Coll.	1852	one term, 1852
Miss Perry,	1853	one term, 1853
Miss Sarah W. Powers,	1853	1853
Rev. Daniel Phillips, A. C. '56,	1854	1854
Miss Elizabeth F. Tobey,	1854	one term, 1854
Miss Felicia H. Emerson,	1854	Fall term
Miss Cynthia M. Pierce,	1855	1855
Miss Juliette Clark,	1855	one term, 1855
Miss Cornelia C. Barrows, m. Rev. Lyman Bartlett, missionary, A. B. C. F. M., to Turkey,	1855	one term, 1855
Miss Clarissa Smith,	1856	1857
Miss Charlotte C. Haskell, teacher Vassar College, m. J. Edwards Porter,	1856	1859
Miss Eliza C. Haskell, m. Edward P. Frisbee, D. D., Pres. Wells College, Aurora, N. Y.	1857	1857
Miss Hill,	1858	1858
Miss Laura R. Johnson,	1858	1860
Miss Lucy A. Cook,	1861	1862
Miss Maria L. Pasco,	1863	1865
Miss Martha R. Gaylord,	1865	1866
Miss Isabella S. Nash,	1867	1868
Mrs. Martha L. Bell,	1868	1869
Miss Abby P. Smith,	1869	1872, '73, '78
Miss Augusta A. Porter,	1872	1873
Miss Emma W. Beaman,	1873	1877
Miss Emma C. Bardwell,	1880	1886
Miss Mary Reed,	1885	
Miss Genevieve Cooley,	1886	1887
Miss Edith J. Ayres, Smith Coll. '82,	1887	one term, 1888
Miss Clara W. Clark, " " '88,	1888	one term, 1888
Miss Alice C. Dickinson, Westfield State Normal School.	1888	1890

CORPS OF INSTRUCTION, SUMMER TERM, 1890.

Elmer Case, Principal.

Miss Mary Reed,
Miss Alice E. Dickinson, } Assistants.

THE ROLL OF HONOR.

These pages have taken note of the desire of Gov. Hopkins that the money given by him might be for the encouragement of hopeful youth in the way of learning for the service of the country in future times. The following roll of honor contains the names of such pupils of Hopkins Academy as have been in various ways conspicuous in rendering such service.

NAMES OF PUPILS OF HOPKINS ACADEMY WHO BECAME MINISTERS OF THE GOSPEL.

Noah Cook.
Parsons Cook, D. D., W. C. '22, minister at Ware and Lynn, Mass.; editor *Puritan Recorder*.
Jeremiah Porter, W.C. '22, home missionary; army chaplain.
Tertius Clark, D.D., Y. C. '24.
Bela B. Edwards, A. C. '24, D. D., tutor, trustee, Prof. Sac. Lit. Andover Seminary.
Sylvester Cook, A. C. '25.
William P. Huntington,
John A. Nash, A. C. '25, principal Hopkins Academy, etc.
Samuel Hopkins Riddle, 1818, Y. C. '23.
Horace Smith.
Elijah C. Bridgman, D.D., A. C. '26, missionary to China.
Dyer Ball, M. D., missionary to Singapore and China, Canton.
Mason Ball.
Sylvester Woodbridge.
Jahlael Woodbridge.
Lucien Farnham, A. C. '27.
Preserved Smith, A. C. '28.
Fordyce M. Hubbard, W. C. '28, D. D., tutor at W. C.; Episcopal minister; Prof. Latin, Language and Literature, Univ. N.Carolina.
Columbus Shumway, minister Townsend, Mass.
Martin Cushman.
Charles C. Corss, A. C. '30.
Lewis Sabin, D. D., A. C. '31, trustee, principal Hopkins Academy; minister at Templeton, Mass.
John Dunbar, W. C. '32, missionary to Pawnee Indians.
William Mason Richards, W. C. '32.
Amos Bullard, A. C. '33, tutor, minister at Barre, Mass.
George C. Partridge, A. C. '33, tutor, minister at Greenfield and elsewhere.

Clinton Clark, A. C. '35, tutor, minister at Pompey, N. Y., and Ridgefield, Conn.
Justus L. James, A. C. '35.
Sylvester Judd, Jr., Y. C. '36, writer of distinction.
Pascal P. P. Kidder, Y. C. '36.
Isaac A. Basset.
Solomon Clark, W. C. '37, minister at Plainfield and Goshen, Me.
George Lyman, A. C. '37, minister at Sutton and So. Amherst, Mass.
Daniel W. Poor, A. C. '37, D.D., minister Newark, N. J., Prof. Eccl. Hist., and Ch. Gov't, San Francisco Theol. Seminary.
Rufus Taylor, A. C. '37, D.D.
Abraham Jenkins, A. C. '38.
Charles Lord, A. C. '38, minister at Whately and Buckland, Mass.
Henry Seymour, A. C. '38, minister Deerfield and Hawley, Mass.
Edward F. Brooks, minister, W. Va.
Leonard Adams.
Elijah H. Bonney, A. C. '39, minister, Pawlet, Vt., Vernon Centre, N. Y., Lenox, N. Y., Clarkson, N. Y.
Dexter Clapp, A. C. '39.
Frederic Dan Huntington, A. C. '39, D. D., minister Boston and preacher at Harvard University, Epis. Bishop, Central N. Y.
Jonathan S. Judd, W. C. '39, minister at Whately.
William Porter, W. C. '39, D.D., Prof. Latin Lang., Beloit.
William B. Stone, A. C. '39.
Simeon Miller, A. C. '40, minister Ireland Parish and So. Deerfield.
Thomas S. Norton, A. C. '40, minister at Dover and Prescott, Mass.
Thomas Spencer, home missionary.
Luther Clapp, W. C. '41, home missionary, Wisconsin.
Loren B. Marsh, minister Chester, Mass.
Dwight W. Marsh, W. C. '42, D.D., missionary to Turkey.
Zephaniah M. Humphrey, A. C. '43, D.D., Prof. Ch. Hist. and Pol. Lane Theol. Seminary.
James G. Bridgman, A. C. '43, missionary to China.
Timothy Lyman, A. C. '44.
Henry K. Edson, A. C. '44, principal Hopkins Acad. and Denmark Acad., Iowa, Prof. Iowa College.
Rodney Gage, Post Chaplain, Alexandria, Va., 1864.
Stephen B. Adams.
John M. Greene, A. C. '53, tutor, D. D., trustee Mt. Holyoke Sem., and Smith Coll., minister Hatfield, So. Hadley and Lowell, Mass.
William E. Dickinson, A. C. '55, minister Chicopee, Mass.

Lyman Bartlett, A. C. '56, missionary to Turkey.
Henry Powers, minister Manchester, N. H., and elsewhere.
Henry M. Bridgman, A. C. '57, missionary to So. Africa.
Richard H. Mather, A. C. '57, D.D., Prof. Greek and German, lecturer in Sculpture, etc.
Laurens Clark Seelye, W. C., Prof. Rhet. Amherst, Pres. Smith Coll.
Edward Clark Porter, Y. C. '58, minister, Racine, Wis.
Henry Porter, M.D., missionary to China.
J. Edwin Tower, A. C. '58, minister at N. Brookfield, not ordained.
Francis L. Nash, minister Sacramento, Cal., and elsewhere.
Myron A. Johnson, Episcopal.
Charles M. Lamson, A. C. '64, D.D., Walker Instructor in Latin, Amherst; minister Brockton and Worcester, Mass., and St. Johnsbury, Vt.
Martin K. Pasco, A. C. '65, minister in Marysville, O., Belpre, O., and elsewhere.
Herbert Jonathan Cook, A.C. '69, principal Hopkins Acad., minister Coldwater, Mich., and Dayton, O.
Arthur Smith, A. C. '77, minister at Scarboro and So. Freeport, Me.
Albert Foote.

PUPILS OF HOPKINS ACADEMY WHO ENTERED THE MEDICAL PROFESSION.

Edward Dickinson.
William Workman.
Chester Johnson.
Moses Porter.
Austin Church, M. D., Y. C. '23.
Orson Osborn, M. D., Y. C. '24.
Lewis Hopkins.
William W. Dwight, Y. C. '26.
Watson Loud.
Marshall D. Perry.
Alonzo Clark, W. C. '28, LL. D., Prof. in sundry medical institutions in N. Y., and elsewhere.
Ephraim Cook, member of Canadian Parliament; sentenced to death for ministering to wounded insurrectionists, but reprieved and banished to the states, and afterwards returned.
Silas Cook.
George H. Batchelder.
Joseph Bates.
Sidney Brooks, A. C. '38.

Levi Dwight Seymour, surgeon at Hampton, Va., during the civil war.
George A. Bates.
William H. Willis (named changed from Orrick.)
Jabez Baldwin Lyman, A.C. '41, instructor French and German, A. C.
George C. Fleming, surgeon in Mexican war.
Franklin Bonney, A. M., A. C. '69.
Charles Robinson, Governor Kansas Territory.
Lucius Lyon, B. U. '69.
George F. Thompson, army surgeon during the civil war.
Edward H. Beaman.
John E. Dwight.
John Chester Lyman.
H. Frederic M. Smith.
George A. Tuttle, A. C. '83.

PUPILS OF HOPKINS ACADEMY WHO ENTERED THE PROFESSION OF LAW.

Henry Chapman.
Aholiab Johnson, entered W. C., class of '23.
George Ashmun, Y. C. 23, M. C.
Edward Kirkland.
Thomas H. Bond, Y. C. '25.
Lincoln Clark, A. C. '25, M. C., Judge, etc.
James A. Shed.
Simeon Nash, Jr., A. C. '29, Judge Court Com. Pleas, Ohio.
John A. Taft, Y. C. '25.
Charles P. Huntington, H. C. '22, Judge C. P.
Edward Bates Gillett, A. C. '39, Dist. Attorney.
Samuel H. Austin, lawyer in Philadelphia.
Erastus Smith Williams, Judge.
Elbridge G. Bowdoin, A. C. '40.
Ithamar F. Conkey, Dist. Attorney.
Joseph S. Curtis, W. C. '52, Judge, Green Bay, Wis.
Henry S. Stockbridge, A. C. '45, State Dist. Attorney, Md.
Louis I. Fleming, A. C. '47.
Maj. James M. Hosford, entered W. C. '47.
John Woodbridge, Jr., A. C. '49.
Matthew McClung, A. C. '55.
John Woodbridge Smith, A. C. '56.
Sylvester Stockbridge.
John Chester Hammond, A.C. '65, trustee of Hopkins Academy and Williston Seminary.
Frederic E. Smith.

YOUNG MEN PUPILS OF HOPKINS ACADEMY WHO ENGAGED IN TEACHING AND BECAME EDUCATORS.

Joseph Lyman Partridge, W. C. '28, tutor.
Francis Phelps, H. U. '37, teacher, Boston.
Joshua F. Pearl, Y. C. '36, founder of Quaboag Seminary, Supt. of schools, Nashville, Tenn.
Merrick Lyon, B. U. '41, LL.D., preceptor Greek Lang., trustee and socius B. U., teacher in Providence, R. I.
Henry K. Edson, A. C. '44, principal Hopkins Academy, principal Denmark Academy, Prof. Iowa College.
Henry Eastman, teacher of music.
William Martin Pierce, A. C. '53, teacher in Virginia and Missouri.
William D. Whitney, W. C. '45, Prof. Sanscrit Lang., Lit., and comparative philology, Y. C., etc., etc.
Newell Wedge, A. C. '48, teacher.
Hon. Levi Stockbridge, Prof. and Pres. Mass. Agr'l College.
William L. Montague, A. C. '55, Prof. Modern Lang., etc., A. C.
Rev. Richard H. Mather, A. C. '57, D.D., Prof. Greek and German Amherst College.
Leicester Porter Hodge, A. C. '50, teacher.
Rev. L. Clarke Seelye, U. C., Prof. Rhet. A. C., Pres. Smith Coll.
Henry Parks Smith, A. C. '60, teacher.
Charles D. Marsh, A. C. '77, Prof. Nat. Science, Ripon Coll., Wis.
Edward Ayres, A. C '78, principal Hopkins Acad., instructor A. C., principal High Sch. and Supt. Schools, Warren and Lafayette, Ind.
Charles A. Tuttle, A. C. '83, instructor Hist. and Polit. Econ., A. C.
Franklin E. Tuttle, A. C. '89, teacher.

PATRONS OF EDUCATION.

Miss Sophia Smith may have been a pupil of Hopkins Academy, but this is not ascertained beyond doubt. If not herself a member of the school a younger sister was, it is believed, and she herself was likely to have caught the spirit that drew hither the young women of her class.
Dea. Eleazar Porter, founder of two prizes at Amherst College.
Dea. George Dickinson, founder of a fund for the increase of the library of the Young Men's Lib. Ass'n, and, in a possible contingency, the library of Hopkins Academy.

PUPILS OF HOPKINS ACADEMY, COLLEGE GRADUATES, WHO ENTERED NEITHER OF THE LEARNED PROFESSIONS.

Loomis Cook, W. C. '28.
Nehemiah Porter, '21.

Paudias T. Ralli, Greek, Y. C. '30.
Theophilus P. Phelps, A. C. '41.
William E. Tyler, A. C. '44.
John S. May, W. C. '51.
Lewis W. West, A. C. '60.
Frederic D. Kellogg, A. C. '79.
George E. Howe, Grad. Mass. Agr'l Coll.
Fred H. Fowler,   "   "   "   "
John R. Callahan, A. C. '89, law student.
Frank B. Doane, A. C. '90.
Edwin A. Richardson, A. C. '90.

PUPILS OF HOPKINS ACADEMY WHO WON DISTINCTION IN CIVIL LIFE, ETC.

George Ashmun, Y. C. '23, M. C., Pres. Rep. Nat. convention that nominated Abraham Lincoln.
Lincoln Clark, A. C. '25, Attorney Gen., Ala., Judge Circuit Court, Ala., M. C.
Roger Hooker Leavitt, state senator.
William Hyde, state senator.
Levi Stockbridge, Pres. and Prof. Mass. Agr'l Coll., representative and senator.
George W. Hubbard, state senator, trustee Smith Charities and Smith Coll.
Francis Edson, representative and senator.
Hinsdale Smith, state senator.
Hart Leavitt, county commissioner, Franklin Co.
Elisha H. Brewster, county commissioner, Hampshire Co.
William P. Dickinson, county commissioner, Hampshire Co.
P. Smith Williams, county commissioner Hampshire Co., representative
Daniel B. Gillett, special county commissioner, Hampshire Co.

John S. Bell,	representative general court.			
Parsons West,	"	"	"	
Leicester W. Porter,	"	"	"	
Theodore Clark,	"	"	"	
Horace Cook,	"	"	"	two terms.
Horace S. Dickinson,	"	"	"	
Franklin Bonney, M.D.,	"	"	"	
Alexander Hyde,	"	"	"	
Charles Cook,	"	"	"	
Henry L. James,	"	"	"	
John N. Pierce,	"	"	"	

Edward B. Gillett, A. C. '39, district attorney.
Ithamar F. Conkey, district attorney.
Samuel D. Ward, controller city Chicago.
Charles Robinson, M.D., governor territory of Kansas.
E. Monroe Wright, W. C. '39, Sec'y Com. of Mass.
Samuel Goode Jones, W. C. '37, Eng. Pres. R.R., trustee University of the South.
Simeon Nash, Jr., Judge Court Com. Pleas, Ohio.
William P. Rawlings, high sheriff.
George W. Bonney, amateur artist.
Capt. Ephraim O. Smith, shipmaster.
Samuel S. Eastman, editor.
John Howard Jewett, editor Worcester Evening Gazette, and poet.
William P. Porter, trustee and treasurer Hopkins Academy.
Elbridge H. Kingsley, distinguished artist in wood engraving.
Henry Worthington Smith, A. C, '59, distinguished life insurance actuary.
William F. Walker, A. C. '86, County Supt. Schools, Vt.
Edward H. Dwight, artist.
Henry M. Seymour, editor.
Clifton C. Johnson, artist.

There is reason to think that the Hopkins School, prior to the charter making it an Academy, was chiefly for boys. From that time onward more young women than young men have enjoyed the advantages of the school. "For forty years Hopkins Academy was a famous fitting school." Dr. Humphrey is quoted as saying that " it educated the girls so as to raise them above their brothers and their brothers' mates so that they went forth as teachers, and then married up." These young women, many of them, became teachers and some subsequently married men in professional life, or otherwise distinguished.

NAMES OF YOUNG LADY PUPILS OF THIS CLASS.

Amy Porter, m. Rev. Joseph D. Wickham, D.D., Y.C. 1815, tutor Burr Seminary, Manchester, Vt., oldest living graduate of Yale.
Lois E. Porter (Coolidge), m.'Rev. Joseph W. Curtis.
Julia Smith, m. Hon. Lincoln Clark, M. C.
Catharine A. Smith, m. Dr. Jones.
Mary D. Ward, m. Rev. Horace Smith.
Lucretia S. Ward, m. Judge Oviatt.
Krissa Kingsley, m. Rev. Eli Moody.

Nancy Dwight, m. Austin Church, M. D.
Elizabeth Dickinson, m. Horace Goodrich, M. D.
Maria P. Dickinson, m. Rev. Lewis Sabin, D. D., principal Hopkins Academy, etc.
Harriet Dickinson, m. Rev. Ebenezer Bullard, 2d wife.
Elizabeth H. Smith, m. Rev. William Harvey, missionary to India, Mahrattas.
Esther Smith, m. Rev. John Dunbar, missionary to Pawnee Indians.
Martha Smith, m. Rev. O. G. Hubbard.
Miranda Smith, m. Rev. Pomeroy Belden.
Margaret Smith, m. Rev. Ebenezer Bullard.
Julia Smith, m. John L. Blodgett, M. D., and afterwards Chas. Howe, Collector, Port Key West, Fla.
Susan Porter, m. Rev. Lucian Farnham.
Sarah Hooker, m. Rev. M. L. R. Thompson, D.D.
Tirzah M. White, m. Judge Williamson of Bangor, Me.
Francis M. White, m. John Kimball, Esq., lawyer.
Abby L. White, m. Rev. William Williams.
Clarissa J. Lyman, m. Rev. John H. Bisbee.
Mary Ann Woodbridge (Hawley), m. Rev. Parsons Cook, D.D.
Rebecca M. Woodbridge, m. Judge Erastus Smith Williams.
E. Octavia Woodbridge, m. Rev. R. H. Richardson, D. D.
Abigail D. Gaylord, m. Wm. Kirkwood, M.D., Nassau, N. Prov.
Lucy Humphrey, m. Rev. Henry Neill, D.D.
Susan C. Belcher, m. Chas. S. Thomson, M. D.
Lucy Stone, m. Henry B. Blackwell.
Eunice W. Bullard, m. Rev. Henry Ward Beecher.
Caroline Daugherty, m. Rev. Wm. M. Richards.
Caroline Phelps, m. Rev. S. G. Bullfinch.
Charlotte Phelps, m. Rev. Mason P. Bartlett.
Adaline A. Spaulding, m. Rev. Moses K. Cross.
Hannah M. Hodge, m. Rev. James Wilcox.
Almira Edson, m. Rev. Mr. Hall, afterward Geo. Atwood, M. D.
Harriet M. Hodge, graduate and teacher at Maplewood, authoress, etc., m. Hon. Thomas F. Plunkett.
Emily Pomeroy, m. Rev. David Eastman.
Lucy Ann Clark, m. Levi Dwight Seymour, M. D.
Lydia Smith, m. Henry E. Ide, merchant, Brooklyn.
Susan H. Smith, m. Edward P. Richardson, M. D.
Maria D. Smith, m. Capt. Joseph Richardson, shipmaster.
Susan S. Seymour, m. Maj. Jas. M. Hosford, lawyer.

Mary Smith, m. —— Phelps, teacher, California.

Sarah W. Powers, graduate Maplewood, m. Rev. Benj. Parsons, missionary to Turkey.

Lucy P. Beaman, m. —— Dayton, M. D.

Sarah S. Wallis, graduate and teacher at Maplewood, m. Rev. F. P. Chapin.

Maria W. Nash, teacher and authoress, m. James H. Hackleton, teacher.

Mary B. Dickinson, m. Rev. James P. Kimball.

Martha G. Hubbard, m. Rev. Francis L. Nash.

Lepha N. Clark, graduate and teacher at Maplewood, teacher at Vassar College and at Bergen, N. Y.

Phebe Whipple, m. Benjamin F. Ayer, Esq., counsel for Illinois Central R. R.

Delia Whipple, m. Gen. Joseph C. Abbott, U. S. Senator, N. C.

Celia Whipple, teacher South and Chicago.

Emma I. Porter, m. Rev. Sereno D. Gammell.

Charlotte W. Porter, graduate Miss Porter's school, Farmington, Ct., principal of "The Elms," Hadley and Springfield.

Mary L. Jewett, graduate State Normal School, Westfield, teacher State Normal School, R. I., m. Chas. F. Taylor, B. U. '63.

Mary E. Beaman, Grad. Mt. Holyoke, m. Sylvester Stockbridge, Esq.

Emma W. Beaman, graduate Mt. Holyoke, teacher Hopkins Academy and elsewhere.

Mina D. Beaman, m. Rev. John D. Willard.

Mattie Metcalf, m. Rev. Herbert J. Cook.

Alice J. Ayres, graduate Maplewood, teacher Tileston Normal School Wilmington, N. C., m. G. W. Baily.

Mary Scott, graduate Mt. Holyoke, teacher A. M. A., Chattanooga, Tenn., and Howard Seminary, Missouri.

Emma C. Bardwell, graduate Mt. Holyoke, teacher Hopkins Academy and Wallingford, Conn., m. Francis J. Heavens, teacher Hopkins Acad., Enfield, Conn., Brookfield, Mass., and Wallingford, Conn.

Helen M. Smith, graduate Mt. Holyoke, m. Henry S. Stockbridge, Jr., Esq., lawyer, M. C.

Mary H. Bonney, graduate Smith Coll., m. Fred E. Smith, Esq., lawyer.

Lizzie Hillman, m. M. Ferguson, M. D.

Louisa H. Smith, graduate State Normal School, Westfield, teacher Hadley and Lawrence, m. Edwin H. Baxter, M. D.

Sarah M. Marsh, graduate Westfield Normal School, teacher Hadley and Michigan.

Alice E. Dickinson, State Normal School, Westfield, teacher Greenfield, Hinsdale and Hopkins Academy.

Edith J. Ayres, graduate Smith Coll., teacher Chicago, No. Brookfield, Hopkins Academy, Brooklyn, Clinton, Northampton.
Emily R. Marsh, graduate Mt. Holyoke, teacher Bertier, Canada.
Alice T. Smith, graduate Mt. Holyoke, teacher No. Hadley.
Lucy McCloud, graduate Smith Coll., teacher Tilden Seminary.
Marion McGregor Dwight, graduate Smith Coll.
Caroline I. Doane, graduate Smith Coll., teacher Ashfield Acad.
Theodora W. Reed, graduate Smith Coll.

PUPILS OF HOPKINS WHO HAVE RENDERED SERVICE TO THE COUNTRY IN THE RANKS OF HER ARMY.

Joseph Hooker, West Point, Maj. Gen. U.S.A., Commander of the Army of the Potomac.
Edwin H. Seymour, served in the Mexican war.
Joseph B. Plummer, West Point, Gen. U. S. A., died in Missouri during the civil war.
Col. John E. Cook, 76th Regt. N. Y. Vol., commanded at Gettysburg after his superior officers were slain.
Maj. James M. Hosford, 112th Regt. Ill. Vol. Infantry.
Capt. Phinehas White, Ind. Cavalry.
Henry K. White, Regt. Mich. Cavalry.
Ezra W. Matthews, Maj. of Battery, Brig. Gen. Gov. Hawley's staff.
Capt. Edwin S. Nash, —th Regt. Kansas Vol.
Lieut. James W. Porter, Battery.
Lieut. James W. Smith, 31st Regt. Mass. Vol.
Rev. Jeremiah Porter, chaplain before, during and since the war, for a long time the oldest chaplain.
Rev. Rodney Gage, post chaplain, Alexandria, Va.
David C. Ayres, hospital steward, Nashville, Tenn.
John W. Beaman, } 2nd Mass. Battery.
Rufus P. Scott,
Edward Johnson, 14th Kansas Cavalry.
John Sullivan, 1st Mass. Cavalry.
Aaron Scott, 96th Regt. Ill. Vol.
George Dickinson, —th Regt. Me. Vol.
Myron Newton, 104th Regt. Ill. Vol., killed at the battle of Hartsville, Tenn., Dec. 6, 1862.
Frederick Brown, 56th Regt. Mass. Vol.
Asa Clark, Jr., 46th Regt. Mass. Vol.
William N. Shipman, 50th Regt. Mass. Vol.
Corp. John A. Morton, Jr., 15th Regt. Ill. Vol.

Lieut. John Howard Jewett,	10th Regt. Mass. Vol.
Corp. John C. Clark, mortally wounded at Spottsylvania,	" "
Corp. Henry Alonzo Dunakin,	" "
Franklin Hubbard,	" "
Wallace A. Hubbard,	" "
Alfred Vanhorn,	" "
Corp. Rufus A. Cook, died in Hospital at Newbern, N. C.	27th Regt. Mass. Vol.
Henry Dunakin, killed June 18, 1864, before Petersburg, Va.	" "
Herbert F. Johnson,	" "
Chas. F. Lyman,	" "
Lucius D. Smith,	" "
Corp. Lewis W. West,	" "
Maj. George N. Jones,	37th Regt. Mass. Vol.
Corp. Levi H. Bartlett,	" "
Edwin Dwight Beaman,	" "
Hosp. Steward Wm. A. Champney,	" "
Levi P. Dickinson,	" "
George F. Enderton,	" "
Charles D. Hodge,	" "
Corp. Samuel Hodge,	" "
George W. Nash,	" "
Samuel D. Smith,	" "
Corp. Sylvester B. Stockbridge,	" "
Francis P. Wheeler,	" "
Daniel H. Bartlett,	52nd Regt. Mass. Vol.
Charles W. Clark, died in hospital at Baton Rouge,	" "
Henry C. Comins,	" "
Alfred L. Cook,	" "
Eleazar Cook,	" "
S. Parsons Cook,	" "
Charles F. Dickinson,	" "
Luther W. Dickinson,	" "
John B. Dunbar,	" "
Corp. Charles S. Enderton,	" "

Edwin C. Gray,	52nd Regt. Mass. Vols.
William H. Hayward,	" "
William H. Hodge,	" "
Sergt. Lewis B. Hooker,	" "
Oscar R. Hubbard,	" "
Benjamin Lombard,	" "
George M. Smith,	" "

Many whose names do not appear in this roll of honor have done good service to their country and their kind and made a worthy record in various lines of useful activity.

Possibly some names that should appear are omitted for the reason that no record could be found and that they could not otherwise be traced.

CHAPTER XIV.

COURSE OF STUDY IN HOPKINS ACADEMY.

NAMES OF GRADUATES WHO HAVE RECEIVED ITS DIPLOMA. PRESENT MEMBERSHIP OF THE SCHOOL.

In the school, as now administered, two courses of study are provided, each to be completed in four years. On completing either course, or its equivalent, the graduate receives the diploma of the institution testifying to this effect.

Instruction is given in the following Departments:

    I. English Language and Literature.
    II. History and Government.
    III. Mathematics.
    IV. Natural Sciences.
    V. Latin.
    VI. Greek.
    VII. French.

I. English Language and Literature.

Reed and Kellogg's Higher Lessons in English. (3 credits.)
Kellogg's Rhetoric. (2.)
Swinton's English Literature, and Brooke's Primer, with memorizing of selections. (4.)
General Exercises, consisting of:
    a. Spelling, daily, through the course.
    b. Reading, on alternate days, during first half of the course, and as much longer as required to attain a satisfactory degree of proficiency.
    c. Rhetorical Exercises: One declamation, one essay, and two impromptu compositions, each term.

II. History and Government.

History of England. (2.)
Primer of Roman History. (1.)
Primer of Grecian History. (1.)
Anderson's Universal History. (2.)

III. Mathematics.

Wentworth's Algebra, to Progressions. (3.)
Wentworth's Geometry, Four Books. (2.)
Mayhew's Book-keeping. (1.)
Natural Philosophy. (2.)
Astronomy. (1.)
Arithmetic reviewed. (1.)

IV. Natural Sciences.

Houston's Physical Geography. (2.)
Morse's First Book in Zoölogy. (1.)
Dalton's Physiology. (2.)
Gray's School and Field Book of Botany, with study of Compositæ. (2.)
Chemistry, with laboratory work. (2.)
Geology and Mineralogy. (1.)

V. Latin.

First Latin Lessons. (3.)
Cæsar, four books, with Jones's Latin Prose Composition, twenty lessons. (3.)
Cicero, seven orations, including Pro Lege Manilia, with Jones's Latin Prose Composition finished. (3.)
Virgil's Æneid, six books, (Georgics and Bucolics, with Latin Prosody. (3.)

VI. Greek.

Greek Lessons. (4.)
Xenophon's Anabasis, four books, and Jones's Greek Prose Composition, twenty lessons. (3.)
Homer's Iliad, three books. (2.)

VII. French.

Sauveur's Petites Causeries. (2.)
Keetel's Elementary French Grammar. (2.)
Les Doigts de Fée. ($\frac{1}{2}$.)
Racine's Athalie. ($\frac{1}{2}$.)
La Fontaine's Fables. (1.)

Unclassified.

Gow's Morals and Manners. (1.)
Mental Science. (1.)

Each student, in addition to the General Exercises, should pursue, at least, three studies. A permanent record is kept of each student's scholarship. Upon the successful completion of any study, credits are recorded in accordance with the foregoing schedule. The recipient of thirty-six credits is entitled to graduation and a diploma. Each branch must be pursued until satisfactory attainment be made, whether the time required be longer or shorter. *Faithful* students, of average ability, will be able to attain three credits each term, and thus graduate in four years. Those who can attain thirty-six credits in less time, will be permitted to do so, and to graduate when qualified.

Students who are absent a part of the time because of sickness, or for other reason, or who absent themselves from examination, must not expect to receive credit for work until they have done the work.

Students who can attend only two terms each year, or even one, may, nevertheless, graduate, when they shall have satisfactorily accomplished the required amount of work. Credit will be given for studies pursued out of school, provided a satisfactory examination be passed upon them. Real equivalents will be accepted in place of authors and text-books named in the course.

The English course consists of all the English Language and Literature, History and Government, Mathematics and Natural Sciences.

The Classical course consists of all the Latin, Greek, French, Algebra and Geometry.

COURSE OF STUDY IN HOPKINS ACADEMY.

YEAR	TERM	ENGLISH.	HISTORY.	MATHE-MATICS.	NATURAL SCIENCES.	LATIN.	GREEK.	FRENCH.	
I.	1.	Higher Lessons.		Algebra.	Physical Geography.	Grammar			Morals and Manners weekly through the year.
I.	2.	Higher Lessons.		Algebra.	Physical Geography.	Grammar.			
I.	3.	Higher Lessons.		Algebra.	Zoölogy.	Grammar.			
II.	1.		of England.	Geometry.	Physiology.	Cæsar.	Grammar.		
II.	2.		of England.	Geometry.	Physiology.	Cæsar.	Grammar.		Book-keeping.
II.	3.	Rhetoric.	of Greece.		Botany.	Cæsar.	Grammar.		
III.	1.	Rhetoric.	of Rome.		Botany.	Cicero.	Grammar.	Petites Causeries and Grammar.	
III.	2.		Civil Government.	Natural Philosophy.	Chemistry.	Cicero.	Anabasis.	Petites Causeries and Grammar.	
III.	3.	Literature.	Universal.		Geology.	Cicero.	Anabasis.	Petites Causeries and Grammar.	
IV.	1.	Literature.	Universal.	Astronomy.		Virgil.	Anabasis.	Petites Causeries and Grammar.	
IV.	2.	Literature.		Natural Philosophy.	Chemistry.	Virgil.	Iliad.	Les Doigts de Fée. Athalie.	
IV.	3.	Literature.		Arithmetic. (Reviewed)		Virgil.	Iliad.	La Fontaine.	Mental Science.

This course of study in the main has been in use since 1882. It is flexible however as respects the order of studies and the particular text books in each, which are subject to change from time to time.

After the new school building was opened in 1865 no class completed the course of study prescribed and received the diploma until 1873, when the first class of three was graduated. The names of those receiving the diploma are these:

Class of 1873.

Charles D. Marsh, Mary N. Shipman, Augusta Hawley.

Class of 1874.

Edward Ayres, Mary H. Bonney.

Class of 1875.

SEMPER AD ALTIORA.

Helen M. Smith, Emma C. Bardwell, Louisa H. Smith.

Class of 1876.

TO MERIT SUCCESS IS THE HIGHEST SUCCESS.

Edith J. Ayres, Alice E. Dickinson, Emma S. Dickinson,
Mary Pelletrier, George A. Tuttle.

Class of 1877.

Caroline Shaw.

Class of 1878. None.

Class of 1879.

CONSTATE NOBIS.

Mary Bell, Annie Cook, Fanny A. Cook,
Helen Hooker, Lucy McCloud, Caroline S. Marsh,
Jennie Pelletrier, Jessie Reynolds, Lettie Smith,
Charles A. Tuttle.

Class of 1880. None.

Class of 1881.

FINIS NOUDUM EST.

Sarah O. Barstow, Prudence C. Richardson, Caroline M. Bell,
Jennie E. Parker, Florence M. Stebbins, Caroline B. Wright.

Class of 1882.

THERE REMAINETH MUCH LAND TO BE POSSESSED.

Lydia A. Cook, Marion Mc.G. G. Dwight, Emily R. Marsh,
Jennie A. Richardson.

Class of 1883.

PERSEVERENTIA ONMIA VINCIT.

Agnes Ayres, Fred H. Fowler, Lizzie J. Spear,
Hattie E. White.

Class of 1884.

John R. Callahan, Mary E. Pellissier.

Class of 1885.
VESTIGIA NULLA RETRORSUM.

Frank B. Doane,   Caroline I. Doane,   Theodora W. Reed,
               Etta L. Sawtelle.

Class of 1886.
NON SCHOLAE SED VITAE DIDICIMUS.

Louise J. Bell,   Nellie G. Burke,   Nellie L. Gray,
Jennie S. Hannum, Thera F. West,   Edwin A. Richardson.

Class of 1887.
AD ASTRA PER ASPERA.

Catherine Callahan, Martha L. Johnson, Julia D. Seymour,
                     Lucy F. Webber.

Class of 1888.
DROIT EN AVANT.

Mary A. Cook,   Sarah D. Doane,   Julia S. L. Dwight,
Hattie E. Enderton, Hattie L. Freeman, Hattie E. Haskins,
Annie S. Lyons,   Gertrude L. Shaw,   Frank L. Smith.

Class of 1889.
STRIVE FOR THE BEST.

Howard H. Bayne,   John E. Lane,   Eugene Pelletrier,
Cotton A. Smith,   Mary L. Cook,   Mary D. Emond,
Bertha H. Gates,   Annie Halpine,   Maria A. Pellissier,
Ellen M. Ryan,   Minnie A. Ryan,   Catharine A. Walsh.

Class of 1890.
SILENCE IS GOLDEN.

Sarah Theodosia Allen,   Alice Martha Belden,
Elizabeth Catherine Collins,   Grace Beaman Howe,
Nettie Louise Johnson,   Eva Lulu Richardson,
Mary Isabella Sanderson,   Catherine Maria Shea,
Jennie Haynes West,   Edward Charles Pellissier.

Of these graduates, eighty-five in all, we number fourteen young men, seventy-one young women, or more than five to one. This is a fact to challange notice and inquiry as to its meaning. Previous to the incorporation of the Academy the school had been for boys almost, if not quite, exclusively. Since that time, and notably in recent years, girls, beyond their brothers, have been ready to enter and remain within these doors that have been set open to all alike. For what good reason should such a fact be a permanent feature of the history of this school?

PRESENT MEMBERS OF THE SCHOOL.

The membership of the school for the winter term 1889-90 is found in the catalogue, that follows:

Seniors.

Sadie T. Allen,	Alice M. Belden,	Lina M. Cooke,
Lizzie C. Collins,	Nellie J. Fitzgerald,	Grace B. Howe,
Nettie F. Johnson,	Edward C. Pellissier,	Eva L. Richardson,
Mary J. Sanderson,	Kate M. Shea,	Jennie H. West.

Juniors.

Nellie S. Bissell,	Margaret A. Conolly,	Jay C. Cooke,
Lina M. Culver,	John E. Dalton,	Mary F. Gates,
Bertha D. Haines,	George E. Johnson,	Kate L. Keefe,
Emma B. Kingsley,	Mary R. Kingsley,	Annie L. Lasalle,
S. Etta McQueston,	Bridget A. Ryan,	Perlia Stevens,
	Kate L. Whalen.	

Sophomores.

Annie E. Cahill,	Edward H. Cooke,	Inez E. Crafts,
Mary J. Davis,	Fannie J. Gaylord,	Charles C. Hunter,
Amy S. Lane,	Anna T. McQueston,	Anna E. Pellissier.
Julia A. Powers,	Helen R. Reynolds,	Mabel L. Shipman,
	Nellie E. Whalen,	

Freshmen.

Lawrence A. Belden,	Earl W. Bryant,	Julia B. Clarke,
Margaret B. Collins,	Floyd S. Crafts,	Theodora Emond,
Alexander T. Ford,	Mary Halpine,	Lucy A. Hickey,
Arthur C. Howe,	Jennie A. Johnson,	Julia E. Johnson,
Edward L. Keefe,	Wallace R. Lane,	Edward S. Marsh,
Edward McGrath,	May L. Morton,	Michael O'Neill,
William J. Pellissier,	Fordyce T. Reynolds,	Susie M. Russell,
Lucy W. Sanderson,	Fred C. Webber,	Martha L. Whalen.

Boys for Winter Term.

Robert J. Ford,	William P. Fowler,	James Gates,
Charles W. Greene,	Edward J. Halpine,	John L. Keefe,
William H. Morgan,	John E. Shea,	Edward C. Smith,
Robert S. Smith,	John H. Temple,	Edward P. West,
	Jesse S. Wilson.	

CHAPTER XV.

CHANGES IN THE FORM AND VALUE OF SCHOOL FUND. PRESENT FORM, CONDITION AND PROSPECTS.

The portion of the Hopkins legacy assigned to Hadley was small, in round numbers only £308. But as we follow the story we are led to exclaim how great a matter a little fire kindleth. The heat of controversy concerning it inspires the exclamation. The feeling rises, likewise, in view of the beneficent work wrought by this means, through two centuries and a quarter. The Fund that had such origin has suffered no serious loss since the burning of the corn mill in 1677. Under wise and careful management it has grown to many times the original sum, and, while furthering the end to which it was devoted, with due allowance for the uncertainty of all material things, its future growth and usefulness seem to be assured.

This growth of value is due in part to the fact that the school land esteemed worth but little when granted at first, by the town, in 1668, appreciated with other property in its neighborhood. This meadow tract, containing sixty acres more or less, with considerable upland adjoining, was bounded by the Connecticut river, and so situated in relation to it that it grew by accretion from Hatfield side and the stream wore for itself a new channel, leaving part of the land an island. This wearing process began as early as 1805 or 1806. In 1825 the new channel had become permanently established. The old bed of the river gradually filled to the opposite bank. The right to the land thus formed was in dispute. The question was submitted by the Trustees to the Supreme Court. At the September term held in Northampton in 1852 the Court laid down the legal principles that should govern in the premises and directed that one or more commissioners should examine the facts, come to a decision and report their doings to the Court. This commission consisted of Joseph Cummings, C. B. Rising and Myron Lawrence, whose award was in substantial accord with the demands of the Trustees. Cushing Rep. 9, 544–553.

Owing to such causes the tract of land which in 1666 was said to contain sixty acres more or less, was by a survey made in 1844 found to contain one hundred and fifty-eight acres and one hundred and eight rods. These lands were for a long series of years rented to people living near them. On some portions buildings were erected. But these tenants did not like to pay rent, grew restive under its burden and longed and sought for ownership. After long delay, in the year 1865, the Supreme Court in answer to a petition for this object in which the Trustees and the town of Hadley united, granted the Trustees leave to sell, at public auction or private sale, any or all the land held by them in trust, the proceeds to be invested in securities of the United States, of the state of Massachusetts, the state of New York or the city of New York or the city of Boston, or upon the security of ample real estate by bond and mortgage.

Sales of most of the lands at North Hadley followed, resulting in a feeling of relief and independence in the minds of those who had been paying rent. The productive value of the fund increased at once. Those of the Trustees who questioned the wisdom of making the sale came to see and acknowledge that it was well that the change took place. The proceeds of the sale were most of them for a time in bonds of U. S. Later these were sold and the proceeds placed in loan and mortgage on real estate in Chicago. After a time, a shrinking of nominal values came, and as an incident, default of interest.

The Trustees took the mortgaged property into their own hands and still hold it and from it receive rent. On one lot they built a house for rental, which has proved a happy disposition of the property, whose value has grown and is likely to be still further enhanced.

The mill privilege at North Hadley—the dam and stream, which had been leased for ninety-nine years, in 1812, at an annual rental of twenty dollars in silver money, was sold and conveyed by deed of quitclaim to L. N. Granger for $300, " it being all the property owned by the Trustees on or near the mill stream at No. Hadley." The estate of Mr. Granger paid for the same Dec. 22, 1877.

GRANT OF A HALF TOWNSHIP OF LAND IN MAINE.

On the foregoing page, 31, the impression is given that no gift was made to the Fund later than the grant of the town in 1678. Exact truth demands notice of the fact that the Trustees were granted a half township of land in Maine by the legislature of Massachusetts on their petition to this end.

Nov. 29, 1817. The Trustees of Hopkins Academy voted to petition the General Court of Massachusetts for a grant of a half township of land, to further the purposes of the institution. Isaac C. Bates, Esq., was to prepare the petition and the prudential committee were required to take all proper means to secure the success of the same.

June 12, 1820, the General Court passed this resolve:

"That there be, and hereby is, granted to the Trustees of Hopkins Academy, their successors in said office or assigns, for the sole use and benefit of said Academy, one-half township, of six miles square, from and of the unappropriated lands in the state of Maine, which on the division of said lands, shall fall to the share of this commonwealth; and to be subject to all the reservations usual in grants of this kind, the same half town-ship to be vested in said Trustees, their successors in said office, and assigns forever, for the sole use and benefit of said Academy, reserving four hundred acres, one-half for the use of schools and the other half for the use of the ministry therein; the said half township to be laid out under the direction of the Commissioners for the Sale and Settlement of Eastern Lands, at the expense of said Trustees. Provided the said Trustees, within five years from and after the laying out and location of said half township, cause ten families to be settled thereon, and provided, also, that said Trustees give bond to the Treasurer of the Commonwealth, faithfully to apply the proceeds and avails of said half township to the sole use and benefit of said Academy.

And be it further resolved that the said half township of land shall be located agreeably to the foregoing provision, within ten years from the first day of January next, otherwise this grant shall be void."

Resolves of the State of Massachusetts, May session, 1820.

Aug. 28, 1820. The Trustees voted to request the President and Secretary to obtain and report such information as may be useful to the Board concerning the half township of land granted by the General Court.

Feb. 27th, 1821. The Trustees appointed a committee, consisting of Isaac C. Bates, Jonathan H. Lyman, William Dickinson, William Porter, and Moses Porter, to contract for the sale of the half township granted by the General Court.

Feb. 26, 1822. The Trustees took the following action:

Whereas, at a meeting of said Board of Trustees held on the 27th day of February, 1821, I. C. Bates, Jona. H. Lyman, William Dickinson and Moses Porter were appointed a committee to contract for the sale of the half township of land granted by the General Court to Hopkins Academy, and, whereas in pursuance of their said commission and authority, a contract has been made with Joseph Whitney, Esq., of Calais, in the county of Washington and state of Maine, which contract has been entered into by Samuel Hubbard, Esq., of Boston, as agent and attorney of said committee, and in the name and behalf of the Trustees of said Academy, which contract is dated the 18th of February, inst., and which the said Trustees are now at liberty to affirm or reject at their pleasure, and said contract being before the Trustees and duly examined and well understood by them, Therefore, voted, We do approve of the doings of our said committee and of the said Samuel Hubbard, Esq., as their agent and attorney, in the name and behalf of the said Trustees; and that we do hereby ratify and confirm said contract, and make it our own, and do hereby direct our Treasurer or Secretary whenever, it shall be necessary and proper to convey said half township, according to our contract and agreement aforesaid, and our covenants therein, and that the Secretary of the Board be directed to transmit to said Samuel Hubbard, Esq., a copy of this vote as his sufficient authority and justification for his doings in the premises.

This land, according to the foregoing contract, was probably conveyed to Joseph Whitney, before named.

The Treasurer's accounts show that he received for Whitney's note, Feb. 28, 1827,	$325.00
Received for J. Whitney's note, due the 18th of February, March 1, 1830.	280.00
Received for Whitney's last note, due Feb. 18, March 16, 1831,	265.00
	$870.00

March 25th, 1822, the treasurer credits S. Hubbard $250 for land. The treasurer's accounts afford only such light as this concerning the proceeds of the sale of the Maine land.

The General Court passed a resolve, Feb. 14, 1825, on petition of Joseph Whitney, directing the agent of the land office to survey and locate the half township of land for the Academy. May 26, 1826, the deed was made to the Trustees of Hopkins Academy, in the town of Hadley, and by them probably conveyed to Joseph Whitney. The condition for the settlement of ten families in the township must have been waived. The land has been held for the timber. It is not settled nor will be for years to come. The impression has obtained without good ground, that the money received from the sale of this land, was used to pay for erecting the Academy building. More probably it was turned into the treasury and employed for the general uses of the institution. The Treasurer's accounts give this impression. The General Court about the same time made a similar grant to the Trustees of Amherst Academy. They sold it to Joseph Whitney for $2,500, date of conveyance Feb. 22, 1821.

Dea. George Dickinson, who died Aug., 1889, left in his will the sum of $200 to the Trustees of Hopkins Academy, to be by them held in trust for the benefit of the Young Men's Library Association, with the condition that, if this Association should cease to exist, the yearly income of this bequest, when it should amount to $500, should be used by the Trustees of Hopkins Academy for the benefit of its library. It was a condition of the bequest that its income should not be used until the principal had grown so as to reach the sum just named.

FORM, CONDITION AND PROSPECTS OF THE HOPKINS ACADEMY FUND AT THE PRESENT TIME.

The inventory, as it appears from the books of the Treasurer, Nov. 27th, 1889, is as follows:

Ten acres of land on Mount Holyoke,	$ 75.00
Five $\frac{144}{100}$ acres of land, Hockanum Meadow, upper,	900.00
Six " " " " lower,	400.00
Four $\frac{1}{2}$ " " Aqua Vitae,	350.00
Five $\frac{33}{100}$ " " Great Landing, upper,	200.00
Two $\frac{117}{100}$ " " " " lower,	75.00
Michigan Avenue property, Chicago, Ill.,	40,000.00
Langley " " "	6,500.00
Rose Park, seven lots, $75 each,	525.00
Harrison Street, Chicago, Ill.	4,000.00
Equal,	$53,025.00
Mortgage loan to Joseph Pellissier,	500.00
" " Benjamin K. Prukey,	700.00
" " John B. Mead,	600.00
" " Edward Stuber,	900.00
" " Fred Mixon,	800.00
Ten shares Rock Island and Peoria R. R. stock,	800.00
	$4,300.00
Estimated value Nov., 1889,	$57,325.00
" " Nov., 1878,	33,231.25
Increase in eleven years,	$24,093.25

It is likely that this property may still grow in value. How soon, or to what extent, it were hardly safe to predict. Definite forecast of the future, contingent on such growth could hardly be wise. It is easy to see that with ample means at command, much might be done to supply the school with facilities which it now lacks and needs, and to render its work broader, deeper and more efficient. Such hope and desire were worthy of any board of trust. Less than this could hardly be asked of them. Such is the spirit of the Board as it now exists. It is looking to a future better than the past has been, to the realizing of the best hopes which its best friends have ever conceived or cherished in its behalf. Among the things possible in this outlook is a new building for the exclusive use of the school, beautiful for situation, plain but ornamental architecturally, itself an inspiring object lesson, all its appointments such as to make the school itself more valuable, and more beneficent as a factor in the system of schools of which it is a part.

CHAPTER XVI.

CONCLUSION.

This history makes the impression that the guardians of this trust through all these years have been careful to cherish the memory of him whose beneficence gave it being, breathe his spirit and further the ends which he proposed to himself. This spirit is alive to-day and in command. One in whom it is not alive might well be sensible that it ill becomes him to have part in the administration of a trust so high and sacred and charged with such power for good. The like spirit has ruled in the young men and women, a goodly company, who have done the teacher's work. The same thing is true very largely of the hundreds of young men and women who have received here in part their training for the work of life. Happy were it for every youth, who leaves these halls in time to come, to feel that he has gained what he has and become what he is in the way of learning, discipline and culture, in order that the meaning of life shall be to render service in highest kind and largest measure to all within reach, since it is evermore true all along the ages as they come and go, that no man liveth to himself.

In this history we trace the tokens of an agency higher than human, "the divinity that shapes our ends." It is not of man that walketh to direct his steps, as he crosses the sea and traverses an untrodden wilderness to make beginnings and lay foundations in this goodly valley. It was not human foresight that brought Wm. Goodwin to Hadley and with him a part of the estate of Edward Hopkins, small according to the reckoning of to-day, to encourage hopeful youth in the way of learning, that on this spot such a good work should begin and continue until now, that so many should share the benefits of this school, to communicate as well as enjoy, that it should be such a boon as it has been to the town of Hadley and its young people and none the less for the reason that so many others have been blessed, that through this period of two and one-third centuries the fund should suffer no other serious loss than that which almost at the first was due to the fortunes of war with the Indians, that from this loss recovery in good degree should come after so long delay; that this stream diffusing good so steadily and so long should still swell as it flows and give promise of growth and doing still better the beneficent work which it has sought to do from the beginning.

Now it has come to pass, in the course of events whose shaping is not of man, that the school is free to the people of Hadley and her children, and its advantages for them to enjoy almost exclusively, a result in some of its aspects to be deplored. This signal privilege should be recognized, and this recognition properly carries with it a sense of responsibility and obligation to prize these blessings, make the most of them and enhance their value for all the years that are to come.

The coming hither of one of the Trustees of Gov. Hopkins and the planting here of the school that ever since has borne his name and done the work for which he studied and planned, were a beginning. Who shall tell what fruit has grown from this planting. What has grown and is still growing on this soil is known and read of all men. Hampshire County is memorable for the institutions of the higher order that cluster here within ten miles of each other and all within sight from the summit of Mt. Holyoke. The eldest of this sisterhood is Hopkins Academy herself, dating from 1816, with a history as Hopkins Donation school reaching still further back one hundred and forty years.

Here are Amherst College and in the same town the Massachusetts Agricultural College. Mt. Holyoke Seminary and College, Smith Academy in Hatfield, Smith College in Northampton and Williston Seminary in Easthampton. The men and women who founded these schools were of like mind with Edward Hopkins and Wm. Goodwin. Out of like regard for God and man, and like desire to set in motion streams of blessing to flow down the centuries, they called these institutions into being and started them on their grand career. These later friends of good learning had the larger wealth and the power that belongs to it. But the spirit that was in them was in these earlier benefactors. Their foresight was clear and far-reaching. They laid their foundations when such examples were rare as compared with what is true to-day. Example they had none in this part of this then new country. They became an example whose inspiration may well be conceived as reaching down to the present hour, and revealing itself in these halls of learning which now gladden our eyes. These later benefactors could but tread in the steps of those who had gone before. Possibly their works had never appeared on this scene had not the like of them been seen here before.

The institutions just named, with the exception of Smith College and Williston Seminary, are within the boundary of the original town of Hadley. Within these limits Miss Sophia Smith had her birth and life-long residence. She was a descendant, in the sixth generation, of Lieut. Samuel Smith, one of the first Trustees of that portion of the Hopkins legacy that was assigned to Hadley by Davenport and Goodwin in their division of the estate, in 1664. It has been thought and said that she was herself among the pupils of Hopkins Academy at its opening. Though this is in question a sister of hers is remembered to have been a pupil. If it came too late for herself to enjoy, there is reason to think she was glad of the opening of the school for her sex to enjoy and that she received an impulse from this source which at length found expression, with the opportunity, linked with duty as she saw it and the desire, in the establishment for the education of the youth of her town and country, of the College and Academy that perpetuate her name.

Hopkins Academy did not open its doors soon enough for Samuel Williston to enter. But he may have felt its influence in the direction of what he became and what he did in gaining and bestowing wealth to found and foster seats of learning, that others might enjoy advantages of this kind that were denied to himself. But his father, the honored pastor of the church at Easthampton, was in intimate sympathy with the first Trustees of the Academy. His sister, Miss Sally Williston, was the first preceptress. In this wise he was within the circle of influence that had its centre here, and may have derived from this source, even if unconsciously, something of the spirit that turned the vision of Edward Hopkins down to future times with the weal of the country and the honor of God, the burden on his heart.

The friends of the school look with hope for a future better than the past and will study to make it sure, supplying as they may be able aids and facilities in the work of instruction, such as a library better furnished than now, illustrative apparatus and the like, and a permanent corps of instruction whose quality may challenge severe scrutiny and comparison. All such endeavor can be only an onward movement in the line of the wishes and prayers and gifts and labors of the school's early benefactors and friends.

APPENDIX A.

THE HOPKINS FUND AT NEW HAVEN.

In the division of the Hopkins legacy by the surviving trustees, Davenport and Goodwin, in 1664, the sum of £400 was assigned to Hartford on certain conditions, that the remainder of the estate "*both that which is in New England and the £500 which is to come from Old England when it shall become due to us after Mrs. Hopkins her decease* be all of it equally divided between the towns of New Haven and Hadley to be, in each of those towns respectively, managed and improved towards the erecting and maintaining of a *Grammar school* in each of them." Out of the part which Hadley hath it was stipulated that £100 should be paid to Harvard College. New Haven's share in this division was £412. Hadley's share £408 less the £100, or £308. The £500 which was to come from the estate to New Haven and Hadley on the decease of Mrs. Hopkins, never came. Her death took place Dec. 10, 1698, more than forty years after that of her husband. At that time the original trustees were long since dead. Their successors in office, whose duty it was to secure this bequest when it became due, failed to do so, hindered possibly by the thought of the difficulty, delay and expense of securing a favorable decree in the English Court of Chancery. After the decree in this court assigning this bequest to Harvard College and the Grammar School at Cambridge, some effort was made to secure New Haven's claim in the premises. But this endeavor was feeble and fruitless. It came too late, and has never been renewed nor apparently has any such purpose or thought been entertained.[*]

On the gift of £412 before mentioned from the Trustees of Gov. Hopkins, the school still known as the Hopkins Grammar School at New Haven was founded. It has continued in being from the time the income of the fund became available in 1664 until this day. [Judd's Hist. Hadley, p. 56.]

[*] See Review of President Quincy's History of Harvard University, in American Biblical Repository for Jan., 1842, pp. 175-185.

During this long career of usefulness it has been chiefly a school for fitting young men for college. The main object of the school is to prepare boys for college, particularly for the Academical Department and Sheffield Scientific School of Yale University, for which it has fitted more boys than any other preparatory school. From it likewise many graduate, who enter into business as their life work.

A long list of young men, mostly recent graduates from college, have been rectors of this school, many of whom have become eminent in other walks of life. On the roll of its alumni many distinguished names are found. The catalogue of 1887-8 gives a list of 97 pupils. The corps of instruction consists of the rector and four other teachers. The cost of tuition is $80 per year, the whole yearly expense ranging from $280 to $430.

The amount of funds held by the Trustees at the present time is $8,000 of productive property, yielding an annual income of $400. A brick school-house capable of accommodating 200 pupils likewise belongs to the school, with ample play-ground attached. Recently something has been thought and said about merging this school in the public school system of New Haven. But the Trustees of the Grammar School seem not inclined to such a measure but to favor the continuing of their own institution and its good work.

APPENDIX B.

THE HOPKINS FUND AT HARTFORD.

The Trustees of Gov. Hopkins, Davenport and Goodwin, in the final division of his legacy in 1664 assigned £400 to Hartford to be managed by Dea. Edward Stebbing, and Lieut. Thomas Bull and their assigns, in accord with the ends of the donor.

A school-house was built in Hartford in 1665, after Hartford had gained £400 from the Hopkins Fund. The date of the beginning of Hopkins school must be set down at 1665. But the name of no teacher appears until 1674 when Mr. Caleb Watson (H. C. 1661) who had been teacher at Hadley, undertook the school and continued to teach it until 1705, when a vote was passed that he be no longer schoolmaster to this town. For the first century of its existence, the school was scarcely more than a primary school for "the children and servants" of the town. It seems to have been the only public school of any sort in Hartford during that period.

The town in 1753 passed a vote providing that the incomes "belonging to the free school (so called) in this town, shall be applied to the use and support of a Grammar School to be kept in the town of Hartford for the future." One who has written a history of the school says, "It sounds very oddly that an institution which for full two-thirds of a century had been on the foundation of a fund for the encouragement of hopeful youth at the Grammar School and College should be *changed* by a vote of the town of Hartford into a Grammar School." The vote, on its very face, seems to be a confession of past delinquency." L. W. Bacon's discourse at New Haven, Appendix pp. 64, 65.

In 1797 the town, at the request of the committee, appointed agents to apply for a charter of incorporation. Such charter was granted in 1798, empowering the Trustees to hold productive funds to an amount not exceeding $20,000, to manage them and the school and appoint forever their own successors. Since then the fund has much increased and a school been maintained whose fame for thorough classical instruction has been surpassed by that of no other school in the country.

A school was in existence in Hartford as early as 1638, supported for the first thirty years in part by appropriations made from time to time by the town and in part by tuition fees of pupils. The first bequest in its favor was made by Wm. Gibbons in 1655, who gave to the town of Hartford thirty acres of land in the town of Wethersfield for the support of a Latin School. In 1659 it received a small donation from John Talcott.

In 1664 the Trustees under the will of Gov. Hopkins gave to the town of Hartford the sum of £400 for the support of the school. It was further endowed in 1673 by a grant from the Connecticut Colony of 600 acres of land in what is now the town of Stafford. In 1680 it received a donation of £50 from James Richards.

The town of Hartford, through committees chosen for the purpose, for more than a century managed the school and the funds accruing from the sources named, until, upon petition of the town, the State Legislature, in May, 1798, incorporated the school under the name of "The Hartford Grammar School," and appointed Trustees with power to fill all vacancies caused by death or otherwise, so that the obligation of the town to maintain a "Latin School" as stipulated in the will of William Gibbons, to provide for the building up of hopeful youths at the Grammar School as stipulated by E. Hopkins, and a Free School " for the schooling of all who should come, in the Latin and English languages," according to the conditions of the colonial grant was performed from 1798 to 1847 by the Grammar School.

Up to the year 1847 the privileges of this school had been confined to boys. During that year the public High School was established by the town of Hartford, for the " free instruction in the higher branches of an English and the Elementary branches of a classical education, for all the male and female children of suitable age and requirements who may wish to avail themselves of its advantages."

This school is now maintained in a building costing, with its furnishings, $285,000. The cost of maintenance for the year ending Sept. 30, 1887, was $27,747. Teachers' salaries $20,015.78. The number of teachers in the corps of instruction is eighteen, nine men and nine women. Whole number of different scholars registered during the year 548.

In this school the salary of the classical teacher is paid from the income of the Grammar School fund which has grown from the beginnings already mentioned, (Gov. Hopkins' legacy chief among them), until its investments amount to $44,042.00; yearly income, $2,337.50. Biennial Catalogue of the Hartford Public High School for 1886–1887.

APPENDIX C.

THE HOPKINS FUND AT CAMBRIDGE GRAMMAR SCHOOL AND HARVARD COLLEGE.

In the will of Gov. Hopkins the sum of £500 was devised to be paid from his estate in England on the decease of his wife, to his Trustees to further the ends which they were already in trust to promote. Mrs. Hopkins died Dec. 10, 1698*—surviving her husband more than forty years. The Trustees under the will were dead. The executor, Henry Dalley, likewise was long since deceased. It has been seen that in the distribution of the estate by Davenport and Goodwin it was agreed that the £500 to come from the estate in England on the decease of Mrs. Hopkins should be divided equally between New Haven and Hadley. Mr. Davenport caused this agreement to be entered in the town record of New Haven.

Everard Exton, Esq., the executor of the executor and his heirs at law, claimed that there were not assets enough to pay the £500. Nothing was done to oblige him to pay over the money or account for its expenditure until 1708. Then proceedings were begun in the Court of Chancery, by the Queen's Attorney General "at the relation of the Corporation for the propagation of the Gospel in New England and parts adjacent in America." The scope of the bill was that the pious design of the donor might be carried out and Trustees appointed for the purpose expressed in the will of Gov. Hopkins. In 1709 Harvard College began like proceedings through its agent in London, Mr. Henry Newman, to whom a remittance of £40 was sent to be used in gaining his end.

The case came to a hearing on the 9th of July, 1709, and reference was made to a master in Chancery to take account of the assets of the Hopkins estate liable to the said £500; and in case the said £500

---

*There is confusion concerning this date. The year is given 1698 and 1699, and the day of the month the 10th, 16th, and 17th in the same paper.

should be received it was ordered that the same should be paid and applied to the school and college in New England for the building up of scholars then in the school and college, according to the will of the said Edward Hopkins. In order thereto the master was to examine witnesses or write to New England to learn if there was any such a school or college there, and, if not, then what school or college was there and on what purpose founded and report the result of his inquiry to the Court.

Feb. 10, 1710–11. The master reported sufficient assets to pay the legacy, also that sixty or seventy years ago there was and is now a school and college at Cambridge in New England and called Harvard College and near by a small building called Stoughton College.

On the 7th of March, 1710, following, the Right Honorable Sir Symon Harcourt, Knight, Lord Keeper of the Great Seal of Great Britain, decreed that within three months the £500 with interest for the same at the rate of five pounds per centum per annum from six months after the death of the said Anna Hopkins, should be brought before the master and by his approval paid out in a purchase of lands in New England, in the name of the Corporation for the propagation of the Gospel, but the trust is to be declared in the deeds to be for the benefit of the College and Grammar School at Cambridge in New England, according to the several portions they shall be entitled unto.

A final decree, however, was made March 19, 1712–13, confirming what was done Dec. 18th preceding, in which it was ordered that the money should be invested in lands in the name of twenty-one Trustees, of whom Joseph Dudley was the first mentioned. In accordance with this decree the £500, with interest added from January, 1700, was sent to Samuel Sewall, one of the Trustees who by the decree was appointed treasurer. He records in his diary July 15, 1715, the receipt of a letter from Sir William Ashurst, bringing the remittance of Mr. Hopkins's legacy. He charges himself with £1104-8s-2d, which was the legacy sent over, and with £147-5s more for difference between 15d and 17d weight, making £1251-13s-2d in all.

These Trustees purchased from the Natick Indians, in 1715, 9266 acres of land and the General Court added by gift 8000 acres more. These lands the Trustees leased for a time, but trouble came. Rents were unpaid and disputes arose concerning terms of lease, so that in 1832, by resolve of the General Court, they were paid $8000 from the State Treasury. The tenants of Hopkinton and Upton in consideration of the release of all claims upon them by the Trustees also paid them $2000 more. This tract of land was incorporated in 1715 as the town of Hopkinton in honor of Edward Hopkins.

The Trustees received from the Legislature in the year 1827 an act of incorporation as the Trustees of the Hopkins Fund. Acts and Resolves of that year.

In the distribution of the Hopkins Bequest by Davenport and Goodwin out of " that £400 that Hadley hath " £100 was to be paid Harvard College. In the gift book of the College, Treasurer Danforth in his account from 1663 to 1668 acknowledges the receipt of £100 in corn and meal and charges for the transportation of the same from Hartford to Boston £7-6d.

Report of School Committee of the city of Cambridge for the year 1885.

The Court of Chancery in the decree before named gave judgment that one-fourth of the income arising from this fund should be paid to the Grammar School in Cambridge, to be given entirely to the master in consideration of his instruction in Grammar learning, of five boys in preparation for Harvard College. The other three-fourths was to be paid in aid of students in divinity in Harvard College under certain limitations.

In 1839 the Trustees by act of the Legislature were authorized to establish the "Hopkins Classical School" from which time payment to the Grammar School ceased. The school thus chartered was opened in 1840. Terms of admission fixed by the visitors, the President and Fellows of the College and the minister of the First church in Cambridge, were the same as those required for admission to the Boston Latin School. Act of 1839.

This school was discontinued in 1854, when an agreement authorized by the act of 1839 was entered into by the Trustees and the city of Cambridge. The Trustees paying annually to the city of Cambridge the one-fourth of the income of their funds on condition that the money so paid over shall be subject to the order of the school committee of said city, to be by them appropriated exclusively to the improvement of the means of classical instruction in the High School under their charge. This agreement is still in force but may be terminated by the will of the Trustees whenever they re-open the Hopkins Classical School. Under this arrangement the treasurer of the city of Cambridge received from the Trustees of the Hopkins Charity Fund from 1855 to 1885 each year, a sum varying from $300 to $958.93, or an average of about $720 yearly. In virtue of such payment, any boys not more than nine approved by the visitors, preparing for the university are to enjoy all the privileges of the High School free of charge. See report of the school committee of the city of Cambridge for the year 1885. From this source chiefly the foregoing statements concerning the Harvard Fund are derived. Here, too, is found a copy of the decree of the Court of Chancery.

Thus the £500 which by the agreement of the Trustees in 1664 should be divided equally between New Haven and Hadley to aid in establishing in each of the towns a Grammar School, was never so divided but found its way to Cambridge to establish the fund whose income has been and still is used in aid of young men, students at the Grammar School or University in that town.

In the year 1840 President Quincey of Harvard University published a history of that institution. In this history the author makes mention of Edward Hopkins as among "the principal benefactors of Harvard College. His noble beneficence stands in bold relief, exceeded by that of none of his contemporaries in original value, Sir Matthew Holworthy and William Stoughton alone excepted, and at the present day greatly surpassing those of both, in amount and efficiency." No copy of the will nor extract from it, nor any allusion to the doings of the Trustees under it, is found in these pages. He speaks of the will as showing the qualities that make a man beloved. He then gives this abstract of its contents: "To numerous friends and domestics he bequeathed legacies amounting to four thousand pounds sterling; to institutions in Connecticut, for the promotion of religion, science or charity, one thousand pounds sterling. For the advancement of the same noble objects in Massachusetts, the bequest of five hundred pounds, vested in Trustees was destined to find its sphere of usefulness in Harvard College or its vicinity. After an unceasing flow of annual benefits for more than a century, his bounty now exists on a foundation of productive and well-secured capital amounting to nearly thirty thousand dollars." This legacy was not readily paid, but was obtained by the decree in Chancery, of which note has been taken.

"In June, 1709, the corporation took measures to secure the legacy of Edward Hopkins. More than fifty years had elapsed since the death of this benefactor and his heirs interposed obstacles which rendered the pursuit of the claims of the College troublesome and expensive and final success dubious. Not deterred by these difficulties, the corporation appointed Henry Newman of London their agent, and remitted forty pounds sterling for the promotion of their rights. The object was pursued with perseverance and a favorable decree in Chancery obtained in March, 1712-13 by which eight hundred pounds sterling, the amount of the principal legacy with the accumulated interest was vested in a board of Trustees and by them laid out in the purchase of a tract of land to which the name of Hopkinton was given in honor of the donor."

History of Harvard University, Vol. 1, pp. 204-5.

In this history repeated mention has been made of the £500 that, by agreement of the Trustees of Gov. Hopkins, Davenport and Goodwin, should come to New Haven and Hadley on the death of Mrs. Hopkins. This event was long delayed and prospect of anything to come from the estate grew uncertain. When it came, little or no note was taken of it. The New Haven Trustees moved in the matter too feebly and too late to accomplish anything. Evidence is wanting that the Hadley committee were in anywise advised of the situation or made any movement in the matter. There was none to contest the payment of the claim to the only party making it.

The equity of the decision, though acquiesced in by those interested, is not universally conceded. *In his letter written Jan. 1, 1759, Col. Israel Williams of Hatfield gives expression to a sense of the inequity of this disposition of this £500 and raises the question whether after so long a time it is too late to have the decree overruled and so have the right prevail. Thus far nothing has come of the suggestion.

See Review of Pres. Quincy's History of Harvard University in American Biblical Repository for Jan., 1842, pp. 175-185. Address of L. W. Bacon at the 200th anniversary of the founding of the Hopkins Grammar School at New Haven, pp. 28-29.

*Col. Israel Williams of Hatfield is the man whose name appears pp. 76-77. He was graduated at Harvard College in 1727. He commanded one of the Hampshire regiments in the French war. He was member of the Council and Judge of the Court of Common Pleas. He was first cousin of Ephraim Williams founder of Williams College. He was a loyalist during the Revolution. He was called the monarch of Hampshire County. Among his papers in possession of Mass. Hist. Society is a draft of a charter by the Governor incorporating himself and eleven others as President and Fellows of Queens College. The charter was never granted. The College had a being only on paper. Col. Williams died in 1788, aged 79. Proceedings of Mass Hist. Soc., Vol. XX., p. 47.

INDEX.

	PAGE
Allen, Rev. Dr. William	85
Allen, John	19
Allis, Lieut. John, heard the case of Robt. Boltwood and school committee,	40, 41, 42, 61
Allyn, Mr. Matthew	20, 24
Adams, Rev. Leonard	147
Adams, Rev. Stephen B.	147
Andrews, Rev. David	143
Ashmun, Hon. Geo., M. C.,	140, 151
Austin, Samuel H.	149
Avery, Rev. William F.	140
Ayres, Rev. Rowland, D. D.,	3, 110, 114, 117, 120, 122, 127, 128, 129, 137, 138, 139
Ayres, Alice J.	154
Ayres, Edward	141, 150
Ayres, Edith J.	145, 155
Ayres, David C.	155
Bacon, Andrew	27, 39, 92
Bacon, Rev. L. W., D. D., Address at New Haven, quoted or referred to	7, 18, 23, 26, 69, 176, 183
Baker, Edward A.	141
Ball, Rev. Dyer, M. D.,	146
Ball, Rev. Mason	146
Ball, Heman,	74
Ballard, Rev. Addison, D. D.,	4, 140
Banister, Rev. S. W.	142
Bardwell, Dea. Baxter E.	138
Bardwell, Miss Emma C.	145, 154
Barker, Edmund P.	143
Barnard, John, Bequest for a school,	28, 29, 30, 31, 43, 49, 50, 53, 55, 90, 93, 94, 103, 104
Barnard, Widow	39, 53, 54, 55
Barnard, Francis	28
Barnard, Henry, Esq., writings referred to,	18, 19
Barnard, Henry, one of town committee to demand rents, etc.,	43
Barrows, Miss Cornelia C.	145

Bartlett, Rev. Lyman . 148
Bassett, Rev. Isaac A. . . 147
Batchelder, George H., M. D., ... 168
Bates, Hon. Isaac C., Trustee, 80; chosen to frame by-laws, 80; to negotiate sale of lands, 167; counsel for Hopkins Academy before supreme court, 97
Bates, Joseph, M. D., ... 148
Bates, George A., M. D., ... 149
Bayne, Rev. John S. 138
Beaman, Rev. W. H. . . 110, 114, 122, 127, 137
Beaman, Miss Emma W. . . . 145
Beaman, John W. 155
Beaman, Miss Mina D., Mrs. Rev. John D. Willard, . 154
Beaman, Edward H., M. D., ... 149
Belcher, Susan C., Mrs. Chas. S. Thomson, M. D., 153
Bell, Rev. James M. 138
Bell, Mrs. Martha L. 145
Benjamin, Prof. Reuben M. 140
Bentley, Mr. Jasper . . . , 74
Berry, Thomas, M. D., . . . ' . 71
Billings, Miss Louisa S., Mrs. Rev. Ezekiel Russell, D. D., 142
Billings, Miss Mary W. . . ' . . 142
Blair, Miss Dolly 142
Blake, Rev. Mortimer, D. D., . . . 139, 142
Blake, Horace T. 143
Boltwood, Robert, miller, rebuilds the corn-mill, 36, 37, 38; negotiatious concerning the mill, his death, ... 41, 59
Boltwood, Samuel, 36; differences with school committee concerning mill adjusted, ... 41, 42, 60, 61
Boardman, Rev. Daniel 70
Bond, Thomas H. 149
Bonney, Franklin, M. D., committee to confer with trustees of Hopkins Academy, 109, 120, 127, 129, 131, 138, 139, 149; building committee, 131
Bonney, George. W. 152
Bonney, Rev. Elijah H. 143, 147
Bowdoin, Elbridge G. . . . 149
Brewster, E. H. 151
Bridgman, Rev. Elijah C., D. D., 146
Bridgman, Rev. James G. . 147
Bridgman, Rev. Henry M. 149
Brooks, Sidney, M. D., 148
Brooks, Rev. Edward F. 147
Brown, Frederick . 155
Bragg, Rev. Jesse K. 142
Brown, Rev. John, D. D.. 137
Brown, Miss Lucy Ann . 142
Bruer, Lycortas L. 142
Buck, Augustus H. 140

Buck, Mrs. C. L.	144
Buerger, John F.	144
Bull, Lieut. John, return to order of court, 19; appointed to manage Gov. Hopkins' estate,	20, 26, 176
Bullard, Rev. Amos	142, 146
Bullard, Eunice W., Mrs. Henry Ward Beecher,	153
Bullard, Rev. Ebenezer W.	142
Case, Elmer	141
Caldwell, Rev. David	142
Chandler, Charles H.	141
Champney, Hosp. Steward, Wm. A.	156
Chapin, Rev. Sewel	74
Chapin, Rev. Horace B.	137
Chapin, Rev. Lucius D.	140
Chapin, L. C., M. D.,	144
Chapman, Henry, Esq.,	149
Chauncey, Rev. Nathaniel	70
Chauncey, "Mr. Chauncey's son,"	71
Chauncey, Israel	71
Chesebrough, Rev. Amos S., D. D.,	139
Chester, Rev. John, D. D.,	75
Church, Austin, M. D.,	148
Church, Miss Hannah B.	143
Clapp, Rev. Dexter	147
Clapp, Rev. Luther	147
Clarke, Henry, 26, 27; legacy, 29, 30, 31, 37, 44, 49, 53, 91, 92, 93, 94, 104, 106	
Clark, William	42, 45
Clark, Rev. Tertius, D. D.,	146
Clark, Alonzo, M. D.,	148
Clark, Lincoln, M. C.,	149
Clark, Theodore	151
Clark, Rev. Clinton	147
Clark, Rev. Solomon	147
Clark, Miss Abigal	142
Clark, Lucy Ann, Mrs. L. D. Seymour, M. D.,	
Clark, Miss Mary	143
Clark, Miss Lepha N.	154
Clark, Miss Juliette	145
Clark, Asa, Jr.,	155
Clark, Corp. John C.	156
Clark, Charles W.	156
Clark, Miss Clara W.	145
Condit, Rev. Joseph D.	137
Conkey, Hon. Ithamar F.	149
Cooley, Miss Genevieve	145
Coolidge, Dea. Nathaniel	136
Coolidge, Miss Sarah P.	143

Cooke, Ensign and Capt. Aaron
   33, 34, 36, 39, 40, 42, 43, 44, 46, 47, 61, 62, 66, 91, 93, 94, 95
Cooke, Westwood, ... 68
Cooke, Capt. Moses 68
Cooke, Mr. Enos 74
Cooke, Rev. Parsons, D. D., . . . 146
Cooke, Rev. Noah. 146
Cooke, Rev. Sylvester 146
Cooke, Ephraim, M. D., . . 148
Cooke, Silas, M. D., . 148
Cooke, Horace . . . 138, 151
Cooke, Charles . . . 138, 151
Cooke, Rev. Herbert Jonathan 141, 148
Cooke, Miss Jane A. . . 143
Cooke, Miss Lucy A. . 145
Cooke, Col. John E. 155
Cooke, Corp. Rufus A. . . 156
Cooke, Alfred L. . . . 156
Cooke, Eleazer . . . 156
Cooke, S. Parsons . . 156
Corss, Rev. Charles C. . . 143, 146
Crossett, Miss Mary A. 143
Cullick, Mr. and Capt. John, trustee under Edward Hopkins' will, .
   10, 12, 13, 16, 19, 20, 21, 22, 23, 24, 26, 28, 38, 90
Curtis, Rev. Joseph W. . . . 110, 114, 115, 116, 137
Curtis, Judge Joseph S. 149
Cushman, Rev. Martin 146
Dalley, Henry, executor of Edward Hopkins' will, 11, 20, 24, 28, 179
Danforth, treasurer Harvard College receives £100, . . 181
Danforth, Rev. Francis 137
Daugherty, Caroline, Mrs. Rev. William M. Richards, . . 153
Davenport, Rev. John, vicar in London, etc., 6; life and character, 13, 14;
   emigrates to America, 13; settles at New Haven pastor of the church, 13;
   friend of Gov. Hopkins and trustee under his will, 18, 21, 22, 23, 24;
   agreement concerning the estate, 25, 27, 28, 29, 33, 38, 39, 67, 90, 91, 92,
                                    93, 100, 103, 173, 174, 176, 179, 183
Davenport, Jesse R. 122, 127, 129, 138, 141
Dickinson, Dea. Nathaniel, 30, 31; chosen by the town 1669 one of committee
   of five, 33; signs Davenport and Goodwin's agreement, . 27
Dickinson, Nehemiah, one of a committee of town to procure a school-master. etc., ... 43
Dickinson, Capt. Elisha 68
Dickinson, Rev. Benjamin 71
Dickinson, Mr. John 74
Dickinson, Dea. William 68, 136
Dickinson, Dea. Elisha 137
Dickinson, Dea. Simeon 137

Dickinson, Elizabeth, Mrs. Horace Goodrich,	152
Dickinson, Maria P., Mrs. Rev. L. Sabin, D. D.,	153
Dickinson, Harriet, Mrs. Rev. E. W. Bullard,	153
Dickinson, Mary B., Mrs. J. P. Kimball,	154
Dickinson, Dea. George	35, 116, 137, 150
Dickinson, Mr. William P.	137
Dickinson, Rev. William E.	147
Dickinson, Edward, M. D.,	148
Dickinson, Miss Alice E.	154
Dickinson, George	155
Dickinson, Levi P.	156
Dickinson, Charles F.	156
Dickinson, Luther W.	156
Dowse, Joseph Perry	144
Dudley, Pres. Joseph, 46; letter to Mr. Russell,	57, 58
Dudley, George	144
Dunakin, Corp. Henry Alonzo	156
Dunakin, Henry	156
Dunbar, Rev. John	146
Dunbar, John B.	156
Dwight, Rev. Daniel	71
Dwight, Nancy, Mrs. Austin Church, M. D.,	153
Dwight, Mr. Timothy	139
Dwight, Rev. E. S., D. D.,	3, 138
Dwight, Miss Mary	142
Dwight, Wm. W., M. D.,	148
Dwight, John E., M. D.,	149
Eastman, Dea. Joseph	68
Eastman, Henry	150
Eaton, Gov. Theophilus, called father by Gov. Hopkins in his will, 10; trustee under the will, 10, 90; sole governor of New Haven colony, 12; character,	12, 16
Edson, Rev. H. K.	140, 147
Edson, Almira, Mrs. Rev. Hall and Mrs. Geo. Atwood, M. D.,	153
Edson, Hon. Francis	151, 171
Edwards, Rev. Bela B., D. D.,	146
Emery, Rev. S. H.	143
Emerson, Miss Felicia	145
Enderton, Corp. Charles S.	156
Farmington,	10, 34, 35
Farnham, Rev. Lucian	146
Ferguson, Rev. John	137
Fisher, O.	140
Fiske, Miss Mary W.	143
Fleming, Geo. C., M. D.,	149
Fleming, Louis I.	149
Gage, Rev. Rodney	147, 155

Gay, Rev. Ebenezer	71
Gaylord, Mr. Samuel	68
Gaylord, Miss Lucy B.	143
Gaylord, Miss Martha R.	145
Gillett, Hon. Edward B.	149, 152

Goodwin, Elder William, arrives in Boston, settles at Cambridge, 14; freeman ruling elder, etc., 14, 15; removes to Hartford, 14; character, 14, 34; trustee under Gov. Hopkins' will, 10; removes to Hadley, 16, 17; dies in Farmington, 34; doings at Hartford concerning the Hopkins estate, 18—27; at Hadley, 32—35, 28, 37, 38, 39, 40, 51, 54, 90, 91, 92, 93, 100, 101, 102, 103, 104, 106, 173, 174, 176, 179

Gould, Rev. Vinson	136
Granger, L. N.	126, 131, 138, 166
Gray, Rev. Mr.	74
Gray, Edwin C.	156
Greene, Rev. John M., D. D.,	147
Grimes, Mr. Samuel	74
Gurley, Rev. John	74

Hadley, town of, grants meadow lands for a school, 30, 31; accepts Mr. Goodwin's proposal, 32, 34; votes to take estates, etc., out of committees' hands, etc., 43; votes to let fall this former vote, 61; selectmen censured and warned by court of sessions, 61, 62; appoints committee to carry out its votes, procure a school-master etc., 43; sundry votes pertaining to the school, ... 64—66

Hadley, town of, vs. trustees of Hopkins Academy, 87—107; in conference with trustees of Hopkins Academy with reference to making the school free to the town Chap. XI, . . . 109—132

Harcourt, Sir Symon, Knight, Lord keeper of the Great Seal of England,	180
Hall, Aaron B.	142
Hannum, Arnold	142
Harvard College, £100 to be paid from the Hopkins estate,	27, 38, 181;
claiming and gaining £500 in court of Chancery,	17, 180, 182, 183
	181, 182, 183
Harvard University, Pres. Quincey's History of	182
Harvey, Rev. Adiel	142
Haskell, Miss Charlotte C.	145
Haskell, Miss Eliza C., Mrs. Rev. Edward S. Frisbee, D. D.,	145
Hawkes, Rev. Theron H., D. D.,	144
Hawley, Joseph	42
Hayward, William H.	157
Hammond, John C. Esq.	138
Hannum, J. Arnold	142
Heavens, Francis J.	141
Henshaw, Marshall, LL. D.,	140
Henshaw, Mrs. Francis J.	144
Henshaw, Miss Almira	143
Hill, Miss	145

Hinsdale, Miss Harriet A., Mrs. Rev. H. L. Hubbell, D. D., 144
Hitchcock, Dea. C. P. 137
Hitchcock, Rev. Roswell, D. D., . . 142
Hodge, Hannah M., Mrs. Rev. James Wilcox, 153
Hodge, Harriet M., Mrs. Hon. Thos. F. Plunkett, 153
Hodge, Charles D. 156
Hodge, Corp. Samuel 156
Hodge, William H. 157
Holmes, Cyrus 139
Hooker, Rev. Thomas, pastor of the church at Newtown and Hartford, 143
. . . . . . 7, 8, 14, 15
Hooker, Gen. Joseph 155
Hooker, Sarah, Mrs. Rev. M. L. R. Thompson, D. D., . 153
Hooker, Miss Mary 143
Hooker, Sergt. Lewis B. 157
Hopkins, Gov. Edward, birth and education, 6; emigration to America, 6; settles at Boston and Hartford, 6; charcter, 6, 7, 9,182; Gov. of Connecticut, successful merchant, 7; returns to England, death, 8; his will, 10, 11; his trustees, their disposal of his estate, 18—27
Hopkins, Mrs. Anna, 8, 9; provision for her in her husband's will, 11; her death, ... 179
Hopkins Fund, sequestered by Gen. Court of Connecticut 18—25; final settlement and distribution by Davenport and Goodwin, . . 24—27
Hopkins Fund and School at Hartford, 176—178; New Haven, 174, 175
Hopkins Fund at Harvard College and Cambridge Grammar school, 179—183
Hopkins Fund at Hadley, agreement of Mr. Goodwin and town concerning, 32—34; early troubles concerning it in court and otherwise, . 35—63
Hopkins Grammar School at Hadley, names of school committee, 67, 68; roll of teachers, ... 69—75
Hopkins Academy, charter asked by committee and town and granted, 78; incorporation, charter and by-laws, . . . 78—83
Hopkins Academy, building erected, 84-86; dedicated and school opened in it, 86: burned, ... 121
Hopkins Academy, trustees 136-139
Hopkins Academy, principal teachers, 139-141; assistants, . 141-145
Hopkins Academy, pupils, roll of honor, 146-157; roll of graduates receiving diplomas, 162-163; present membership, Jan. 1, 1890, . 164
Hopkins Academy in the supreme court, town of Hadley vs. trustees of Hopkins Academy, report of the case, . . . 87–107
Hopkins Academy, in conference with the town with reference to making the school free to the town Chap. XI, . . . 109--132
Hopkins Academy, changes in the fund, etc., 165 et seq; present and former condition, estimated value of property, . . 169-170
Hopkins, Rev. Samuel, D. D., ... 77
Hopkins, Lewis, M. D., ... 148
Hosford, Rev. Henry B. . . . 140, 144

Hosford, Miss Louisa	144
Hosford, Maj. James M.	145
Hovey, Lieut. Thomas	68
Howard, Chauncey	142
Hubbard, Mr. Edmund	68
Hubbard, Rev. John	70
Hubbard, Moses	74
Hubbard, Dea. George W.,	4, 151
Hubbard, Fordyce M., D.D.,	146
Hubbard, Wallace A.	156
Hubbard, Franklin	156
Hubbard, Oscar R.	156
Humphrey, Rev. Zephaniah M., D.D.,	147
Humphrey, Miss Lucy, Mrs. Rev. Henry Neill, D.D.,	153
Hunn, Rev. David L.	137
Huntington, Rev. Dan	136, 139
Huntington, Judge C. P.	149
Huntington, Rev. William P.	146
Huntington, Theodore G.	128, 138
Huntington, Rt. Rev. Frederic D., D.D.,	147
Huntington, Miss Elizabeth P.	142
Hutchinson, Rev. Horace,	140, 142
Isham, Rev. Austin	143
James, Rev. John	71
James, Rev. Justus L.	147
Jenkins, Rev. Abraham	147
Jewett, Lieut. John Howard	152, 156
Jones, Major George	156
Johnson, Aholiab, Esq.,	149
Johnson, Chester, M. D.,	148
Johnson, Miss Laura R.	145
Johnson, Rev. Myron A.	148
Johnson, Edward	156
Johnson, Herbert F.	156
Johnson, Clifton C.	152
Judd, Rev. Sylvester, Jr.,	147
Judd, Rev. Jonathan S.	147
Kellogg, Joseph	67
Kellogg, Giles C., Esq.,	75, 141
Kellogg, Rev. Gardiner	74
Kellogg, Rev. Bela	75
Kidder, Rev. Pascal. P.P.,	147
Kilburn, Mr. Hezekiah	71
Kingsley, Krissa, Mrs. Eli Moody,	153
Kingsley, Elbridge	152
Lamson, Charles E.	138
Lamson, Charles M., D.D.,	148

Lane, Rev. John W.	138
Little, Miss Mary Ann	142
Lobdell, Rev. Henry, M. D.,	140
Lord, Rev. Henry	136
Lord, Rev. Charles	143, 147
Loud, Watson, M. D.,	143
Lyman, Rev. Joseph, D. D.,	80, 136
Lyman, Hon. Jonathan H.	136, 167
Lyman, Clarissa J., Mrs. Rev. John H. Bisbee,	153
Lyman, Rev. George	147
Lyman, Jabez B., M. D.,	149
Lyman, John Chester, M. D.,	149
Lyman, Rev. Timothy	147
Lyman, Charles F.	156
Lyon, Merrick, LL. D.,	150
Lyon, Lucius, M. D.,	149
McClung, Matthew	149
Mann, Rev. Asa	143
Marsh, Ensine Moses	68
Marsh, Job	68
Marsh, Rev. Jonathan	70
Marsh, Rev. D. W., D.D.,	147
Marsh, Rev. Loren B.	147
Marsh, Prof. Charles D.	150
Marshall, Jonathan B.	143
Mather, Rev. Cotton. His Magnalia quoted concerning Gov. Hopkins, 7, 8, 9; concerning Mrs. Hopkins, 8; concerning Gov. Eaton, 12.	
Mather, Judge Warham	70
Mather, Rev. Nathaniel	71
Mather, Rev. Richard H., D.D.,	150
Mayhew, Miss Abby C.	144
Melyen, Rev. Samuel	70
Merrill, Miss Eliza	142
Mighill, Samuel	70
Miller, Rev. Simeon	147
Mitchell, Walter G.	141
Mitchell, W. W.	141
Montague, Prof. William L.	150
Morse, Rev. John	70
Morton, John A.	138
Morton, John A., Jr.,	155
Morton, L. M.	144
Mosely, Miss Sophia	141
Murdock, Miss Thankful	142
Nash, Lieut. Enos	68
Nash, Dea. Enos	68
Nash, Rev. John A.	139, 146

Nash, Samuel, Esq., committee of the Town to confer with the Trustees of Hopkins Academy,	109, 120
Nash, Judge Simeon, Jr.,	149
Nash, Miss Maria W., Mrs. James H. Hackleton,	154
Nash, Capt. Edwin S.	155
Nash, Rev. Francis L.	148
Nash, Miss Isabella S.	145
Nelson, Rev. William F.	142
Nichols, George	139
Newman, Henry, agent of Harvard College to secure legacy of £500,	179, 182
Norton, Rev. Thomas S.	147
Orr, William, Jr.,	143
Osborn, Orson, M. D.,	148
Packard, Miss Louisa	142
Palmer, Francis L.	143
Partrigg, Samuel, Colonel, Representative, Judge of Probate, etc., taught Hopkins School, 70; favored an English School, 45; reasons given, 52-57, 41, 42, 43, 44, 46, 47; dismissed from school committee, 59.	
Partrigg, John	70
Partridge, Joseph L.	150
Partridge, Rev. George C.	146
Pasco, Miss Maria L.	145
Pasco, Rev. Martin K.	148
Pearl, Prof. Joshua F.	150
Penney, Rev. Joseph, D.D.,	137
Perkins, Rev. Nathan	136
Perry, Marshall D., M. D.,	148
Perry, Miss	145
Phelps, Caroline, Mrs. Rev. S. G. Bullfinch,	153
Phelps, Charlotte, Mrs. Rev. Mason P. Bartlett,	153
Phelps, Mr. Charles	68
Phelps, Francis	150
Phelps, Theophilus	151
Phillips, Rev. Daniel	145
Pierce, Master Josiah, teacher, preacher, town clerk, etc.,	71, 72
Taught Hopkins Grammer School, covenant with school committee,	72, 73
Taught in Amherst, Northampton and South Hadley,	73, 74
Pierce, William Martin	150
Pierce, Dea. John N.	138
Pierce, Miss Cynthia M.	145
Pomeroy, Miss Emily, Mrs. Rev. David Eastman,	143, 153
Poor, Rev. Daniel W., D.D.,	147
Porter, Samuel, Esq.,	67
Porter, Hon. Eleazer	68
Porter, Mr. Eleazer	68
Porter, William, M. D.,	68, 136

Porter, Col. Moses	68, 136
Porter, Mr. Elisha	68
Porter, Rev. Aaron	70
Porter, Miss Amy, Mrs. Rev. Jos. D. Wickham,	50
Porter, Dea. Eleazer,	138
Porter, James B., Esq.,	135
Porter, Rev. Jeremiah	146, 157
Porter, Lois E., Mrs. Dea. Coolidge and Mrs. Rev. J. W. Curtis,	152
Porter, Susan, Mrs. Rev. Lucian Farnham,	153
Porter, Miss Lucretia	142
Porter, Miss Augusta A.	145
Porter, Rev. William, D.D.,	147
Porter, Moses, M. D.,	148
Porter, Henry, M. D.,	148
Porter, Rev. Edward C.	148
Porter, Miss Charlotte W.	154
Porter, William P., Esq.,	138
Porter, Miss Emma T., Mrs. Rev. Sereno D. Gammell,	154
Pratt, Rev. Levi,	137
Pratt, James O.	144
Proctor, Miss	142
Powers, Rev. Henry	148
Powers, Miss Sarah W., Mrs. Rev. Benj. Parsons,	145, 154
Pynchon, Major John, heard the case of Sam'l Boltwood, 41; letter to Mr. Russell, 45; return to President and Council, 46, 47, 58, 59, 61, 62.	
Quincy, President Josiah, History of Harvard University,	174, 182, 183
Read, Hanson L.	144
Reed, Miss Mary A.	143
Reed, Miss Mary,	145
Richards, Rev. William M.	146
Riddle, Rev. Samuel Hopkins	146
Robbins, Rev. Alden B., D. D.,	143
Robinson, Gov. Charles, M. D.,	149, 152
Rogers, Daniel W.	141
Ruggles, Rev. Samuel	70
Ruppaner, Anton, M. D.,	144
Russell, Rev. John, first minister of Hadley, 62, 63; school committee, 27, 30, 32, 33, 34, 35, 36, 39, 40; reasons to Pres't and Council, 48 et seq., 43, 44, 45, 92, 93, 94, 95.	
Russell, Rev. Samuel	69
Russell, Rev. Ezekiel, D.D.,	4, 133, 139
Scott, Aaron	155
Scott, Rufus P.	155
Sabin, Rev. Lewis, D.D.,	139
Sanderson, John P.	139, 143

Sanford, Hon. John E.	144
Seelye, Rev. L. Clark, D.D.,	148
Seymour, Rev. Henry	4, 143, 147
Seymour, Susan S., Mrs. Maj. James M. Hosford,	153
Seymour, Edwin	155
Seymour, Rev. John A.	144
Seymour Henry M.	152
Seymour, Levi D., M. D.,	149
Shed, James A., Esq.,	149
Sherman, George	141
Shumway, Rev. Columbus	145
Shipman, William S.	122, 126, 127
Shipman, William N.	155
Smith, Lieut. Samuel, school committee,	27, 31, 32, 33, 34, 35, 92, 93, 173
Smith, Dea. Philip	39, 67, 93
Smith, Chileab, 63; appointed by Court,	60, 67, 95
Smith, Sargeant Joseph	68
Smith, Dea. John	68
Smith, Dea. David	68
Smith, Dea. Oliver	68
Smith, Dea. Seth	68
Smith, Windsor, Esq.,	85
Smith, Dea. Jacob	68, 136
Smith, Rev. Joseph	70
Smith, Mr. John	74
Smith, Rev. Worthington, D.D.,	139
Smith, Dea. Sylvester	137
Smith, Dudley, Esq.,	137
Smith, Capt. Elijah	137
Smith, Dea. Rodney,	138
Smith, Catharine A., Mrs. Dr. Jones,	152
Smith, Oliver E.	138
Smith, Hon. Hinsdale,	151
Smith, Rev. Henry B., D.D.,	85
Smith, Miss Sophia	150, 173
Smith, Miss Mary D,	143
Smith, Miss Sarah A.	143
Smith, Miss Miranda	144
Smith, Julia, Mrs. Lincoln Clark,	152
Smith, Elizabeth H., Mrs. Rev. William Harvey,	152
Smith, Esther, Mrs. Rev. John Dunbar,	153
Smith, Martha, Mrs. Rev. O. G. Hubbard,	153
Smith, Miranda, Mrs. Rev. Pomeroy Belden,	153
Smith, Margaret, Mrs. Rev. E. W. Bullard,	153
Smith, Julia, Mrs. John W. Blodgett, M. D.,	153
Smith, Lydia, Mrs. Henry E. Ide,	153
Smith, Susan H., Mrs. E. P. Richardson,	152

Smith, Maria D., Mrs. Capt. J. Richardson,
Smith, Mary, Mrs. Phelps,
Smith, Helen M., Mrs. Henry S. Stockbridge, Jr., 154
Smith, Alice T., Mrs. Gerry, 155
Smith, Louisa A., Mrs. Edwin H. Baxter, M. D., 154
Smith, Horace M. 144
Smith, John Woodbridge, Esq., 149
Smith, John 144
Smith, Miss Abby P. 145
Smith, Miss Clarissa 145
Smith, Rev. Horace 146
Smith, Rev. Preserved 146
Smith, Henry Parks 150
Smith, Rev. Arthur 148
Smith, Lieut. James W. 155
Smith, H. Fred, M. M. D., 149
Smith, Frederic E., Esq., 149
Smith, Lucius D. 156
Smith, Samuel D. 156
Smith, George M. 157
Spaulding, Adaline, Mrs. Rev. M. K. Cross, 153
Spear, Rev. C. V. 140, 141
Spencer, Rev. Ichabod S. 137
Spencer, Rev. Thomas 147
Stanwood, Miss Joanna 144
Stearns, Rev. J. G. D. 139
Stebbins, Dea. Edward 19, 20, 26, 176
Stebbins, Edward 131
Steele, Rev. Stephen 71
Stockbridge, Hon. Levi 151
Stockbridge, Henry S., Esq., 149
Stockbridge, Henry S., Jr., M.C., 154
Stockbridge, Sylvester 149
Stone, Rev. Samuel, teacher of the church at Newtown and Hartford
                  he and Mr. Goodwin do not agree, 14, 15, 16
Stone, Rev. William B. 147
Stone, Lucy, Mrs. Henry B. Blackwell, 153
Strong, Gov. Caleb 79
Strong, Mr. 74
Strong, Hon. Joseph 136
Strong, Miss 142
Strong, Charles L. 142
Stuart, Judge William Zephaniah 142
Taft, John A. 149
Taylor, Mr. 73
Taylor, Oliver S., M. D., 139
Taylor, Rev. Samuel A. 143

Taylor, James A. 143
Taylor, Rev. Rufus, D.D., ... 147
Thomson, George F., M. D., ... 149
Tilton, Dea. and Hon. Peter. A first Trustee under Gov. Hopkins' will. 27, 30; choice of the town at the instance of Mr. Goodwin, 32, 34; defendant in Court vs. William Goodwin, 34, 35, 36, 39, 44, 45, 46, 47, 91, 92, 93.
Tobey, Miss Elizabeth 145
Todd, Rev. John, D. D., . . . 137
Tower, Rev. J. Edwin 148
Tracy, Mr. Fanning, . . . 74
Train, Miss 144
Treat, Rev. Salmon 70
Tuttle, George A., M. D., ... 149
Tuttle, Prof. Charles A. 150
Tuttle, Franklin Elliot 150
Tuxbury, Rev. Franklin 122, 127, 137
Vanhorn, Alfred 157
Walker, Rev. G. L., D.D., History first church Hartford referred to, 15-17
Ward, Nathaniel, Engagers meet at his house, . . 29
          His legacy, . . 29, 39, 50, 53, 94, 103
Ward, Lucretia S., Mrs. Judge Oviatt, . . . 152
Ward, Mary D., Mrs. Rev. Horace Smith, . . . 152
Ware, Lauriston, Builder, ... 132
Warner, Dea. Andrew . . . 14, 30, 31
Warner, Capt. Oliver 137
Washburn, Charles E., M. D., . . . 143
Waterbury, Rev. J. B., D.D., . . 136
Watson, Caleb, first school master, . 53, 54, 56, 69
Webber, Rev. George N., D.D., . . . 145
Wedge, Newel 150
West, Parsons, Esq., . . 114, 122, 126
West, Lewis W. . . 151, 156
Whitaker, Mr. Augustus . . 144
Whitaker, J. Edwin . . . 144
White, Mr. Ebenezer . . . 74
White, Tirzah M., Mrs. Judge Williamson, . 153
White, Frances M., Mrs. John Kimball, Esq., . 153
White, Abby L., Mrs. Rev. William Williams, . 153
White, Prof. George H. 141
Whitney, Joseph, Esq., ... 167, 168
Whitney, Miss Sarah 142
Whitney, Prof. William D. . . . 150
Wilcox, Nathaniel F. 141
Wilder, Samuel C., committee of town to confer with Trustees,
          121, 122, 123, 124, 138
Willis, William H., M.D., (name changed from Orrick) . . 149

Williston, Miss Sally	141, 173
Williston, Hon. Samuel	141, 173
Williston Seminary,	173
Williams, Col. Israel, letters concerning Hopkins School,	77
Concerning Hopkins Fund,	183
Williams, Rev. Elisha	71
Williams, Rev. Stephen	71
Williams, Rev. Solomon	71
Williams, Miss Emily H.	142
Williams, Judge Erastus Smith	149
Williams, Rev. Charles N.	144
Williams, Hon. P. Smith, committee of Town to confer with Trustees of Hopkins Academy, 109-120; Building Committee, 131, 148; School Committee, 117.	
Winthrop, History quoted,	6, 8, 9, 14
Winthrop, Gov. John, Jr., corresponds with Davenport and Goodwin concerning the estate, 22-24; Mr. Dalley deals with him,	24-25
Witherell, Rev. Isaac	140
Woodbridge, Mr. Ephraim or Samuel	70
Woodbridge, Rev. John, D.D.,	86, 110, 116, 137
Woodbridge, Miss Mindwell	144
Woodbridge, Mary Ann, Mrs. Hawley and Mrs. Rev. Parsons Cook, D.D,	153
Woodbridge, Miss Susan A.	144
Woodbridge, Rebecca M., Mrs. Judge E. S. Williams,	144, 153
Woodbridge, John, Jr., Esq.,	149
Woodbridge, E. Octavia, Mrs. Rev. R. H. Richardson, D.D.,	153
Woodbridge, Rev. Sylvester	146
Woodbridge, Rev. Jahleel	146
Workman, William, M. D.,	148
Younglove, Rev. John	65, 69

ERRATA.

Page 4, seventh line from the bottom, after members, insert, or teachers.
Page 17, line 11, for opposed read approved.
Page 51, last line but one, for Hopkin,s read Hopkins,s.
Page 63, note, for ater, read after.
Page 142, for Stewart read Stuart.
Page 145, for Alice C. Dickinson read Alice E. Dickinson.
Page 160, after Henry Parks Smith, &c., read John B. Dunbar, Prof. Latin and Greek, Washburn College.

www.ingramcontent.com/pod-product-compliance
Lightning Source LLC
Chambersburg PA
CBHW020925230426
43666CB00008B/1568